The Bombay House Heist
& Other Forgotten True Crime Stories of India

The Bombay House Heist

& Other Forgotten True Crime Stories of India

Sunil Nair

JUGGERNAUT BOOKS
C-I-128, First Floor, Sangam Vihar, Near Holi Chowk,
New Delhi 110080, India

First published by Juggernaut Books 2026

Copyright © Sunil Nair 2026

10 9 8 7 6 5 4 3 2 1

P-ISBN: 9789353458911
E-ISBN: 9789353458676

Typeset in Adobe Caslon Pro by R. Ajith Kumar, Noida

Printed at Thomson Press India Private Limited

*For my father, P. Karunakaran Nair, who always reminded me
that being a good human being was far more important
than being well-read.*

Contents

Introduction

To begin with, this book is not for the average doom-scrolling, brain-fogged true-crime junkie. There are no brides-chopped-into-thirty-seven-pieces or lovers-butchered-and-buried-in-a-blue-drum stories, as in the current news cycle, to be found here. It is, nevertheless, a work on serious crime – sometimes banal, often outrageous and almost always deadly.

I began working on this book as a sequel to my earlier work on crime in colonial India, focusing only on crimes committed in my hometown, Mumbai. Conversations with city police historian Deepak Rao on some of the great crimes in Bombay during the decades before and immediately after Independence helped develop the essential structure of this work. I had to trawl through rare and out-of-print works on the history of Mumbai, recollections of colonial police officers, official police histories, little-known books in the genre from my personal collection and the Internet. My work was made somewhat easier when I fortuitously stumbled upon a digitized edition of the life and times of Khan Bahadur Mir Abdul Ali, head of the Detective police, Bombay, which dwelt on some remarkable crimes in the city in the late nineteenth century, the details of which I found in the century-old issues of the *Times of India* in the archives of the Asiatic Society of Mumbai.

My intention, at first, was to produce a book on the most famous (or more correctly, infamous) crimes in Mumbai alone, over the course of about a century, beginning from the 1870s. It was only later, while looking for a publisher, that the idea of a pan-India book took hold. I have thrown in a few stories from all across India, though admittedly the book is still largely Mumbai-centric. I must confess that for want of time, this was done rather randomly. A reviewer of my first book had been peeved that I had not included the famous Elokeshi case from Bengal in that work, and so that had to be added. The Alavandar case from Chennai has always been one of my favourite crime stories, and hence, it made the cut as well. There is another case from Raj-era south India – the murder of an English schoolmaster by his Indian pupils – where the perpetrators were never brought to book. I did, however, make a departure from individual crimes with my retelling of the life and times of Jambulingam, a Robin Hood-like desperado whose depredations in the Tirunelveli district in the 1920s made him a household name in south India. Much like Veerappan's escapades in our time, Jambulingam's exploits are the stuff of legend and remain a part of local Tamil Nadu folklore even today, the way Sultana Daku's do, in the north. Jambulingam's story, I felt, was no less interesting and deserved to be shared with a wider audience.

Some of the stories included in this book, such as that of the notorious serial killer Raman Raghav and the Nanavati case (both done to death – to use a bad pun), could not be avoided as they're simply too popular to leave out of a work of this nature. For my timeframe, I took the 1970s as my cut-off point, given that accounts of the famous crimes beyond that decade are now easily accessible on the Internet. The Swami Shraddhananda case is from much later, though, and I must confess that it was included so as to have at least one story from my current home, Bengaluru. I also felt that Shraddhananda's story, with its elements of the bizarre and the brutal, would stand on its own in this fairly blood-soaked work. Also, as it happens, the swami is the only one among all the criminals mentioned in this book who is still alive.

I have concluded the book with a whodunnit – the Rajabai Clock Tower case. It is by far my favourite crime story, and one which I spent a great deal of time researching and writing. As I had no access to the actual case papers or court records, my account is based largely on the testimonies of the witnesses that the *Times of India* reported on, at great length, during the course of the trial. The tragedy of the Godrej girls – who fell, jumped or were thrown from the tower – reverberated through British India during the 1890s and was talked about for years after the event. Most recently, the case was also the subject of a fictional account titled *Murder in Old Bombay* by the US-based author, Nev March. The story, which loses nothing through repetition, is certainly worthy of celluloid production. There are other accounts that I would have liked to include, such as the Pagla murder case, involving the notorious criminal Khoka, who terrorized Calcutta in the mid-1930s, but time constraints, as well as the difficulty of researching obscure crimes (given the paucity of reliable sources) has meant that some otherwise interesting stories had to be left out.

True crime as a genre, both in books and films, is truly captivating. Blood, gore and shoot-outs apart, these stories are, at the end of the day, about our own selves – and the passions and imperfections that often drive us to unspeakable deeds. Almost everyone loves a good crime story, and I hope the few that I have narrated here make every page of this book worth turning.

1

The Bombay House Heist*

It was early in the morning of 10 January 1949, and Jamshedji Pirojsha Surti, an invoice clerk at Tata Group's head office in Bombay, was understandably nervous. With good reason too, for over the next few hours, he would have to ensure the safe transfer of a large amount of cash to the group's textile mill in the suburbs. It was a set routine, but that did not make his task any easier. On the ninth or tenth of each month, a truckload of cash made its way from the group's Bombay House headquarters on Bruce Street (now Homi Mody Street) to the Tata Mills premises at Parel, there to be distributed to the hundreds of textile workers eagerly queuing up for their month's wages. Arriving at the office a little after 6.30 a.m., Surti ran some last-minute checks to

---

* *The Times of India* – 11, 12, 14, 15, 18 January 1949; K.L. Gauba, *Sensational Trials of Crime*, Hind Pocket Books (P) Ltd, Delhi; Vikas Kumar Jha, *The Queen of Indian Pop: The Authorised Biography of Usha Uthup*, translated by Srishti Jha, Penguin Random House India, 2022, pp. 73–77; Mumbai Police, *Urbs Primus in Indis*, Commissioner of Police, Mumbai, 2006; Kulamarva Balakrishna, *A Portrait of Bombay's Underworld*, P.G. Manaktala & Sons Pvt. Ltd, Churchgate, Bombay, 1966.

ensure that everything was in order. As it turned out, he was doubly keen that day to ensure everything went according to plan – one that had been in the works for some months. The trusted Tata employee would rob his employer on that fateful day, pulling off what was up until then one of the most daring heists in the history of the country's commercial capital. Not for him the ethos of his Zoroastrian faith – *Humata, Hukta, Huvarsta* (good thoughts, good words, good deeds) – by which the group's founder Jamsetji Nusserwanji Tata had built his vast empire. Surti would throw it all out of the window that Monday morning.

The routine in the days leading up to pay day at the mills was time-tested and unvarying. The day for payment of wages to the textile mill workers each month was fixed by the Bombay Millowners' Association. In the first week of each month, this date would be made known to the Tatas and other mill owners, who would then make arrangements with their banks to collect the cash for disbursal to their employees. In the case of the Tatas, sometime during the first week of every month, the manager of Tata Mills would inform his bosses at Bombay House about his cash requirement for the month. This usually varied between 4.5 lakh and 5.5 lakh rupees, a princely sum in the late 1940s. The accountants at Bombay House would then prepare two cheques – one to be presented to the Imperial Bank of India (now State Bank of India) for around 10,000 rupees in small change, and the second for a larger amount to make up the balance – around 4.5 lakh rupees in currency notes, which would be drawn from the Reserve Bank of India. The cash, after being collected from the banks by officials from the Tatas' accounts department, would be divided into small bundles for ease of distribution. These would then be put into yellow bags, sealed and locked up in a safe, to be removed only on the day of shipment. The bags would then be placed in steel trunks and delivered by a truck to the mill compound. On 6 June, 9,100 rupees in petty cash was obtained from the Imperial Bank, and 4,75,000 rupees in currency notes of denominations ranging from one rupee to 100 rupees, were received from the Reserve Bank. The cheques had been drawn by J.J. Tata, the chief cashier, and countersigned by B.M. Batliwalla, an assistant secretary. As was customary, the money was put into the yellow bags and locked up in the safe, to be taken out only on the tenth. Surti, who oversaw the whole operation, would be riding in the truck that day to ensure that everything went smoothly. Surprisingly, given the large amount of cash being transferred, there were no security guards in the truck. Bombay was not known for Chicago-style hold-ups and no one seemed to have given the possibility of a robbery much thought.

The truck was outside Bombay House at around 7.40 a.m. Three *hamal*s (labourers), Jyoti, Gangaram and Rajaram, who had arrived in the truck, went into the building with five steel trunks while the two drivers, Maruti and Sajnu, waited outside. The bags of cash were placed in the trunks, which were locked by Surti's assistants, who then handed him the keys. The hamals were then told to take the trunks down and place them in the truck.

The trunks were not too large and each could easily be carried by a single person. When three trunks had been kept in the back of the truck, Rajaram and Jyoti began arranging them while Gangaram went back into the building to get the fourth. It was then that something entirely unprecedented happened. A large black car suddenly came up the narrow street and pulled up a little behind the truck. The Mercury sedan had barely come to a halt when four men, brandishing revolvers, jumped out. A man dressed entirely in black – later identified as Sher Khan – threatened Jyoti with a revolver saying, 'Don't shout or create an alarm, or here is a revolver' or words to that effect. His accomplices, meanwhile, covered the other men standing around. Jyoti got the message and raised his hands. Miya Gul Khan, the Pathan watchman stationed at the entrance to Bombay House, watched in silence as the three trunks were moved into the car.

Maruti, who had decided to lend the hamals a hand, then emerged from the building carrying the fourth trunk. Obviously unaccustomed to having a revolver pointed at his face early in the morning, he panicked and dropped the trunk. To everyone's surprise, the lock on the trunk came off and one of the bags, containing about a lakh of rupees, tumbled out. Sher Khan, who had now grabbed Maruti by the collar, moved fast. Bending down, he quickly scooped up the bag and jumped into the car. His underlings followed suit, the driver hit the accelerator, and the sedan raced down the road towards the Imperial Bank and into the crazy warren of streets beyond. Unobserved by anyone, a man who had been waiting on a bicycle outside the (now defunct) West End Watch Company on the corner of Bruce Street, watching the robbery unfold, slipped away quietly.

The brazen daylight raid, which the press quickly named the 'Bruce Street Dacoity', held the city in thrall. To pull off a fast one on the venerable Tata Group in the heart of India's commercial capital certainly called for audacity of a high order. And it was quite a haul: the dacoits had made away with nearly 3.5 lakh rupees.

Whoever had done it certainly had a lot of guts; they could also be said to have been a little foolhardy, for they could expect the full force of the law to descend on them in short order. And that is exactly what happened. The top bosses at Tata Sons, one suspects, would have been apoplectic. The phones would have rung furiously in Bombay House, and calls to political bigwigs were surely made. Police Commissioner J.S. Bharucha,[1] the first Indian police chief to hold that office and a Parsi to boot, could not have welcomed such a development in the second week of the new year.

Within minutes of the crime, a posse of policemen descended on Bruce Street. The case was entrusted to the Bombay City Criminal Investigation Department (CID) and a team led by Deputy Commissioner George W. Quilter, including Inspector Hansraj Ghaie, Inspector Vaidyanath Sami and Sub-inspector Basil Kane,[2] soon got cracking. Surti, the accounts staff, the watchman and all other witnesses to the robbery were questioned and detailed descriptions of the criminals were taken down. The police suspected that it was an inside job right from the start, and the hamals and two clerks were detained by the Detection Branch of the CID for interrogation. Strangely, nobody seemed to have had the presence of mind to note down the number of the getaway car. But a big car like that was not easily hidden and would eventually be traced. Details of the criminals obtained from the witnesses would be circulated to the local police stations, for beat constables or officers would probably know someone fitting the description. In cases like these where the culprits could not be identified, the police relied largely on their network of informers for leads. Over time, someone would talk. Of the four men involved (plus the driver), at least one was bound to eventually boast about his part in the robbery, and word would be out on the street. It was loose talk that brought many a criminal to book. A slip of the tongue after a peg too many, an attempt to impress a prostitute with an expensive piece of jewellery, or simply the irresistible urge to spend the big fat wads of newly acquired cash – any of these could prompt a nudge to the local head constable or sub-inspector or a call to one of the bigwigs of the Crime Branch. Indeed, for the most part, this was how cases of robbery or dacoity were often solved. A few well-placed blows or the swing of a heavy, brass-shod lathi also helped loosen tongues. Crime detection was not always done the Sherlock Holmes way, with a magnifying glass in hand.

The public always loves a good crime story, and the Bombay-wallah was no different. News of the dacoity was met with shock and awe around the city and one suspects, also with a measure of glee and grudging admiration. It was almost like something out of the movies, the city's other great draw. Surprisingly, the *Times of India* did not think the news merited a place on the front page and only gave it a fairly longish single column on page five with a very tame headline that did not mention the Tata name at all – 'Armed Men's Coup in Bombay'. The report did have all the essential details though, and noted that the booty was the 'largest to be collected in a single coup in Bombay's crime records'.[3] It was also probably the first time since Independence that a dacoity on such a scale had been carried out anywhere in India.

The press could dine on a story like this for a week, and further developments were not long in coming. As the Crime Branch got into its stride, names of likely suspects were whispered and the police soon had their first breakthrough.

The hot tip came in just a day after the robbery: a young man had been seen walking around Crawford Market, trying to exchange a big wad of cash. Ghulam Ahmad, one suspects, was either not aware of the source of the money or was simply a dimwit, doing this just a stone's throw away from the Bombay Police headquarters. He was promptly hauled in and low-value currency notes worth 1,534 rupees were found in his pockets. Ahmad was quick to sing, though. The money had been given to him by his uncle Said Khan, a taxi driver living in Marwari Chawl.

A raid on Khan's residence turned up 13,106 rupees in cash, a huge sum to be found with a humble taxi driver in those days! The money had been tucked into a leather belt, and included five bundles of one-rupee notes, all unopened and fresh from the bank. The serial numbers on the notes were found to tally with those issued by the Reserve Bank of India on 6 January and were clearly part of the Bombay House loot. Khan was a tough customer, however, and insisted that he'd saved up the money after years of taxi-driving. And try as they might, the police could not budge the thirty-year-old Pathan from his stand.

Following another tip, a second taxi driver, Lawrence 'Larry' Pinto, said to be one of the principal organizers of the robbery, was also picked up for questioning. Miya Gul

Khan, the watchman at Bombay House, and five employees of the Tata Mills were also remanded in police custody a day after the crime on suspicion of having facilitated the hold-up.

The plot began to unravel as the suspects were interrogated. Larry Pinto, who had planned the raid for over a couple of months, made a startling disclosure: Jamshed Surti had a role in the crime. While the cops were almost certain that the culprits could not have pulled off the raid at Bombay House without inside information, the direct involvement of their own staff was bound to have come as an unpleasant surprise to the Tatas. The conglomerate had always been known for regarding every one of its employees as a member of the larger Tata family and this betrayal by a fellow Parsi would have come as a big shock. Surti was formally arrested two days after the dacoity.

Some more of the looted cash was found that Friday. Acting on a tip-off, a team of officers led by Deputy Commissioner Quilter raided a building in Colaba and nearly 40,000 rupees was recovered from the premises. While the police did not reveal where exactly the money was found for fear it would jeopardize the investigation, they were now quite certain they were on the 'right track', the *Times of India* reported.[4]

The investigation threw up yet another stunner. The Mercury sedan used in the heist belonged to Justice S.K. Tendolkar of the Bombay High Court and had been provided by his driver John, a friend of Larry Pinto's. John, who had been promised and received 4,000 rupees for the use of His Lordship's car in the heist, could not have been particularly bright. There are surely not many quicker ways of cooling one's heels behind bars than committing a dacoity using a

High Court judge's car – particularly one so large and likely to attract attention. Maybe the crooks – who, while daring, turned out to be quite amateurish – just wanted to make a grand entrance!

Another Parsi was also found to be involved in the plot. Cawas Irani, who ran a transport business, had been deputed to wait at the corner of Bruce Street on his bicycle and warn of approaching danger with a wave of his hand. He got 30,000 rupees for his role in the dacoity, but had expected more. As this was not forthcoming, he bore a grudge against his fellow conspirators and later turned approver.

The alleged ringleader of the plot and the main accused in the case was a Pathan by the name of Sher Mohammad Khan (alias Sher Dil). A man of great nerve and undoubtedly bold, Sher Khan was a reckless desperado who had served several spells in jail for a string of criminal offences. He was said to have taken more than one lakh rupees for himself from the Bombay House loot and had immediately absconded to Pakistan but was soon extradited to stand trial in India. Meher Gul, who was said to be a roommate of Said Khan's, also managed to get away to Pakistan with a substantial sum.

Finally, following a prolonged investigation and several more arrests, the case came up for trial in the sessions court, with a special jury being sworn in. Four of the accused – Sher Mohammad Khan, Lawrence Pinto, Rustom Dhanjishah and Shamshul Rehman – were found guilty in the main dacoity case and received stiff terms of imprisonment. Kawas Irani, the disgruntled cyclist who ratted on his friends in return for a pardon, walked out a free man.

Jamshed Surti and some of the other smaller players accused in the case were charged and convicted for abetting the crime and drew relatively minor sentences. There was, however, a sole exception. Said Khan, the taxi driver from whom some of the stolen money was recovered, was not charged with commission of the dacoity or its abetment. Instead, the case against him was in connection with possession of the alleged proceeds of the crime. In his deposition, Sub-inspector Basil Kane, who was the main witness for the prosecution, told the court that Said Khan had pointed out to him, the place at Warden Road where he had received the money from one of the accused. However, Jamshed Surti, while deposing on the details of the dacoity in the courtroom, did not mention anything about Said Khan's role in the plot.

Said Khan, on his part, vehemently disputed the prosecution's charge. He insisted that the money found in his leather belt was part of his savings, accumulated over years of taxi-driving. While he could not give any reasonable or convincing explanation for the five one-rupee bundles that were identified as having come from the Reserve Bank of India, he was advised by his legal team that there was no need to show how the money came into his possession. Indeed, it could be argued that the money had been planted by the police to incriminate him! What worked in Said Khan's favour also was the fact that there was nothing linking the higher-denomination notes found in his possession with the dacoity, as their serial numbers had not been recorded. Said Khan was therefore discharged by Presidency Magistrate K.C. Thakore, but the cash found in his house was impounded.

Said Khan, however, was not satisfied with the verdict and decided to appeal.

Renowned Bombay lawyer K.L. Gauba was retained to argue the matter before the High Court. The appeal was admitted and the two judges on the bench that finally decided the case, Chief Justice M.C. Chagla and Justice P.B. Gajendragadkar, accepted the arguments of the defence. They agreed that while it was proved that the wads of one-rupee notes, part of the 14,640 rupees recovered from the accused and his nephew, were issued by the Reserve Bank of India on 6 January, there was nothing to conclusively establish that those were the very same notes given to the Tatas. They could well have been given to some other customer, the judges observed. The order passed by the presidency magistrate was therefore set aside by their Lordships and the impounded amount of 14,640 rupees was returned to Said Khan.

Sher Khan, the main accused, got into more trouble while the dacoity case was being heard. According to Gauba, the Pathan was being produced before the presidency magistrate on another charge — that of having escaped from his police escort on an earlier occasion. Given his formidable reputation and propensity for violence, Sher Khan had been handcuffed and surrounded by several policemen as he was brought into the courtroom. The handcuffs, however, were no deterrent to the Pathan, and Sher Khan managed to assault Sub-inspector Basil Kane before he was overpowered and dragged away. The next day, when he appeared before Oscar Brown, chief presidency magistrate of Bombay, Sher Khan could hardly walk or speak. The police had beaten him up in the lock-up, he claimed. While this was probably true, Brown was not impressed and added a further six months of imprisonment to Sher Khan's numerous jail terms.

Said Khan, the only accused in the Bruce Street dacoity who evaded punishment, later migrated to Pakistan. A few days before leaving India, he visited Gauba to bid farewell. As the story goes, he was accompanied by another Pathan carrying a tray covered with a silk handkerchief. 'A Pathan never forgets an act of kindness,' Said Khan told Gauba, offering him the tray with sweets for the *begum sahiba* (Gauba's wife). Under the handkerchief were a box of sweets and a few unopened bundles of currency notes. The proceeds of the Bruce Street Dacoity? That was something Gauba could never be certain about.[5]

2

The Alavandar Murder Case*

C. Alavandar was a cad, and an unlucky one at that. Most men (an overwhelming majority, I would suggest) who violate the Tenth Commandment get away with it, with the aggrieved party none the wiser. But Alavandar paid the supreme price for having coveted another man's wife. And to rub it in, the woman he seduced connived in and actively abetted his murder.

Alavandar first met twenty-two-year-old Devaki Menon at Gem & Co.,[1] a once-popular Madras landmark on China Bazar Road, where he was employed. The shop mostly dealt in plastics, with a sideline in fountain pens, and Alavandar's

---

*Maddy, 'The Alavandar Case', *Maddy's Ramblings*, 4 June 2016, https:// maddy06.blogspot.com/2016/06/the-alavandar-case.html, accessed 20 February 2025; T.V. Antony Raj, 'Murder Most Foul: Part 4 – The Trial and the Judgement', *Wordpress*, 19 October 2013, https://vara. wordpress.com/2013/10/19/murder-most-foul-part-4-the-trial/, accessed 20 February 2026; S. Rajagopalan, *Famous Murder Trials*, N.M. Tripathi Pvt. Ltd, Bombay, 1968; S. Muthiah, *Madras Miscellany*, East West Books, 2011; 'Chilling Tales from Old City,' *The New Indian Express*, 16 May 2012, https://www.newindianexpress.com/cities/chennai/2009/aug/24/chilling-tales-from-old-city-80014.html, accessed 20 February 2026.

professional standing was admittedly not one to impress the opposite sex. However, it enabled him to befriend a number of young women he would otherwise not have had access to. The ex-serviceman was a natty dresser and though not tall (at 5'4"), was something of a charmer; and, like all seducers, an extremely smooth talker.

The affair can be said to have begun sometime in August 1951 when Devaki walked into Gem & Co. one evening to buy a fountain pen. Never one to let his matrimonial vows come in the way of having a good time, and always keen on pretty young things, Alavandar engaged her in conversation. He worked his charm, and soon the Hindi tuition teacher from Adam Sahib Street was a frequent visitor at the store. Alavandar had been about a bit during his two-year stint as a sub-divisional officer with the Military Engineering Services during the Second World War, and he probably had some tall tales to tell. Dates followed, sweet nothings were whispered, and within weeks the forty-three-year-old Lothario had managed to bed the young girl at a hotel in nearby George Town.

Some months later, in May 1952, Devaki (who seems to have been somewhat naïve and impressionable) met and fell in love with P. Prabhakara Menon, a former clerk with Premier Insurance Company. The twenty-four-year-old Menon had good prospects, having been recently appointed, at a monthly salary of 100 rupees, to solicit advertisements for a magazine (*Freedom*) launched by one of his directors. The young couple hit it off and were married within a month, on 6 June.

But Alavandar was destined to come into Devaki's life again. A few months after the marriage, as her husband sought advertisements for his fledgling magazine, Devaki suggested they approach her 'friend' from Gem & Co. An introduction followed, during which Alavandar congratulated Menon on his choice of a wife. There may have been something in Alavandar's tone as he said this, for the compliment made Menon distinctly uncomfortable. The pen-and-plastics seller seemed to have known Devaki a little too well . . .

Though Devaki had stopped seeing Alavandar some months before her marriage, the meeting revived old memories and lusts in the serial philanderer, and he began pursuing her again. Alavandar told Devaki he would place an advertisement in her husband's magazine only if she agreed to spend some time with him. They met again, and on one occasion Alavandar tried to force himself upon her, but Devaki managed to fend him off and get away.

Menon, who had been watching his wife more closely since his introduction to Alavandar, had been growing uneasy. The green monster had entrenched itself in his mind. Finally, he decided to have it out with her one day. How well had she in fact known Alavandar, he demanded to know. Had she had an affair with him before their marriage? He'd had his own share of affairs, he said, but he had to know. Devaki, playing it safe, denied having anything to do with Alavandar. She had known him casually since she'd often visited his store and she insisted that was all there was.

But this did not put Menon's mind to rest, and he kept after her. Finally, after a long time, as the couple sat watching a film at the Minerva Talkies one evening, Devaki confessed. It was all in the past, she said, but now Alavandar was chasing her again. Unable to stomach the tale of his wife's dalliance, a furious Menon choked down his anger and stalked out of the theatre.

His rage had not abated by nightfall and his thoughts now turned to revenge. Was that scumbag harassing her again? Well, he'd fix him good and proper.

One does not know if Devaki willingly went along with what was to come next, but she eventually agreed to get Alavandar to their house one day. The couple, who had been staying at her father's house after the marriage, had by now shifted to new premises at Cemetery Road – an ominous name, one might add, in light of what was to follow.

A few days later, around noon on 28 August, Devaki was seen at Gem & Co., talking to Alavandar. She left in a few minutes, followed shortly by Alavandar. The not-so-model father of three young kids was never seen alive again.

But Alavandar was missed. When he failed to make it home that night, his wife was alarmed and made enquiries. The next day, Alavandar's friend M.C. Cunnan, one of the partners of Gem & Co., landed up at Devaki's door (he must have been up to date on his philandering buddy's conquests) to inquire about Alavandar. She admitted meeting him the previous afternoon, but said she had not seen him since. S. Venkatarangam, the other partner at Gem & Co., also enquired about the missing employee, whom he'd seen the previous afternoon talking to Devaki. Alavandar had agreed to meet him and Cunnan at the Chamber of Commerce for some election-related work that morning, and his absence was puzzling. Later that day, with Alavandar failing to turn up anywhere, a 'missing' report was filed at the Law College police station.

While the hunt for Alavandar was underway at Madras, a remarkable incident occurred some 300 miles south at Manamadurai when the Indo-Ceylon Express[2] pulled in at 11.45 a.m. on 29 August. At the insistence of some passengers, the travelling ticket examiner, J. Alexander Fleury, called the guard to pull out a green steel trunk from under the seat of a third-class compartment. A foul smell was emanating from it and there were little pools of what looked like blood around. The railway police were summoned, the carriage was detached from the train and, with a sub-inspector in attendance, the lock on the box was forced open. Inside, and presumably to no one's surprise, was a corpse, but minus the head. The limbs had been severed and packed in with the man's bloody torso. There were no unique identification marks on the victim, who had been circumcised and so was thought to be a Muslim. The trunk, the police surmised, had in all probability been placed in the compartment at the train's point of departure at Egmore itself. A report was duly filed, the post-mortem was conducted and the body buried in Manamadurai. However, the vertebra connecting the head to the torso was retained, in case the head turned up elsewhere.

The head, or what was left of it, was not long in coming. A couple of days later, on 1 September, it surfaced on the Royapuram beach near Bower Kuppam, incidentally while a police party was scouring the area for any signs of hasty burials on the beach. Crime Branch Head Constable N.C. Jayarama Aiyar saw the head being washed in with the tide and quickly took possession of this vital piece of partly decomposed evidence. Alavandar's relatives were shown the head, but could not be certain it was his. The police, however, had some joy as Cunnan positively identified what was left of the head as Alavandar's by the two punctures on the left earlobe and a tooth which overrode another on the right side of the upper row. What, after all, one might ask, are friends for?

Cunnan, good friend that he was, had not paused the search for his missing chum. He had landed up again at Devaki's door on the morning of 30 August but found it locked and was told the couple had gone away. He then visited her father, a retired Permanent Way inspector with the Southern Railway, at Adam Sahib Street a little distance away, only to be told that the couple were not there either. Not satisfied, he went to see the deputy commissioner of police (Crime Branch) and voiced his suspicions about the couple. He was certain they were somehow involved in Alavandar's disappearance. Now that Alavandar's head had been identified, the headless corpse found on the train at Manamadurai was recalled. A special officer of the Crime Branch was sent to bring back the body and the steel trunk. The corpse being already buried, special permission was obtained to exhume it and get it back to Madras. The Tanjore Railway Police, who were conducting their own investigation into the Case of the Headless Corpse, sent Inspector Ratnaswamy to Madras to ascertain whether the head and the body belonged to the same individual.

Alavandar's wife was called to identify her naughty spouse's gruesome remains. His waist thread, circumcised penis and green socks confirmed that he was indeed her missing husband. The stomach analysis of the corpse revealed the presence of opium – to which, along with the circumcised penis, the press attributed the victim's heightened sexual prowess.

The Madras City police were now moving fast. Menon's servant, thirteen-year-old K.T. Narayanan, was questioned. The boy identified the trunk as the same one that his master had removed from the house on 28 August. Karthavarayan, the rickshaw-puller hired by Menon in Egmore to carry the trunk that evening, was located and his statement taken. To carry the trunk in and place it in the railway carriage, it was later revealed, Menon had hired a porter, paying him five rupees. Another rickshaw-puller, Arumugam, stated that he had been waiting at the junction of Cemetery Road and Adam Sahib Street on the afternoon of 28 August when a gentleman carrying a bundle had engaged him around 4 p.m. to drop him at the seashore near Bower Kuppam. Later, he had seen the same man coming back, but now empty-handed.

Devaki's father was questioned and he revealed that the couple had suddenly decided to move to Bombay as Menon had apparently landed a good job there. On the morning of 29 August, they had left their furniture and some personal items at the home of her brother, a surgeon at Stanley Hospital, and had departed immediately, ostensibly for Bombay.

The police also got in touch with Menon's employer, one of the directors of Premier Insurance, who told them that the couple had approached him in Mysore on 30 August. Menon had asked for some money as they were going to attend a wedding in Bombay. Menon had also met *Freedom* editor N. Somashekhar in Mysore on the same day and had told him that he was leaving for Bombay where he had secured a good job.

While the investigation continued, an essential legal proceeding, the inquest on the severed head of a man, 'mutilated and decomposed beyond recognition', was held by Inspector A. Ramanatha Aiyar of the Crime Branch on 7 September. The *panch* witnesses, after hearing the evidence and examining the head, returned a unanimous verdict that 'death was caused by violence' and expressed the opinion that 'from the presence of two punctures on the right ear lobe and one on the left, and a slightly twisted tooth in the upper row, the severed head was that of Mr Alavandar, reported missing'.

Twelve witnesses were examined in all, including M. Loganathan of Pudumanikuppam, Royapuram, who deposed to having seen a severed head washed ashore at Bower Kuppam on 1 September and to the fact that the police removed it to the General Hospital mortuary for post-mortem examination.[3]

Meanwhile, the birds had flown the coop, but the hunt for Prabhakara Menon and Devaki was on.

It took the police a few days, but the fugitive couple were finally tracked down to Bombay. Menon was arrested on 10 September.[4] They had been staying with one of his relatives, an army officer, and Menon had even managed to find a job with a company in Bombay. To alter his appearance, he had shaved off his moustache before leaving Madras. A search of Devaki's possessions also turned up a watch and pen belonging to Alavandar. Produced before the city presidency magistrate, Menon admitted to the murder but said he had committed it as Alavandar had attempted to seduce his wife and had also threatened him with a knife. He also pleaded that Devaki, who had recently undergone an abortion, should not be sent to Madras unless in the custody of her relatives.

The couple were flown back to Madras and questioned.

The large-bladed weapon (a so-called Malabar knife) that Menon had used to kill Alavandar and dismember his body and thrown away in a park at Broadway, Madras, was also recovered. It had been found by the park attendant, who had gifted it to his mistress! Devaki's *sari*, stained with blood as she helped her husband cut up the corpse and clean up the resulting mess, was also found. The police also got together nearly 50 witnesses to be examined in the case.

A preliminary chargesheet was filed on 24 September and the two accused were produced before the chief presidency magistrate, Egmore. Both were charged with having agreed and conspired, between 25 August and 29 August, to intentionally cause the death of Alavandar, and also cause the disappearance of evidence of the murder with the intention of evading legal punishment.

Evidently uncomfortable with his changed circumstances, Menon requested that he not be handcuffed on the way to court. He also wanted the couple's clothes (presumably retained by the police) to be returned to them, a request the magistrate said should be made to the jail superintendent.[5]

While the police charged Menon on three counts – conspiring to kill Alavandar, committing the murder and trying to destroy evidence of the crime – Devaki was offered a chance to turn approver in return for being charged only with conspiracy and destruction of evidence. The couple discussed this and initially Devaki had agreed, but during the hearing at the magistrate's court, she changed her mind and refused to testify.[6]

This turnaround by the spirited young wife created a sensation, for she could potentially go the gallows if convicted, and heightened public interest in the case had already stirred up the good citizens of Madras, most of whom were solidly behind the couple. Alavandar, most people felt, had only got what had been coming to him for a long time. Interest in the trial was not confined to Madras alone. Alavandar came from the mercantile Chetti community, and its members from the Tamil diaspora in Malaya and Singapore keenly followed the trail, every stage of which was covered by the correspondent of the *Indian Daily Mail* in Madras.

The spirited Devaki also objected to her confessional statement being read out in court, saying she had been compelled to make it.[7] Her defence counsel pointed out that if the confessional statement was published, especially in a jury case, it would create havoc. The magistrate then said that he would appeal to the press not to publish it.

Prabhakara Menon could not sit quietly either. He briefly went on a hunger strike[8] in mid-November, saying he had been ill-treated in jail. He had been kept handcuffed and was not allowed to meet his wife and relatives, he claimed. Devaki had therefore been produced in court alone. The magistrate then asked counsel for the defence to file a formal complaint regarding this, and adjourned the hearing.

When the case came to trial at the Madras High Court on 13 March 1953, a large throng of people crowded into the courtroom, delaying the proceedings. On the second day, the press of people in the verandah prevented entry into the courtroom, and the police had to call in additional reserves to keep order. Given the public interest in the case and the sympathy voiced by some for the accused young couple, the prosecution was never going to have an easy time. The public prosecutor was Govind Swaminadhan,[9] son of the distinguished Dr S. Swaminadhan who had argued for one of the defendants in the infamous Newington College murder case of 1919. The Menons' defence was also ably conducted by S. Krishamurthy and B.T. Soundararajan. A.S.P Ayyar,[10] the judge presiding over the trial, was known for having an elevated mind. A stern moralist, the former ICS officer had never been popular with the British, who had denied him a promotion in his younger days. The fact that he was also from Malabar (as was the accused) cast some doubts on his leanings, but to all who knew him well there was never any doubt about his integrity.

It was difficult to say with absolute certainty what had actually transpired in the house at Cemetery Street on the afternoon of 28 August. According to the prosecution, Menon was waiting in the bedroom when Alavandar entered the house, decoyed by Devaki. The eager Casanova was just getting down to business trying to undress Devaki when Menon sprang upon him, knife in hand (obtained earlier that day, when he also skipped work, so he probably meant to do him in). As the two men grappled, Menon was bitten on his finger and Alavandar received fatal stab wounds on his belly. The couple then hacked up the body (not an easy task by any means) and Menon then disposed of the head at the Royapuram beach. He came back home by 5.30 p.m., having purchased a green steel trunk. The torso and severed limbs were packed in the trunk and Menon then hired a rickshaw to take it to Egmore, where he left it on the 8.30 p.m. Indo-Ceylon Express. The couple also cleaned up the bloody floor with Lux soap to snuff out the smell of blood. The crime had been premeditated; it was a well-thought-out plan.

According to the couple's statement, Alavandar had followed Devaki home after she left his store and attempted to molest her after she let him into the house. Menon arrived just then and knocked on the door, which was opened by Alavandar. The two men exchanged words and then got into a fight. Alavandar was stabbed by his own hand as the two men fell to the floor. It was not a premeditated attack; Menon was only defending his wife's honour after the rogue had tried to assault her.

The prosecution's attempts to get Devaki to turn approver in return for a pardon also did not succeed. She stood by her man. The defence, for its part, tried hard to blacken Alavandar's character (which did not really need much doing), but it was obvious what had really taken place inside the Menon's residence that fateful afternoon. Whatever the provocation, the couple were undoubtedly guilty of culpable homicide and it was hard to believe that Menon at least, had not intended to finish off his wife's former lover.

At the lengthy trial that included a long parade of witnesses and exhibits (including Alavandar's skull), the defence sought the death penalty for Menon. Justice Ayyar then summed up the case for the jury, for it was important to take in all the relevant evidence and circumstances of the case before deciding whether the accused could be convicted of culpable homicide not amounting to murder (if the jury felt the murder had not been planned or intended), or if in fact, the killing had been premeditated. He accepted the grave and sudden provocation theory put forward by the defence, and his sympathies were clearly with the accused, for in his opinion Alavandar was a scoundrel who deserved his end. The jury of nine, however, was not swayed and brought in a unanimous 'guilty' verdict against both the accused.

On 13 August, Justice Ayyar, accepting the verdict, sentenced Prabhakara Menon to seven years of rigorous imprisonment on a charge of culpable homicide, while Devaki drew a milder prison term of three years. Menon wanted to appeal but was dissuaded from taking that course by his counsel, who convinced him that he had in fact got away lightly. In the event, both husband and wife were released from prison before the expiry of their sentences on grounds of good behaviour.

And what happened to the Menons after their release? They were both in their late twenties when they came out of prison and went back to their native Palakkad (in the newly formed state of Kerala) to start a new life. The couple are said to have started a tea-shop (which, it is said, prospered and expanded into a big hotel) and lived happily ever after. It was also said that the couple had, in their *puja* room, a framed photograph of Justice Ayyar, along with pictures of other deities.

3

The Dadar Triple Murder*

The evening of 18 October 1888 was one of frenzied activity on Lady Jamshedji Road in lower Mahim, not too far from Bombay's bustling Dadar railway station. As a gaggle of bystanders watched, a posse of policemen descended on a bungalow, occupied by a Parsi widow and her large family. Rattanbai, as the woman was known, had been brutally done to death along with her daughter and grandson. It was, to quote the *Times of India*, 'one of the most shocking triple murders within the memory of the oldest living inhabitant of Bombay'.[1]

The fifty-eight-year-old lady had presided over a large household that included her two sons, three daughters and the six-year-old boy. Once fairly well off, the family was known to be in slightly straitened circumstances after the death of

---

*S.M. Edwardes, *The Bombay City Police: A Historical Sketch 1672–1916*, Oxford University Press, 1923; *A Biographical Sketch of Sardar Mir Abdul Ali, Khan Bahadur, Head of the Detective Police, Bombay, with an Account of Interesting Criminal Cases*, Bombay Gazette Steam Printing Works, 1896; *Gazetteer of the Bombay City and Island*, Vol. 2, The Times Press, Bombay, 1909, *The Times of India*, 19, 20, 22, 23 October, 1888.

its patriarch, Framjee Cowasjee Mehta, a bullion-keeper at H.M. Mint. The sons were employed as clerks at business establishments in the city while two of the daughters were teachers at the government Gujarati School in Charni Road. The widow, her twenty-year-old daughter Banoobai, the boy Aspandiar and a newly appointed servant, Rama, were the only occupants of the house that fateful Thursday.

Around 5.30 p.m. that day, Rattanbai Karaka, a friend of the family, called at the bungalow, which stood in a large compound fronted by a grove of palm trees. The front door was open, but as nobody seemed to be there, she went around to the back of the house where there was a small cookhouse or kitchen. Looking through the cookhouse door, which was slightly ajar, she was greeted by a horrible sight. On the floor, lying in a large pool of blood, their heads smashed, were the bodies of her friend and the little boy. The old woman had evidently been preparing the midday meal when she was attacked, as the cooking pots containing meat and rice were still on the fire. Karaka must have been a woman of some nerve, for she then went back to the house to look for Banoobai, who she knew must be somewhere around. A further shock awaited her. In a small sitting room in the front part of the house was the body of the young woman, her skull battered to a pulp.[2]

Rushing out of the house, she made her way to the Dadar Distillery nearby to summon help. Nusserwanji Desai, an *abkari* (excise) inspector, and two of his colleagues immediately accompanied her to the house. The victims being very obviously beyond all help, the police were called.

By the time Deputy Commissioner H.G. Gell arrived,

the neighbourhood was in an uproar and the compound was besieged by a mob of agitated spectators, mostly Parsis. A triple murder was not an everyday occurrence in late nineteenth-century Bombay, though the city did have its fair share of violent crime. The Bombay City police were always kept on their toes by the lawless elements of the country's premier metropolis.

The *Times of India*, reporting on the 'Horrible Triple Murder at Dadar' the next day, devoted an entire column running the length of a page to the crime. Incidentally, the same page also carried a little report that said Police Commissioner Colonel W.H. Wilson had left the city for the salubrious environs of Mahabaleshwar the previous afternoon, having obtained a month and five days of privilege leave.

Wilson had taken over the reins of the city police from the legendary Sir Frank Souter only a few months ago. His five-year tenure was beset with the same problem faced by his illustrious predecessor – a chronic lack of manpower. The city police force then numbered 1,621 officers and men – certainly not enough for a population of 8,80,000. Detection and prevention of crime was not easy under the circumstances and many cases of house-breaking were recorded in 1888.[3]

The commissioner had chosen an inopportune moment to be away from the city. But he needn't have worried much, for the investigation was in safe hands. Khan Bahadur Mir Abdul Ali, the head of the city's Detective Branch, had an impeccable track record. The son of an equally famous policeman, Abdul Ali had joined the city police in 1865, rising through the ranks to become an inspector and later the head of the detective force. Highly regarded by his superiors, he had been awarded the title of Khan Bahadur in 1873 on the recommendation of Sir Frank Souter.

While it was obvious to the police that robbery was the main motive (the house had been thoroughly ransacked), it was the appalling brutality of the crime that set it apart from other homicides. The widow's head had been severely fractured by repeated blows from a very heavy object. The wounds on the boy's head were similar and 'judging from the agonized expression on the poor little fellow's face, it is evident that he died an extremely hard death', the *Times* reported.

Curiously, someone seemed to have moved the boy's corpse. 'When found, he was lying with his face on the ground, but before the police arrived his position had been changed, and when our reporter saw him, he was on his back with one of his tiny arms across his breast and the other hanging stiff by his side,' the paper said. The boy could well have been in his death throes when the crime was discovered, for he had been 'weltering in his own gore'. The abkari inspectors, in an attempt to help, may have turned the body on its back, but this is entirely a matter of conjecture.[4]

The report also said Rattanbai Karaka had seen all the three bodies before calling for help, but at the coroner's inquiry the next day, the abkari inspector said the lady said she had seen two bodies severely hurt in a house in lower Mahim. So, while it is not clear from the newspaper reports whether the victims were actually dead when found, it's quite unlikely that they were alive given the violence of the blows inflicted on them. Dr Sidney Smith, the coroner's surgeon, was certain that all three victims had died very quickly. The coroner's report on the numerous injuries inflicted on the victims makes for very disturbing reading. All three victims had been killed by blows from a heavy, blunt instrument wielded by someone with great strength and their skulls had been completely smashed. Inspector E.H. Grennan, who arrived at the scene within minutes of the crime being reported, found a heavy wooden pestle (used for pounding spices) and a pickaxe, both stained with blood, outside the cookhouse. An inquest was held the next day, after which the bodies were handed over to the family. The last rites, held at the Towers of Silence, were attended by a large congregation from the Parsi community.[5]

The servant Rama, now nowhere to be found, was naturally the prime suspect. However, the possibility that a gang of robbers was involved could not entirely be ruled out. To all those who visited the scene of the crime, it was simply inconceivable that one man alone had killed all three members of the house and, instead of making a quick getaway, had gone about smashing every single cupboard and trunk in the house. He would have been at it for an hour at least! The rooms on both the lower and upper floors had been littered with clothes, empty boxes and papers. A large teakwood chest with an enormous Chubb lock had its top smashed to splinters and a wardrobe was completely wrecked, its contents scattered on the floor. Almost every article of value had been taken away, including gold bangles, diamond earrings and brooches, saris embroidered with silk and gold, besides several other items of apparel. Also missing were silver dishes, a set of silver spoons and table knives, a silver tea set and vases, incense burners, copper kitchen tongs and a pair of spectacles. According to the *Times*, 'the hand of a most determined housebreaker was to be traced in every apartment.[6] Altogether, property worth about 2,020 rupees had been stolen.

Carrying away so much booty would not have been easy, and the murderer was quite likely to have had one or more accomplices. The crime in itself was a daring act as the bungalow was not situated in an isolated spot but was only a few yards away from the main road. Also, in the compound in which it stood was another house, separated from it only by a very low wall. There was also a hut occupied by workmen along the wall, and behind the house were some huts or sheds occupied by some dyers. That three people could be murdered in fairly inhabited surroundings without an alarm being raised or any suspicion being aroused, was in itself astonishing. The local police station (not necessarily a deterrent) was not too far away either. Was this a well-planned and premeditated affair or did the missing servant (or someone else) commit this dastardly crime on a sudden impulse? No answers were immediately forthcoming.

Rama had begun working with the family just a few weeks prior, the Mehtas told the police. A young man, around eighteen years old, had arrived at their doorstep, seeking a job. Introducing himself as a *mali* (gardener) he claimed to have worked for the Wadia family in Mazgaon, where he said he now resided. Rattanbai had agreed to employ him as a house servant for four rupees a month, his working hours being 6 a.m. to 6 p.m. He gave his name as Krishna Lakshman, but said he was called Rama. He had not given the family any real cause for concern while he was with them, but they now recalled a couple of events that should have set off alarm bells. Some days ago, Rama had moved a heavy box containing valuables from a room without being asked to. On being questioned, he said he had shifted it while cleaning the room. That seemed plausible, so they had let it pass. But more ominously, he had once questioned Aspandiar as to where his grandmother kept her valuables. The boy, who had not taken to Rama at all, had told Rattanbai about this but the widow did not make much of it, only asking the boy to keep an eye on the servant. The old lady must have been quite naïve or a very gullible soul to have kept Rama on after this![7]

If it was indeed the servant who had done the deed (as seemed most likely), he probably had a few accomplices, the police reasoned. As the killings had occurred before noon (the midday meal had not been taken), the murderer or murderers had had a good few hours to decamp with their loot and could have even left the city by now. Another theory being floated was that the killings occurred while the servant was away on an errand, and Rama, on discovering the bodies, had panicked and run away, fearing he would be arrested for the crime.

All this was very much within the realm of possibility. Bombay was also home to a large floating population, including vagrants and men from so-called 'criminal tribes' who had no fixed abode. The latter were a nuisance, and hard to pin down – moving as they did from one city to another, committing petty thefts and burglaries. But some of them would also resort to violence when confronted or if they were disturbed while committing a crime. Had any of these men been keeping a watch on the house, and upon finding it occupied by only two women and a child on that day, decided to rob the house? There were no easy answers to these questions.

Meanwhile, the absconding servant had to be found. The men in the nearby huts and the dyers were questioned, but no one seemed to know anything about the missing Rama, which was obviously an alias. The sole clue or lead he left behind was the reference to the Wadia family at Mazgaon. Losing no time, Acting Superintendent G.H. Cobb was at the Wadia residence within hours of the murder coming to light. Here he found that the family did have a servant by the name of Rama. The man was however, unaware that his name had been used by the Mehtas' househelp to seek employment. He had absolutely no idea who his namesake was and had never heard of him. Cobb was truly stumped. This was indeed a bummer! But there was nothing to be done about it and the police would have to look elsewhere. Pressure on the authorities to round up the culprit or culprits was intense, and the Bombay government, no doubt anxious to have the case solved at the earliest, announced a reward of 300 rupees to anyone, for information that could help solve the case.

While the investigation seemed to have hit a dead end, Mir Abdul Ali was not quite convinced that the Wadias' servant Rama had been telling the truth and so he was summoned for a further round of questioning. The police may have slapped him around a bit to refresh his memory, for Rama now recalled that he had once mentioned his master's name and place of residence to two brothers he was acquainted with. One of them was named Dhanji and the description by the Mehtas' servant in fact matched that of Dhanji's brother Nanoo Narayan. Nanoo also went by the name of Krishna Lakshman – the alias used by the Mehtas' servant. The Khan Bahadur's hunch had been right and at last the police seemed to be on the right track. Narayan's last known address was at Mount Road in Mazgaon, but he was not to be found there. However, the police had a description of the suspect and a manhunt was launched. Soon, word came from an informer that Nanoo Narayan had been seen entering Dr D. Rozario's bungalow at Mazgaon where his brother was employed. The police were at the bungalow within minutes and the absconding servant was apprehended. The good doctor, shocked to find the police at his door, had no idea that the city's most wanted man had been taking shelter in his premises.

Nanoo Narayan turned out to be a tough cookie. He stoutly denied any involvement in the murder or that he had been employed by the Mehtas. The police did not buy any of this. A quick check of the suspect's clothes showed traces of blood, despite obvious attempts having been made to wash them off. Also, he'd tried to change his appearance by shaving his face and cutting his hair quite short. But Nanoo kept up his act. When confronted with the family of his late mistress at Dadar, he refused to recognize them. The Mehtas, however, immediately identified him as their missing servant.

He was taken to the Byculla police station for further interrogation, but remained adamant. The police eventually wore him down and after several hours of questioning, Narayan finally admitted to having stolen some jewellery from the house. He'd thrown away some of the stuff (which he thought worthless) and had sold the rest to a goldsmith in Mazgaon. This worthy was immediately summoned and revealed that Narayan had pawned five articles of jewellery with him on 18 October, for which he had been given one rupee on account.

A few hours later, realizing that the game was now up, Narayan made a full confession to Deputy Commissioner Gell and admitted to having committed the murders.[8] He did not however seem to feel any sense of guilt or remorse. Willingly and with admirable sang froid, he walked the police over the scene of the crime and 'reconstructed' it for their benefit.

It was around 11 a.m. and he had been cleaning some plates in the house, he said, when he suddenly 'felt determined' to kill the old widow, Banoobai, and the child Aspandiar. Armed with a wooden pestle, he had entered the front sitting room, where Banoobai was sleeping on a large wooden chest, and dealt her a blow on the forehead, which stunned her. Dragging her to the floor, he had then bashed her head in. He then made his way to the cookhouse and killed the widow, who had been peeling potatoes, with a single blow of the pestle. However, just to make sure she was dead, he rained a few more blows at her. Just then, the boy Aspandiar had run into the cookhouse and was killed in the same manner. The family were a little sceptical when informed about Narayan's confession. Banoobai's relatives said she was a well-built lady and would have easily resisted and overpowered the slightly built Narayan had she been awake. She'd complained of a headache earlier and had been lying down. The killer, however, said she had not offered any resistance.

Narayan then went upstairs and started to break open chests and cupboards with a pickaxe, taking away as many valuables as he could lay his hands on. He seemed to have worked himself into a frenzy as he went about ransacking the house. The coroner, Dr Thomas Blaney, had observed during the inquest that, 'from the disordered state of the rooms it appeared as if a maniac or a number of maniacs had been at work'.[9]

While Narayan accepted his guilt, two other witnesses gave statements to the police that were starkly at variance with the servant's confession. A toddy-tapper working in the compound of Rattanbai's house said that between 12 noon and 1 p.m. that Thursday afternoon, he had seen a party of five men entering the house and shutting all the windows of the upper storey while a sixth man remained outside, seemingly keeping a watch, at the gate of the compound. Another witness, a man operating a steamroller on the road outside the compound, said he had heard cries from the house but had ignored them as he thought some children inside were being punished for being naughty. In the face of Narayan's confession however, these claims were dismissed by the police.[10]

In the end, it seemed like such a senseless crime. Narayan could have surely robbed the family without killing three helpless persons. He may have plotted the crime over a long time, and whether his intention was merely to rob the house is not known. It may be that one of the women caught him when he was in the act of stealing and he decided to silence her, and then killed the other two members of the household as well so as to leave no witnesses.

The toddy-tapper's statement too could have an element of truth though. Narayan may have had accomplices but for some reason had decided to take the blame himself. Or the police, failing to get hold of anyone else, had made him the fall guy.

Police inquiries and a perusal of the records revealed Nanoo Narayan to be a singularly cold-blooded criminal.

He'd been earlier held for the murder of a boy for the trifling sum of five rupees but was not convicted. The boy had been knifed and the body thrown into a gutter, in the compound of a cotton mill at Tank Bunder. Narayan was also suspected of stealing a gold watch while working as a *punkha*-boy at the home of Lady David Sassoon, and had also robbed a doctor in whose house he had been employed.

The *Times of India*, which followed every twist and turn of the case, treated its readers to a detailed description of the murderer:

Narayan, who is good looking, is quite a youth, he being barely 20 years of age. He stands about five feet three inches, and although he is of slim build, his limbs are well developed. His complexion is fair, and he wears a slight moustache. His features are a little sharp, his thin lips when closed and his penetrating deep brown eyes denoting a character of considerable determination. Looking at his age and stature, it is hard indeed to believe that he could have committed the crime single-handed, but the manner in which he has confessed his guilt leaves little if any doubt in the mind of the police as to the genuineness of his statement.[11]

For good measure, the *Times* also commended the policemen who cracked the case. Acting Superintendent G.H. Cobb, Inspectors J.P. Dillion, G.S. Briscoe and Erenan, Khan Saheb Mir Abdul Ali and Subedar Roshan Ali were all 'deserving of serving of the warmest praise', it said. 'Every step taken towards discovering the murderer,' the *Times* said, was 'characterized was something more than mere intelligence.

Generous tribute indeed, and something notably lacking in the newspapers of our day.

At his trial in the sessions court, Narayan withdrew his confession but the jury returned a verdict of guilty and he was sentenced to death. During his cross-examination, a member of the victim's family contended that it was impossible for one person to have carried out the crime and carry away so much property. The jury and judge too felt that Narayan was probably assisted by others in the crime. This put the police in an awkward position, as only a fraction of the items looted from the house had been recovered, and questions were asked as to what had happened to the remainder of the missing jewellery. Colonel Wilson, distressed by the insinuations made against the police, asked the Khan Bahadur and Rao Bahadur Daji Gangaji to clear up the matter with Narayan before he was hanged. Mir Abdul Ali, in a final interview with Narayan just two days before his execution, questioned him again about the missing property, but the killer stuck to his story. He had acted alone and the five pieces of jewellery found with the goldsmith were the only items stolen by him. The mystery of the missing jewellery was never satisfactorily explained.

The condemned man also seemed to have undergone a change of heart towards the end of his days. Expressing repentance for what he'd done, Narayan requested Abdul Ali for the services of a brahmin to assist him in prayers before his execution. The next day, offering prayers with the assistance of a priest, he sought forgiveness for the murders of Rattanbai, Banoobai and Aspandiar, and also for killing the boy in Tank Bunder.[12]

On 23 February 1889, Nanoo Narayan, alias Krishna Lakshman, alias Rama, achieved the dubious distinction of being possibly the first man to be hanged for a triple murder in the city of Bombay.

4

The de la Hey Murder[*]

The year was 1919 and autumn had just set in over Madras. The Great War, which had officially ended a year earlier, was slowly receding from memory in the city that had been shelled

---

[*] Edwin P. Hoyt, *The Last Cruise of the Emden,* André Deutsch, London, 1967; 'Painful Tragedy in India', *The Straits Times,* 27 October 1919, p. 11; 'Tragedy in Court of Ward's Institution', *Pinang Gazette and Straits Chronicle,* 28 October 1919, https://eresources.nlb.gov.sg/newspapers/browse/pinangazette, accessed 22 February 2026; 'An extrordinary case', *Pinang Gazette and Straits Chronicle,* 29 October 1919, p. 3, https://eresources.nlb.gov.sg/newspapers/browse/pinangazette, accessed 22 February 2026; 'Tragedy at Madras', *Malaya Tribune,* 3 November 1919, p. 6; 'The Shooting Tragedy: Second Accused as Approver', *Pinang Gazette and Straits Chronicle,* 1 November 1919, p. 8; 'Newington Tragedy', *Pinang Gazette and Straits Chronicle,* 8 November 1919, p. 3; 'De la Hey Murder', *Pinang Gazette and Straits Chronicle,* 16 February 1920, p. 1; 'The De La Hey Murder', *The Singapore Free Press and Mercantile Advertiser* (1884–1942), 5 March 1920; 'De La Hey Murder Case', *The Straits Times,* 3 February 1921, p. 7; 'Mrs de la Hey's Claim: The Newington Murder Recalled', *Pinang Gazette and Straits Chronicle,* 18 April 1922, p. 11; *Andhra Patrika,* 4 February 1920; Lady Pentland, *The Right Honourable John Sinclair,* Methuen & Co Ltd, 1928; P.B. Vachha, *Famous Judges, Lawyers, and Cases of Bombay,* N.M. Tripathi, 1962; *The History of the Madras Police (1859-1959),* Inspector general of Police, B.N.K. Press Pvt. Ltd, 1959; S. Muthiah, *A Madras Miscellany,* East West Books, 2011;

by the German light cruiser SMS Emden in the opening months of the war in 1914.[1] The premier metropolis of south India had made headlines then, being the only one in the country to come under direct German fire. The Emden's shells did nothing worse than setting the Burmah Oil Company's storage tanks ablaze, though three people were killed. But now Madras would make news again – for the unsolved murder of an Englishman, which would roil British India, and for the subsequent trial that was then said to be the most expensive in the country's history.

Around 12.30 a.m. on 16 October, the stillness of the night was shattered by a loud shotgun blast. Dorothy de la Hey, wife of the principal of the Newington School in Teynampet, sleeping in her cot on the second-floor verandah, woke up with a start. She called out to her husband, Clement, who was asleep on another bed nearby, but got no response. There was a whiff of cordite in the air, and then she heard a thud, as if

---

Maddy, 'The De La Hey Case', *Maddy's Ramblings*, 12 March 2022, https://maddy06.blogspot.com/2022/03/the-de-la-hey-case.html; C. Hayavadana Rao, *The Indian Biographical Dictionary*, Creative Media Partners 2015; Aananth Daksnamurthy, 'Zamindar of Singampatti, an LIC agent and last of 'crowned' rulers left in India, dies', *ThePrint*, 26 May 2020, https://theprint.in/india/zamindar-of-singampatti-an-lic-agent-and-last-of-crowned-rulers-left-in-india-dies/429741/, accessed 22 February 2026; 'The Zamins of Tamil Nadu', *Facebook*; https://www.tamildigitallibrary.in/admin/assets/book/TVA_BOK_0015038_History_of_Singampatti_Zamindari.pdf; Jaya Menon, 'Lording over a shrinking fiefdom', *The Times of India*, 4 August 2016, https://timesofindia.indiatimes.com/blogs/tracking-indian-communities/lording-over-a-shrinking-fiefdom/; accessed 22 February 2026. 'Singampatti Group Manjolai Hills', *Crazy Tea Maker Blogs*, 2 July 2017, https://crazyteamakerblog.wordpress.com/2017/07/02/singampatti-group-manjolai-hills/, accessed 22 February 2026.

something heavy had been thrown outside. The mosquito net around her husband's bed had caught fire, and what she saw in the faint light made the woman scream her head off. Clement lay dead in a pool of blood, the left side of his head blown off. Dorothy's cries soon brought some of her husband's students rushing into the room. One of them, it was later alleged, had plugged the tutor with a shotgun at very close range. But no one would ever be convicted of the crime.

The Newington School found itself embroiled in scandal. For an institution that had been founded to improve the moral character of its students, the murder of a tutor by one or more of his wards was an egregious distinction it could have done without.

It had all begun well enough though. The school had been set up by the British government's Court of Wards to educate the sons of the minor princes and *zamindars* of south India (known as *zamins*), and was loosely modelled on the lines of the Rajkumar colleges in the north. It was supposed to function somewhat like an English public school, and the boys would be groomed to be 'gentlemen' and taught all the etiquette and social graces that the British deemed essential for persons of a certain class. Whether this was in any measure achieved is debatable, for many of the Newington wards were later found to be quite an unsavoury lot, with not much in the way of morals to speak of.

Newington, however, had never been short of official patronage. The erstwhile governor of Madras, the progressive and reformist John Sinclair (later Lord Pentland), had taken a benevolent interest in the school's affairs.[2] He made several informal visits to the school, had the boys over at

Government House for tennis, and even organized cricket matches between them and his staff at Chepauk.[3] Always sympathetic to the interests of the landed aristocracy of the Presidency, he visited their homes while on tour and was keen on providing the minor zamins with 'educational facilities suitable to their position and equal, if not better in quality than any they can now obtain anywhere in India'.[4] Pentland hoped to develop Newington along the lines of the elite Rajkumar colleges and had laid the foundation stone for a proposed larger institution in January 1919, only two months before his departure from Madras after a six-year spell there. The rulers of Bobbili, Venkatagiri and Parlakimedi had together donated three lakh rupees for the proposed new school, with the government committing an equal sum. The de la Hey murder, however, scuttled this altruistic venture and the government eventually refunded the amount.

Despite the governor's support, Newington did not draw the cream of the south Indian aristocracy and talented pupils were lacking. Staffed by both European and Indian tutors, the school provided accommodation for its wards in its three-storeyed building (generally referred to as the 'Minor Bungalow', as its up-and-coming pupils were called 'minors').

The principal who would thrust Newington into the limelight – for all the wrong reasons – had been in place for many years. Clement Theodore Radcliffe Oldridge de la Hey had come to India in his early twenties, having graduated from Keble College, Oxford, in 1901. By 1919, he had been a tutor at Newington under the Madras Court of Wards for 15 years. In 1918, during a spell of home leave in England, he married twenty-six-year-old Dorothy Phillips and brought her to Madras. The couple soon became parents to a baby boy, Anthony.

Clement was passionate about cricket and was fond of hunting, shooting and the outdoor life. But he was also a strict disciplinarian. This did not always sit well with his wards, who one assumes were always under his watch. Wealthy heirs to large estates, and accustomed to deference from those around them since early childhood, they could not have relished being ticked off by anyone, let alone an Englishman. Regular classes apart, the wards were taught to hunt and shoot, and play English games like cricket and tennis. Two native teachers, Dharma Rao and Rangaswamy Iyengar, also taught the children languages and science. At the time of Clement's murder, in addition to his family, their maid Harriet and attendant Ponnusamy, nine minor zamins and some of their personal servants were present at Newington.

The minor zamins were addressed not by their given names, but by the estates or principalities they came from. Five of these – Kadambur (aged eighteen), Singampatti (aged sixteen), the Urkad brothers (aged seventeen and twelve) and Talavankottai (aged thirteen) came from the Tinnevelly district. The other four wards were from the Andhra zamins of Chundi (aged nineteen), Berikai (aged eighteen), Saptur (aged eighteen) and Pedamerangi (aged fourteen). Of these, Singampatti was the richest, while the Urkad boys were related to the influential Raja of Ramnad.

The murder put these otherwise little-known boys and their shenanigans in the spotlight. Singampatti and Kadambur, the prime suspects, were arrested. Dorothy, in her deposition, said both had come into the bedroom some minutes after the gunshot was heard, though they were not among the first to arrive. Singampatti had appeared to be frightened while Kadambur had stared blankly at her all the time, his hands firmly clasped behind his back. For good measure, she also added that among his students, Clement had liked Kadambur the least. Tellingly, she recalled having observed a hole in the curtain (she meant the mosquito net) before turning in for the night.[5] Had someone cut out a hole in the net to push in the barrel of a gun?

One of the boys had telephoned the police, and the civil surgeon, Major C.A.F. Hingston, was at the spot in about 10 minutes but could do nothing except certify that the victim was dead when he arrived. C.L. Withinshaw, the deputy commissioner of police, was next on the scene. He immediately went upstairs to the boys' rooms and found a 12-bore shotgun on the outer verandah. On opening the breech, he saw that both chambers were loaded but only the cartridge in the right one had discharged. The inner part of the barrel was fouled with the explosion. Some cartridges were also found in Kadambur's room, but this was not unusual, as the weapons and ammunition were stored in his room on the ground floor. Later, in the morning, a second gun was found in the carriage driveway, both chambers loaded with No. 3 shot, and a few loose cartridges were lying around. These, the defence would later argue, had been planted by the police to validate Dorothy's claim about a thud being heard moments after the gunshot. Samuel Nurse, a gunsmith from Oakes and Co., also rubbished the police's version of events. There was no way, he affirmed, that the gun could have be thrown from a height of some 40-odd feet (the third floor) without suffering any damage. Also, the cartridges, if thrown from that height, would have been scattered all over and not lying around the gun, where they had obviously been placed by someone.

The minors were questioned, and the picture that emerged of the school and the events leading up to the shooting was quite murky. It would muddy the subsequent trial enough to cast doubts on the investigation and on the veracity of the witnesses' claims, finally culminating in a serious miscarriage of justice.

Clement had been running a tight, but not very happy ship. For someone who ought to have set a good example to the students, he was certainly wanting. For one, his opinions seemed to be clouded by racial prejudice, and he evidently looked down on his students and the society they came from. He had apparently referred to the Ramnad ruler as a 'bloody nigger prince' and had also abused the boys using racial slurs, calling some of them 'Tamil barbarians'. Clement had also written to Kadambur's mother complaining about her son's behaviour.

The master was not popular with Madras officialdom either. Lord Pentland, none too pleased with the complaints he received about Clement's conduct and with some encouragement from the Raja of Ramnad, had drawn up plans to set up another school for the wards. Clement's position was apparently temporary and he was only standing in for his predecessor, Cameron Morrison who had gone to England on home leave. Interestingly, his sister, also named Dorothy, was well-respected by the establishment and had been appointed the first principal of the Madras College for Women (now Queen Mary's College) that had come up in 1914 on Mount

Road, not too far off from Newington.[6] Dorothy said her brother was, 'a very outspoken man. If he disliked a person, he would say so to his face.[7]

While the *dorai* (master) was decidedly unpopular with his wards, the *memsaab* apparently was not. The much younger and dishy Dorothy (Dorrie to the boys) was more approachable and freer with the boys. One of the wards, Urkad Senior, was said to have visited her often, the suggestion being that they had been intimate. The boys, teenagers for the most part, had not been amenable to discipline and got into several scrapes despite their watchful master. One of them was said to have got into trouble over a girl (a grass-cutter) while on a school visit to Ooty and another confessed to petty thievery at the school. Morals had been distinctly lacking at Newington.

The two main suspects in the case were the tall and swarthy Seeni Vellala Siva Subramaniya Pandia Thalaiwar of Kadambur and T.N. Sivasubramania Sankara Teerthapathy, the minor zamin of the fabulously wealthy Singampatti estate, who had joined Newington only seven months before the murder. It was revealed later that there was an unusual link between the two zamins. Kadambur had earlier been proposed as a potential husband for a sister of the Urkad brothers but had turned down the alliance and Singampatti's hand was now being sought for the girl. The Kadambur lad was apparently the only one in the school interested in studies, but his request for a recommendation to study at a school in England had been turned down by Clement. Was this rejection a strong enough motive for murder? Kadambur, like most studious kids, was also probably not very popular among his fellow pupils, as he had complained to the principal about some of them.

Withinshaw, aided by a jury, held an inquest on the morning of the murder to ascertain the facts. The minor zamin of Berikai, the first witness, said that after hearing the shot that fateful night, he had seen Kadambur and Singampatti come running up to the third floor. Kadambur had a gun in his hand and Singampatti was behind him, but was not carrying a gun. The minor zamin of Talavankottai said the plot to kill Clement had been hatched in the billiards room on the evening of 15 October by Kadambur and Singampatti. Kadambur said that he had made up his mind to shoot de la Hey – he'd had enough of the dorai's insults. Talavankottai claimed to have seen both the accused later that night, cleaning the double-barrelled shotguns and examining the cartridges. He had told both Chundi and Berikai about this, but none of them (including Urkad Junior, who was also present) could muster the courage to inform the principal, as they were afraid of Kadambur's wrath. Withinshaw informed the jury that he was not going to examine Singampatti as he would be made a co-accused in the case, but the jurors might want to hear his story for their own satisfaction. Singampatti told the jury that he had been forced into this nocturnal adventure by Kadambur, who had threatened him. But his statement was not recorded. Both Kadambur and Singampatti were held on a charge of culpable homicide amounting to murder. Major Hingston's statement to the police also weighed against the accused. The surgeon said Berikai had told him that Singampatti and Kadambur were the perpetrators.

For Dewan Bahadur P. Parankusam Naidu,[8] the police commissioner of Madras, the murder could not have come at a worse time. The first Indian to hold the prestigious post, he was also due to retire shortly, after a distinguished career. The de la Hey affair kicked up a storm across the Madras Presidency in the coming months and fingers were pointed at the police for not having done enough to put together a watertight case against the accused.

The case itself did not fall short on sensation: an Englishman with his head blown off, minor princelings and a beautiful woman who probably had had liaisons with the 'natives' was juicy stuff indeed. Not since the Emden shot up the city five years ago had there been such excitement. The press predictably went into a frenzy, with outlandish and smutty theories being bandied about by an incredulous citizenry. Was the attack motivated by racial hatred, or was it an outcome of jealous rage? Were all the boys involved in the plot to finish off de la Hey? There was certainly no love lost between them. Had the principal caught his young wife canoodling with one of the minors? She was known to be a bit of a tease, after all. A harried Dorothy, who could not stand the finger-pointing and poisonous whispers, soon scooted off to England, just weeks after the shooting, along with her sister-in-law. Major Hingston later told the court that she had left the country on his advice as her health had deteriorated to such an extent that she could not possibly stay in India without endangering her life. This was surely an exaggeration. The widow had probably been packed off home to avoid embarrassment if any salacious details about her relations with the boys were revealed during the course of the trial.

Singampatti's loaded father spared no expense to free his son from custody. An English lawyer, T. Richmond, was retained, following which Singampatti turned approver. Testifying before the court on 24 October, the minor zamindar of Singampatti said it was Kadambur who had who shot de la Hey, while he had been forced to go along under duress. Kadambur had threatened to shoot him otherwise. He also added that Kadambur had attempted to kill himself after the deed:

As soon as dorai was shot, I ran away. Kadambur came running behind me. Fearing he was coming to shoot me, I ran fast and came to the place where the minors were sleeping. Kadambur went to the spot where the chamber pots were placed. There Kadambur stood up and pointed the gun, the muzzle, to his chin and pulled the trigger. The gun did not work. There was only the noise of a click.[9]

With Singampatti turning King's Evidence, Kadambur was left to face the music alone. The Kadambur family then brought in Dr S. Swaminadhan, a leading criminal lawyer (a doctorate in law from Harvard) who had practised both in London and Madras, ably seconded by the equally distinguished V.L. Ethiraj[10] to defend their boy.

By now, the case had become the talk of Madras, and passions ran high, fed by the newspapers which launched into a frenzy of mudslinging, innuendo and finger-pointing. This turned out to be a godsend for Kadambur. Swaminadhan, claiming that his client could never receive a fair trial in the highly-charged atmosphere of Madras, petitioned the viceroy, seeking a change in venue. The Governor Lord Willingdon, also weighed in, and so, by mutual consent, it was decided to hold the trial in Bombay. This was an extraordinary step, and the ensuing legal battle pushed the de la Hey murder into the list of historic cases tried at the Bombay High Court.

Interest in the murder spilled over to other British settlements. Across the South China Sea, the Tamil mercantile diaspora avidly followed the twists and turns of the case as the *Straits Times*, *Malaya Tribune*, *Pinang Gazette and Straits Chronicle* kept their readers updated about the events back home.

The case went to trial at the First Criminal Sessions of the Bombay High Court in February 1920. In an unusual proceeding, Chief Justice Sir Norman McLeod decided that he would preside over the trial himself and, in a first, entered the courtroom in sartorial splendour – red gown, knee breeches, silk stockings and pump shoes, topped by a full-bottomed wig. The stage was quite literally set for one of the most spectacular cases ever tried in Bombay.[11]

As the trial went on, it quickly became clear that none of the witnesses could be taken entirely at their word and that there was no real evidence to back up their statements. Talavankottai, testifying for the prosecution, said that the evening before the murder he had seen Singampatti and Kadambur handling the cartridges and taking the guns into the bathroom. The other wards were also aware of the suspects' plans but had done nothing to stop them. The Urkad brothers and Chundi confirmed that the plan was hatched between Singampatti and Kadambur that evening. Singampatti did not deny this but said Kadambur had threatened to shoot him if he did not follow him to the dorai's room. Kadambur had also asked him to be ready to shoot the principal in case he missed, and also to shoot Dorothy or any others who appeared on the scene. They had both run upstairs after Kadambur had fired the shot and lay on their beds until they were later roused and arrested by the police. This last bit at least was patently false as both Dorothy and Berikai had confirmed that Singampatti had come into the room a few minutes after the shot was fired. Berikai testified that Singampatti had thrown his gun down from the third floor, but this claim was demolished by the firearms expert's opinion that the shotgun would have shown some signs of damage had this been the case.[12]

There was more that did not add up – an exchange of letters in Tamil between Kadambur and Singampatti while both had been in jail. Singampatti testified that he had written the letter at the instigation of Kadambur, who had informed him that Swaminadhan and Ethiraj had obtained a letter from minor Chundi saying that while Kadambur and Singampatti had planned the murder, it was minor Berikai who had actually done the shooting! Also, Singampatti Senior had apparently told Kadambur during a visit to the jail to keep his mouth shut and that he would first make his son an approver and then get Kadambur out of jail too!

The defence was led by the eminent R.N.D. Wadia of the Bombay bar. A skilled cross-examiner, he tore the witnesses' testimony to shreds, bringing out their inconsistencies and questioning the veracity of their statements. He also dwelt on the possibility of Urkad's involvement in framing Kadambur who had rejected his sister's hand. Also, the prosecution had been unable to put forward any motive for the murder. While de la Hey had on occasion humiliated the boys, there had been no immediate provocation for one of them to shoot him. And surely, it was a little far-fetched of the prosecution to assume that the boys had nurtured their grievance for months and finally decided to act when they did. The prosecution seemed to have no convincing answer to his vital point. Was the murder something to do with Dorothy's alleged trysts with the minors, in particular Urkad Senior? Wadia also implied that the conspiracy and shooting were planned by Urkad Senior, with Singampatti as the shooter since he was known to be a good shot. Chundi had said he'd seen a tall man with curly hair, purportedly Kadambur, going upstairs with a gun, but that description could apply to Singampatti as well. Wadia also proved that Berikai could not have seen what he did on a dark night as he was not wearing his glasses. He also brought out that most of the witnesses held a grouse against Kadambur for having complained to the principal about their misdeeds.

There was another suggested motive. Could the link between the Urkads and the Raja of Ramnad have something to do with the murder? The Raja's views on Home Rule and his opposition to Clement's appointment as principal of Newington were no secret. Also, de la Hey was known to have used a racial slur against the Raja. Could this antagonism have prompted Urkad Senior to gang up with the accused in a plot against their tutor? There were no clear answers to all these questions.

All this cannot have impressed either judge or jury The minors seemed to be a set of lying scoundrels, and for all one knew the whole bunch could have been in the plot together. The testimony of Singampatti, who was both witness and approver, was tainted and unreliable. Urkad Junior's (the youngest witness, aged twelve) claim that Berikai and Talavankottai had earlier got into trouble with the principal over their conduct with the grass-cutter in Ooty did not show the wards in a favourable light either.

Justice McLeod summed up the case for the jury, advising that they could not find against the accused unless the prosecution presented a complete and satisfactory picture of the crime and the role of the accused. He pointed out that the standard of truthfulness amongst the Newington boys was not very high. Talavankottai's testimony could not be depended upon as he was, according to the other boys, 'the champion liar of the school', implying that the others were liars as well.[13] The jury deliberated for just three minutes, after which the foreman informed the clerk of the court that they had unanimously found the accused not guilty. The verdict met with loud applause in the packed courtroom and was accepted by Justice McLeod, Kadambur walked out a free man.

The English establishment at Madras was outraged by the verdict and the authorities were criticized for bungling the case. However, while there had obviously been a miscarriage of justice, there was nothing to be done about it. To no one's surprise, Newington House, for which Lord Pentland had nurtured great hopes, was closed down shortly after. After all the bad press it received, there could not have been any other outcome.

While Singampatti and Kadambur were acquitted, Dorothy would not let them get away lightly and sued the two minor zamins in the Madras High Court, claiming damages worth 10 lakh rupees. After some legal wrangling, Dorothy's lawyers managed to secure a compensation of two lakh rupees from Singampatti to settle the case. The court also ordered the Kumara Raja of Singampatti to pay Dorothy de la Hey the cost of the suit, including the costs of the two counsel.[14]

The de la Hey case effectively ruined the Singampattis. The prohibitive litigation costs (they apparently paid their lawyer 1 lakh rupees for each appearance in court) ate up most of the family's vaunted wealth. Portions of their estate were leased to the Bombay Burmah Trading Company to meet the expenses of the trial. The family also lost 74,000 acres of land when the zamindari system was abolished in 1950. T.N.S. Murugodass Teerthapathy, crowned as the thirty-first (and last) Raja of Singampatti, took over the family estates when his father (the former minor zamin) died in 1934. Educated briefly in Ceylon, he grew up to be a talented sportsman. A crack shot with a rifle and an excellent fencer, he was also a good rugby and football player and a ballet dancer. Well-regarded and respected for his numerous charitable works, despite his diminished means, he administered what remained of his family's once-vast estates till his death in May 2020. Not one to hold a grudge, he invited de la Hey's descendant, Matt de la Hey to visit him at his palace (a rambling old bungalow) at Singampatti in 2013. The young man later wrote a blog about his visit to Tamil Nadu, including a chapter on the de la Hey murder.

The de la Hey case also had repercussions for Dr S. Swaminadhan, the lawyer who defended Kadambur. Once a part of Madras high society, living in a huge house in Gilchrist Gardens, his family was socially ostracized by the British after the trial. His children had a tough time at their English convents and had to be moved to government schools to complete their education. Swaminadhan's daughter, Lakshmi, moved to Singapore before the outbreak of World War 2, and went on to achieve fame as Captain Lakshmi Sehgal of Subhas Chandra Bose's Indian National Army, while his other daughter, Mrinalini, became a noted dancer and later married Vikram Sarabhai, the pioneer of India's space programme. Swaminadhan's son Govind followed in his father's footsteps, joining the Madras bar. A formidable lawyer who later became advocate general of Tamil Nadu, he was destined to be involved in the notorious Lakshmikanthan and the Alavandar murder trials.

Not much is known about the other zamins, but they all struggled to survive after the enactment of the Zamindari Abolition Act of 1950, which took away all their powers and much of their land. Their way of life had anyway become an anachronism after the British departed India in 1947.

5

The Lloyds Bank Robbery*

Lawrence Cardoso was probably bored as he sat in his taxi outside the Lloyds Bank head office in Bombay on the morning of 20 April 1951. Summoned for a ride to the Reserve Bank of India, he had been asked to wait at Lloyds rear entrance on Bastion Road (now A.K. Nayak Marg). The Reserve Bank's head office was only a little distance away, behind the Horniman Gardens in the Fort area, and Cardoso would have expected to get it done and over with quickly. He'd done this beat earlier as well, as Lloyds invariably hired him to ferry cash to and from the Reserve Bank. There was not much traffic so early in the day, and it would be an easy ride.

It was now nearly 10.45 a.m. Inside the bank, the four men, who were to escort a bag loaded with 12 lakh rupees in cash to the RBI, were ready to move out. They had done

---

*'Ramkishan Mithanlal Sharma vs The State of Bombay', *Indian Kanoon*, 22 October 1954, https://indiankanoon.org/doc/423598/, accessed 22 February 2026; *The Bombay Chronicle*, 21 April 1951; *The Times of India*, 7 October 1952; *The Townsville Daily Bulletin*, 21 April 1951, https://trove nla.gov.au/newspaper/article/63134581, accessed 22 February 2026

this often enough, and the standard operating procedure put in place by Lloyds was always followed on such occasions. The bank regularly sent large amounts of cash to the Reserve Bank whenever the head cashier thought there was a surplus. A day before the money was to be dispatched, the currency notes, tied up in bundles, would be counted and checked by the assistant cashiers, who then put their signatures on the top and bottom notes of each bundle of 100-rupee notes. The cash would always be delivered by a party of four men – a senior official of the bank, two assistant cashiers and a peon. On the day fixed for the delivery, the bundles would be put into a leather bag, which was then attached by a chain to the peon's belt. The escort party would then proceed by taxi to the Reserve Bank to deposit the money.

Lloyds had received a large cash deposit from the Bank of Iran some days earlier and accordingly it was decided to transport the money to the RBI on 20 April. For the official in charge of the consignment, Brightling, the two assistant cashiers, Sarkari and Shiavax Doctor, and the peon Rama Madura, to whose belt the cash-filled bag was attached, it was a big responsibility. Like Cardoso, they too would have hoped for a quick run to the RBI and back. If all went well, they would be back at the office within an hour.

The four men filed out of the rear entrance and moved towards the waiting taxi. There were a quite a few people on the street by this time, including the watchman, Balgopal Kadam and Sarwar Khan, a driver who was seated on the pavement close to the taxi. Presumably, no one paid much attention to the Ford Mercury car parked a few metres away, and so were not in the least prepared for the mayhem that was to unfold in the next few minutes.

Brightling got into the rear seat followed by Rama Madura, while Sarkari went round in front of the taxi and sat next to the driver. Doctor, the second cashier, was about to get into the rear seat when, suddenly, all hell broke loose. The doors of the Ford Mercury opened and five men armed with revolvers rushed towards the cab. Sarkari, in the front passenger seat, heard two loud bangs as a man pulled open the door on the driver's side and pumped a couple of bullets into Lawrence Cardoso at point-blank range. Death was instantaneous as the slugs slammed into Cardoso's chest, and the unfortunate driver's body almost tumbled out of the door head first. The killer, later identified as Anokhelal Ranjit Singh, then ran round the front and got into the seat next to the driver, which was now unoccupied as the terrified Sarkari jumped out and ran down the street. Another man, later identified as Rubidas Radhelal, pulled Cardoso's body out onto the road and got behind the steering wheel. More shots were fired as three other gunmen, Harnarayan Nanakchand, Ramkishan Mithanlal Sharma and Bankelal Devisingh, closed in.

As gunshots and screams rent the air, Brightling, in the rear seat, acted swiftly. He was out of the door in a trice and, dodging the gunmen, ran towards the junction of Bastion and Outram Roads (now Purshottam Thakurdas Marg). Doctor, a little slow to move, or perhaps less agile, took a bullet in the palm of his left hand as Harnarayan fired at him. Amidst all the noise and confusion, only one man held his nerve and attempted to hit back. Raising his baton, Balgopal Kadam rushed at Harnarayan, only to be shot in the face at a few yards' distance. The impact of the bullet knocked the brave watchman off his feet and he toppled over. Rama Madura was also shot at close range in the abdomen, and the leather bag attached to his belt seized. The peon's limp body (for he had fainted) was then hauled out on to the road by Harnarayan and Bankelal. Sarwar Khan, watching all this unfold as he sat on the pavement, moved forward to help Cardoso – who was now lying dead in the street – but was threatened with a revolver by Ramkishan. Wisely, he backed away. Sarwar Khan would later identify Ramkishan as one of the assailants on that day.

The action was not over yet. As the five men piled into the taxi and began to drive away, the quick-thinking and resourceful Brightling made a desperate attempt to stop them. Dragging out a motorcycle parked near the corner of the Parsi Lying-in Hospital a little distance away, he threw it in the path of the oncoming taxi. But Rubidas, formerly a motor driver for the Pan American Airways in Delhi, skillfully managed to get around this obstacle (though he clipped the fender in doing so) and the taxi sped away.

However, Brightling was not done yet. A man who obviously took his job seriously, he rounded up a few Lloyds employees and commandeering a private car parked nearby, drove around for a while hoping to spot the taxi. They had no luck, which was just as well, for the men who had robbed the bank were a desperate lot and would not have hesitated to fire at anyone who got in their way. Brightling then reported the incident to the Esplanade Road police station, but they had already been informed and news of the attack was now being relayed to police outposts across the city. The bank's telephone operator, a Mrs Patterson, who, along with Vida Palmer, a clerk, had witnessed the robbery from the window of the mezzanine floor, had called the police within minutes of the crime.

The police were quick to respond. Senior officials, including Commissioner M.B. Chudasama, and sleuths from the CID, were on the scene within five minutes of the crime, the *Bombay Chronicle* reported. A crowd of over 2,000 people, mostly office-goers and passersby, soon gathered and the police had to cordon off the area. Also, rather belatedly, given what had transpired, armed guards were posted around the bank – surely a case of shutting the stable door after the horse has bolted.[1]

Cardoso's body was moved to an improvised first-aid post at the Parsi Lying-in Hospital, and later moved to the morgue.[2] His licence papers revealed the number of the taxi (BMT 1829), which was flashed across the police wireless network. The three injured men – Doctor, Kadam and Rama Madura, were provided first aid and later taken to the St George Hospital nearby. Kadam, shot in the face at almost point-blank range, was lucky to survive but would be completely blind in his right eye.

The getaway taxi was soon found a few hours later, abandoned just over a kilometre away near the Kashmir Hotel (which still stands, though now in a very dilapidated state) at Dhobi Talao. The front fender had been dented, probably from the collision with the motorcycle, and the bonnet was a little ajar. The leather bag, with the bank's stamp on it, was also found in the taxi.[3]

The Lloyds Bank Dacoity was big news the next day. Minor snatch-and-grab raids did occasionally occur at moneylender and pawnbroker shops across the city, but a bank robbery on this scale was unheard of, and probably a first for Bombay. Given the confusion surrounding the sequence of events that morning, and depending on who their correspondents spoke to, it was not surprising that the newspapers got a few of the details wrong. Some of the evening papers had reported that more than one man received fatal injuries, and that Rama Madura had been bundled into the car by the attackers. This, the *Bombay Chronicle* informed its readers, was incorrect. While the unfortunate taxi-driver had succumbed on the spot, the injured bank staff, including the peon, had been taken to the St George Hospital where their condition was reported to be satisfactory. [4]

News of the robbery was reported even as far away as Australia, where the *Townsville Daily Bulletin* carried a report the next day that was a little exaggerated and not entirely accurate, with the headline: 'Gun Attack in Bank Robbery'

BOMBAY, April 20 – Five gunmen today killed a taxi driver and wounded three workers outside Lloyds' Bank before escaping with 90,000 pounds in the biggest robbery in the city's history. The gunmen sprayed bullets into a crowd of onlookers before driving off in the taxi. Chests containing the money had been loaded into the taxi at the bank's entrance in the main Bombay thoroughfare for transfer to the reserve bank. [5]

For the Bombay City police, this was both a slap in the face and a challenge. Not since the Bombay House dacoity on Bruce Street a couple of years ago had anyone pulled off a heist this big. And this just about 200 yards away from the site of the first one. The culprits at that time had been locals and the police had managed to nab them within days. This time though, it would take longer.

The robbery was clearly well planned and it was believed that the gang had prior information about the cash delivery. The descriptions given by the witnesses were not of much help and, in fact, some of them were not sure of the number of men involved in the attack (a point that was discussed at great length during the trial and the subsequent appeal). Brightling, Vida Palmer, Mrs Patterson and Sarkari thought at least five men had participated in the raid. So did Baburao Raje, a passerby who happened to be on the street when the attack was in progress. But another witness, a Major Casey, differed. The taxi had whizzed past him as he stood on the footpath and before it picked up speed, Casey had noticed four men sitting inside – two in the front and two in the rear seats. A sub-manager of Lloyds Bank had also witnessed the robbery from an upstairs window but could not be certain about the number of attackers.

The Bombay CID quickly got to work, the police informer network was activated and discreet inquiries made. Hotel receptionists, lodging-house proprietors and taxi-drivers were questioned. The police were faced with an uphill task and it was some time before they realized that the dacoity had been carried out not by local goons but by men from outside the city. Slowly, more details emerged. The bank robbers were said to have laid a *chaddar* worth a whopping 10,000 rupees at the Haji Ali Dargah in Worli to seek the blessings of the fifteenth-century Sufi saint whose mortal remains are buried at the shrine. The word on the street was that a couple of men from the gang had come from the notorious Chambal valley, a hotbed of crime in the central Indian state of Madhya Pradesh. That made sense. The ruthless manner in which the attackers had gone about shooting four men without any qualms betrayed a familiarity with violence.

It was not very long before the police knew who they were looking for. Anokhelal, the ringleader, was said to be from Delhi. He had arrived in Bombay by train early in April and was followed by four other men, Harnarayan Nanakchand, Rubidas Radhelal, Ramkishan Mithanlal Sharma and Bankelal Devisingh. They had initially stayed at the Astoria Hotel in Churchgate and then shifted to the Kashmir Hotel at Dhobi Talao a few days before the raid on the bank. All five men had now left the city and were probably hiding out in their native villages along the Uttar Pradesh–Madhya Pradesh border. Getting them back to Bombay would not be easy.

However, descriptions of the men were now available, and the first arrests soon followed. Anokhelal (accused No. 1 in the case) and Harnarayan (accused No. 2) were apprehended in mid-May, within a month of the robbery. The Chambal connection turned out to be true. Part of the loot was found at the house of Anokhelal's wife in the village of Bhagwasi, in the Bhind district of Madhya Pradesh. A steel trunk hidden inside the house was found to contain six large bundles and five smaller ones of 100-rupee notes to the value of 6,47,400 rupees. A tin box containing three revolvers and two tins of live cartridges, buried under the mud floor, were also unearthed. The revolvers by themselves did not constitute valuable evidence, for it could not be proved that the bullets found at the scene of the crime were in fact fired from those very same weapons. The currency notes, however, brought the crime home to the accused as some of them bore the signatures of the assistant cashiers of Lloyds Bank.

Anokhelal, it emerged, was a movie buff and claimed to have produced a Hindi film called *Ek Teri Nishani*. The robbery, he told the police, was inspired by the Hollywood film, *Highway 301*.[6] Anokhelal was also something of a dandy and had in fact gone to the Taj Mahal Hotel at Apollo Bunder for a haircut after conducting a recce of Lloyds Bank a few days prior to the raid. He liked to do things in style. Little wonder then that he thought it fit to arrive at the scene of his desperate venture in a high-end car. But Anokhelal did not hang around after the robbery and left the city that very night for Allahabad, along with Ramkishan, by the Calcutta Mail. Rubidas, accused No. 3, was also arrested, but despite strenuous efforts by the police, Bankelal was never found and Ramkishan was apprehended only nine months after the robbery.

At their trial and during the appeals that followed, Anokhelal, Harnarayan and Ramkishan claimed to have had nothing to do with the dacoity on 20 April. Anokhelal admitted to having visited Bombay, but said he had left the city on the night of 18 April for Allahabad, and Ramkishan claimed to have left a day or so earlier. Both the accused also filed affidavits to that effect at the First Class Magistrate's Court at Allahabad. Harnarayan said he had stayed at the Astoria Hotel at Churchgate with Ramkishan for a few days, but had moved to the Kashmir Hotel in Dhobi Talao on 18 April and stayed there until the night of 20 April, when he left for Delhi. He said he had nothing to do with the robbery and had come to Bombay to make some purchases for his wedding.

Five men were accused in the case and all were charged under Section 397 of the Indian Penal Code with having committed dacoity using deadly weapons and also under Section 396 IPC for the murder of Lawrence Cardoso during the course of the dacoity. Initially, only Anokhelal, Harnarayan and Rubidas were charge-sheeted and committed for trial at the sessions court, followed by Ramkishan, who was arrested at Bareli railway station on 25 December. Rubidas died on 3 August, 1952, and Bankelal Devisingh, the accused No. 5, was never apprehended.

In the end, only Anokhelal, Harnarayan and Ramkishan stood in the dock for the Lloyds Bank Dacoity and the murder of Lawrence Cardoso. The trial took a considerable amount of time, and over 100 witnesses gave evidence before a special jury. The summing-up by the judge took nearly three days and the jury deliberated the matter at length before returning unanimous verdicts of guilty against each of the accused on both charges. On 6 Oct 1952, Sessions Judge J.M. Shelat sentenced all three accused to imprisonment for life. Commending the investigating officer, Inspector Hujur Ahmed Khan and other officers of the Bombay CID for having carried out the investigation with 'considerable amount of efficiency and expedition', the judge also cleared the police officers of all the allegations made against them by accused during the trial.[7]

An appeal was made to the Bombay High Court, but was summarily dismissed on 12 January 1953. The accused had, however, not exhausted their legal resources and obtained special leave for an appeal to the Supreme Court. This was granted, but no relief was forthcoming and the appeal was dismissed by a three-judge bench of the apex court on 22 October 1954.

While the Lloyds Bank Dacoity made headlines in India, another robbery at the bank's office in London captured the world's imagination two decades later. On the night of 11 September 1971, the Lloyds Bank branch on Baker Street was burgled by a gang that tunnelled 40 feet into the banks vault from a shop two doors away. While the exact amount stolen is not known, the gang is thought to have got away with cash and other property valued between 1.25 million and three million pounds. The case also fuelled rumours that the government had put out a so-called 'D Notice' to gag the press as compromising photographs of Princess Margaret were thought to have been taken from one of the safe deposit boxes in the bank's vault. While many of the records relating to the case were released in 2013, some 800 pages of information are still closed and will be available for public viewing only in January 2071. Said to have been inspired by a Sherlock Holmes story, the 'Red-Headed League', the burglary also featured in the Jason Statham thriller, *The Bank Job*.

6

The Kishori Case

John the driver had seen and heard quite a few interesting things in his otherwise dull life as chauffeur to Hamida Banu, a one-time film actress in pre-Independence Bombay. Kishori, as the lady was otherwise known, was a social butterfly, and so John was privy to many juicy secrets whispered in the backseat of her car as he drove her numerous guests around town. Of late, he had been doing double duty, having to ferry one of the memsaab's boyfriends around on a regular basis. And this one was unusual. Dattatreya Sadashiv Nadkarni, a traffic manager with Trans World Airlines, was not the type of man Kishori usually picked up. She generally preferred rich Marwari *seths* with pockets full of cash. Moreover, Nadkarni had once been a police inspector. John had always wondered how someone like Nadkarni, a Maharashtrian brahmin, typical of the middle-class men that Kishori sedulously avoided, could have fallen in love with his scheming mistress. But the deed was done – he had fallen for her – hook, line and sinker. From what he heard from the servants, the love-struck ex-policeman now wanted to marry madam! Indeed, he had been pestering her about this for some time.

The events of the morning of 9 February 1949 would stay for long in the driver's memory – and while interesting to others, it caused him a lot of grief over the coming months. John had just completed his morning ablutions when he was called by one of Kishori's servants to attend to Nadkarni, who had been found lying unconscious in the driveway of Kishori Court, the famous bungalow at Worli that bore his mistress's name. He had run upstairs to get some water to revive the sahib, but was dissuaded from doing so by Kishori madam.

If the driver was a little disconcerted or puzzled by these instructions, he didn't let on. There had certainly been some unusual developments since last night, when a raucous party had been on in full swing on the first floor, where a couple of millionaires from Delhi were being entertained by some dancing girls. He had driven the girls back to their homes a little after midnight, and then had made another trip to drop off madam's sister Razia at her home in Matunga. He had been putting the car back into the garage when someone called out to him. Looking up, he saw a bundle of clothes being thrown down from Kishori's first-floor rooms. Nadkarni then came down the back staircase leading to the garage. Asking the driver to put the clothes in the car, he said he would be going back home when Kishori called out from the upstairs balcony and asked Nadkarni to come back. Mohan Alvarez, one of Kishori's servants, also repeatedly asked him to stay back. Nadkarni then went back up the stairs and Mohan told John that the couple had just had a quarrel. Lovers' tiffs being none of his concern, the driver then went off to sleep in the car.

Sometime later, a disturbed-looking Nadkarni woke him up and said he would like to rest for a while in the car. He then took a ring off his finger and asked John to go and give it to Kishori. An unusual request, by any means, but the driver was probably used to these dramas and went upstairs to do this. Kishori, however, would not accept the ring and told him to take it back. Now another servant, Rampal Chouhan, appeared and cajoled Nadkarni to go back to the house to sleep. The distressed lover complied and went upstairs. John, presumably having had enough excitement for one night, handed over the ring to Rampal. Asking him to return it to Nadkarni, he turned in for the night.

Seeing Nadkarni sprawled senseless on the ground next morning, must have come as a surprise to the driver. Given the events of the previous night, John would have been a bit uneasy as well, but there was not much he could say to his mistress, who suggested that Nadkarni had fallen down the front stairs following an epileptic fit. A whitish fluid was dripping out of the side of Nadkarni's mouth. Had he really suffered a fit? John had no way of knowing, but it was probably best not to pour any water down his throat. By now the servants had gathered around and Nadkarni was carried to a room upstairs and placed on a sofa. Later, he was moved to Kishori's own bedroom and when all attempts to revive him failed, her personal doctor was sent for. He too, could do nothing and Nadkarni was then shifted to St George Hospital. Kishori madam, however, did not deem it necessary to accompany her admirer to the hospital. Instead, Rampal and another servant, Jagdish Kumar Shetti, were dispatched to complete the necessary formalities. Nadkarni's family was also informed.

When Nadkarni's younger brother Shivanand arrived

at the hospital, he found Jagdish and Rampal sitting by the patient. Nadkarni had slipped down the front staircase of the Kishori Court bungalow and hurt himself, they explained. Shivanand found this story a little hard to swallow, particularly after he noticed his brother's ring on one of Jagdish's fingers. Suspecting foul play, he immediately lodged a complaint with the Delisle Road police station, and a case of attempted murder was filed against Kishori and her servants. The local police, however, did not seem to be taking the case seriously enough, and so Shivanand (who probably pulled a few strings, his brother being a former police officer) had it moved to the General Branch of the CID. Meanwhile, Nadkarni had been moved to a private nursing home. He had been unconscious since he had been brought in. But five days later, he regained consciousness and was briefly coherent. Questioned by the CID officers, he shook his head when asked if he had slipped down the staircase. However, when asked if he had been beaten, he nodded in the affirmative and gave the names of Kishori and Mohan. There was not much else to be got out of him as he was not always lucid, and despite all efforts, Nadkarni expired a few days later.

The case was now one of murder. The medical report clearly showed that Nadkarni had been roughly handled, to put it mildly. All the ribs on his left side were fractured and there was evidence of a haematoma in the left temporal region and the left ear of the deceased. While there were not many visible external injuries, the patient had been admitted to the hospital in a very grave condition. According to Dr Vinayak Bhajekar of St George Hospital, the injuries were consistent with those sustained after a severe physical assault or a fall from a height of about 15 to 20 feet. The patient could well have been thrown to the ground from that height, breaking all his ribs. Dr A.V. Baliga, who operated on Nadkarni, said the left half of the body had been paralysed.

By now the suspects had all been arrested for attempted murder under Section 307 of the Indian Penal Code. Jagdish had been arrested on the ninth and Rampal on the eleventh. Mohan Alvarez was picked up while boarding a boat for his native Goa at Ferry Wharf a couple of days later. Meanwhile, Kishori had fled but eventually surrendered before the police on 15 February and was immediately arrested. She, however, secured bail from the High Court but was ordered to stay away from Bombay as the CID felt she would tamper with the witnesses. Kishori then moved to Poona, from where she kept track of things before she and her servants were charged with murder under Section 302 IPC following Nadkarni's death. She again sought bail (and there were several influential people willing to stand bail for her), which the police stoutly challenged as Kishori was the prime accused in the case. Her servants, who had obviously acted on her instructions, were small fry.

If the Kishori case was a headache for the police, it was cause for much titillation and gossip in the upper echelons of Bombay society, where Kishori madam was widely known as a procuress. A minor actress who played two-bit roles in Hindi films in the early 1940s, she had arrived from Lahore as Mumtaz Allahditta, and within six years, had amassed a considerable fortune. While she did not shine on the big screen, her looks and charm won her many admirers who, in the long-honoured tradition of besotted lovers, lavished her with money and diamonds. She was said to have had several bank lockers stuffed with cash and jewellery, and reputedly owned an interest in a cinema hall in Karachi. During much of the 1940s, she held court in the lounge of the Taj Mahal hotel where the good and the great of Bombay congregated for drinks, and much else. Kishori apparently made good conversation, helped in cutting business deals and comforted lonely souls, either with her own charms or those of others – for a price.

Not shy of flaunting her wealth and with no false professions to modesty, she lived in the lavishly appointed Kishori Court. The one-storey Art Deco building fronting the Worli Seaface was a watering hole for high-flyers who were not unduly burdened by morals. Here, Kishori would host parties and soirées where well-heeled men willing to lighten their wallets were treated to wine, women and song. The house had several rooms for entertaining guests. Plush sofas, gleaming chandeliers, and paintings that could not be viewed in respectable company, served to set the mood for an evening of unbridled pleasure. Kishori's own bedroom, to which only a chosen few were admitted, was said to contain a glass cabinet with 500 bottles of the world's most expensive perfume brands. The police were aware of her activities, but her proximity to men in high places allowed her to operate with impunity.

This is not to say that she was always successful in staving off trouble. Some six months before the Nadkarni episode, she had been arrested for aiding and abetting prostitution under the Bombay Prevention of Prostitution Act, 1923, and for possessing more than four bottles of foreign liquor under the

Bombay Abkari Act of 1872. Found guilty in both cases, she was obliged to spend a few months behind bars. However, the brief spell in prison did not serve to chasten her and Kishori was soon back in business again.

The Nadkarni murder was a good opportunity for the police to put Kishori behind bars for a considerable length of time. The case was taken up and investigated very thoroughly by the CID; watched closely and no doubt with some trepidation by those in the upper echelons of Bombay society. One never knew how many skeletons would tumble out of the cupboards in Kishori Court!

The police investigation soon unravelled the details of what had transpired on the night of 8 February. Nadkarni had arrived at the bungalow at around 11 p.m., intending to spend the night there, and sat down in one of the reception rooms on the first floor. The party, which was then in full swing in one of the other rooms, went on well beyond midnight, when Nadkarni (who had downed a few drinks and was probably tired) barged in and called a halt to the celebrations. Two Delhi millionaires at the party, not wanting any trouble, left immediately. Kishori, however, was furious at the way her clients had been treated and insisted that Nadkarni pay off the two dancing girls who had been hired for the night. This he did, giving them 100 rupees each after which they were dropped off at their homes by John.

It was after John's second trip to leave Razia at Matunga that a nasty altercation had broken out between Nadkarni and Kishori. She was still fuming about the abrupt end to her party, and so Nadkarni had gone down to sleep in the car. At some point after Nadkarni had gone back upstairs to sleep in Kishori's room, he had been assaulted by Jagdish and Rampal. The duo then picked him up and flung him from the first-floor balcony onto the ground below – a drop of nearly 15 feet. That could very well account for the broken ribs on the left side. Later in the morning, after Nadkarni had been carried upstairs to Kishori's bedroom, she had instructed all the servants, including John, that in case of a police inquiry, they were to say that Nadkarni had suffered a fit and fallen down the front staircase.

When the case came up for trial at the sessions court, Mohan, who had initially agreed to turn approver in exchange for a pardon, backed out. However, two other witnesses stood their ground and testified against the accused. Malanna, the gardener, and his son Chinnanna, told the court that they had seen Jagdish and Rampal throwing Nadkarni from the first-floor balcony on the north side of Kishori Court. Jagdish had been holding Nadkarni by his neck and Rampal by his legs. Jagdish had also threatened to cut Malanna's throat if he told the police what he had witnessed. The prosecution's case was also backed up by the driver John, who deposed to having been instructed by Kishori to say that Nadkarni had fallen down the stairs after having a fit.

Kishori, who seemed to think no lawyer from the Bombay bar was competent enough to defend her, obtained the services of the renowned Sir Iqbal Ahmad, a former chief justice of the Allahabad High Court. Sir Iqbal did his best, which was not good enough, but he did get the prosecutor B.M. Mistry to concede to the accused a charge of culpable homicide not amounting to murder. Kishori and the other accused thus avoided the more serious capital charge of murder. Kishori,

Jagdish and Rampal were each sentenced to seven years' rigorous imprisonment on a majority verdict (6:3) by the nine-member jury. Mohan Alvarez was acquitted.

The verdict was appealed, and the Bombay High Court on 16 February 1950 ordered a retrial on the grounds that the jury had been misdirected. This time the defence managed to obtain a split verdict in Kishori's favour from the seven-member jury. However, the presiding judge held this to be no verdict under the law and directed that a second retrial be held, subject to the approval of the local government.

A third trial was therefore held, involving detailed and prolonged cross-examination of all the prosecution witnesses. According, to K.L. Gauba, who was briefly involved in the appeals process, Kishori wept on the shoulders of her junior counsel A.L. Agarwal, but her tears did not move either the judge or the jury. Given her colourful background and previous convictions, it is not surprising that the verdict went against her. All three accused were held guilty as charged, and sentenced to five years of rigorous imprisonment.[1]

Gauba, for his part, thought the prosecution's case was very weak and that the defence, which involved several changes of counsel, had not been very well conducted. It was simply a case of too many cooks spoiling the broth. He also made a valid point: that it would have been physically impossible for two men to lift and throw a fully grown man from a balcony with a railing three-and-a-half feet high so that the body fell clear of the two-and-a-half-foot parapet running below. This was a point the defence lawyers had not sufficiently stressed upon. One of the judges who heard the appeals, and to whom Gauba later mentioned this, seemed to agree and said that had the defence emphasized this point, they might well have secured an acquittal.[2]

The sessions verdict was appealed, but was upheld by the Bombay High Court on 19 June, 1951. Kishori then filed an appeal with the Supreme Court under Article 136 of the Constitution, but this too was dismissed in February 1953.

As befitting a case involving a former actress, the trial and the subsequent retrials (in themselves unusual proceedings) provided much drama and were closely followed in Bombay and also by Indian audiences elsewhere.[3]

Kishori, having exhausted all her legal resources, served out her sentence in Pune's Yervada Central Jail, and migrated to Pakistan after being released. The by-now-infamous Kishori Court was then taken over by the government and held by the Custodian of Enemy Property before being auctioned off. The building still stands on Worli Seaface.[4]

7

The Temple View Murders*

Hughes Road is a well-known thoroughfare in south Bombay, inhabited by the more prosperous gentry of the city. Linking Kemps Corner to the famous Royal Opera House near Chowpatty, the road cuts through an upmarket neighbourhood that still houses some fine old colonial-era mansions and apartments. It was here in late October 1967 that a little-known building called Temple View found notoriety as the site of the famous Chunawala murders.

The Chunawalas were a prosperous family from the city's mercantile Bohra community. Sixty-year-old Mohammed Siddique Chunawala owned an automobile parts business called Car Mart, located only a little distance away from his residence at Temple View, a two-storeyed structure standing

---

* *The Times of India*, 24–26 October 1967; *Benedict Costa, Bombay – The Twilight Zone*, Hind Pocket Books, Delhi, 1972, pp. 58–60; Samuel T. Sheppard, *Bombay Place Names and Street Names*, The Times Press, Bombay, 1917; Mumbai Police, *Urbs Primus in Indis*, Commissioner of Police, Mumbai; Vikas Kumar Jha, *The Queen of Indian Pop: The Authorised Biography of Usha Uthup*, Penguin Random House India, Gurgaon, 2022, pp. 64–65.

on Owen Dunn Street (now Krishna Sanghi Path), off the main Hughes Road (which, incidentally, has long been mispronounced as Huge-is Road).[1] The old man was known to be quite wealthy, and his children were comfortably settled abroad – a son lived in Germany and a daughter in Aden.

The Gamdevi police station on Grant Road, under whose jurisdiction the Temple View building fell, was alerted to the murders on the Monday morning of 23 October. A watchman from Car Mart, seeing smoke coming out of his employer's ground-floor flat, had rushed in to investigate. Opening the front door and stepping into the room, he was greeted by a horrible sight. Heaped up in the passage leading to the main door, beside a smouldering heap of clothes, were the bodies of Mohammed Chunawala, his forty-five-year-old wife Fatima, eight-year-old grandson Sajid, and their forty-year-old housemaid, Annie Fernandes. Their throats had been slit and all the bodies bore multiple wounds. The brutality of the crime indicated that it was in all likelihood an act of deep-seated hatred.

The police arrived at the spot within minutes. Some of the blood on the floor had been wiped clean, and the killers had taken their time about it for some reason. The assailants had done the deed, probably early in the day, or maybe even late on the previous night. They had left no trace, no clues. It could not be immediately ascertained if cash or other valuables had been taken from the flat. Indeed, the ornaments on Chunawala's wife's body had been left intact. Robbery, it seemed, was not the primary motive for the murders. The neighbours and their servants were questioned, but no one seemed to have heard or noticed anything unusual or suspicious early that morning. Unfortunately, there was no watchman or guard at the entrance to the building, so no one could say if any strangers had been seen lurking around or if there had been any suspicious callers at the Chunawala flat early in the day.

As was customary in such cases, the men from the Fingerprint Bureau went through the flat with a fine-tooth comb looking for prints and hoping for some luck. The Bombay Police Dog Squad was also roped in. Two of its famous canines, Akbar and Lala, picked up the scent of the assailants and tracked them for nearly a kilometre to the Grant Road railway station, where the trail went cold.[2] The murderers had possibly taken a cab or, what was most likely, boarded a train to some distant destination. This was what a gang of robbers would usually do. It was not uncommon for men from other states to commit a burglary or dacoity in Bombay and go back to their native villages to lie low till the heat from the police had worn off. The stolen articles would then be disposed of through a middleman, either in Bombay or elsewhere.

It could well have been an attempted robbery gone horribly wrong, the police reasoned; but then, nothing seemed to have been taken from the flat. Why would anyone want to kill an old man and his family, including a small child, and also their servant? One thing was clear: the murderer or murderers were known to the family. The flat had not been broken into, and whoever committed the murders had been let in by the victims – so everyone had been silenced to make sure that there would be no witnesses to identify the perpetrators. Personal or business rivalry was a possibility, but the family did not seem to have any enemies, at least not any that their friends or relatives were aware of. The pile of burnt clothes near the door was also a curious and unusual feature of the case. They did not belong to any of the victims and so could only have been worn by the as-yet-unknown killers. The only explanation seemed to be that the murderers had changed into Chunawala's clothes and burnt their own, which were probably saturated with blood, to avoid drawing attention to them as they exited the building. However, as it turned out, it was these charred remains that would help the police nail them.

The fingerprint men did not have much luck. Scores of prints were lifted from the room, but these belonged to the victims or to those who regularly visited the house. They did, however, manage to lift two unidentified fingerprints from a blood-splotched meat safe in the kitchen. These did not match those of the victims or persons known to them, or indeed any of the prints of known criminals in the Fingerprint Bureau's records. While moving the body of the servant girl, who seemed to have been killed in the kitchen, one of the assailants had apparently rested his hands on the glass top of the meat safe, leaving very clear prints. But without a suspect to whom these prints could be linked, there was not much to go on.

The Temple View killings made the front page of the *Times of India* the next day. 'Family of three & maid servant done to death', the newspaper proclaimed in bold type, and for good measure carried a photo of the burnt pile of clothes on its front page, and another of the blood-soaked passage in the Chunawalas' flat on page 10.[3] The last such incident in recent memory had occurred some five years ago when a businessman, his young wife and their child had been killed by a servant in their Churchgate flat.

The brutal killing of eight-year-old Sajid Khan roused the public to a fury. The boy's mother had left for Aden a few weeks ago, leaving him in the care of his doting grandparents as the child was undergoing treatment for a liver ailment. There was some tension around the Hughes Road area following news of the murders, and a curfew was also temporarily enforced in the locality.

Incidentally, as the *Times* reported, there had been yet another murder on the same day, and not too far from Temple View. A sixty-year-old woman, Laluben Turakhia, was stabbed to death in her flat at Gowalia Tank, allegedly by her newly employed servant, who had decamped with her gold bangles and necklace. The police were certainly kept busy that day.

The seriousness of the affair and the need for quickly apprehending the culprits was not lost on Police Commissioner A.G. Rajadhyaksha. Away from the public gaze, the men in uniform had not been idle, and diligent police work was quietly underway. The Crime Branch of the Bombay CID was roped in and Deputy Commissioner Vaidyanath Sami, one of its finest officers, was promptly on the scene with his best men. The Crime Branch officers quickly latched on to the one real clue the murderers had left behind. The policemen who had initially combed the flat had probably not given much thought to the burnt clothes that had been left behind, but Inspector V.V. Vakatkar and Sub-inspector T.B. Gaud went through the charred remains very carefully.[4] And there, among the scorched bits of cloth, was what would eventually prove to be the key to the whole mystery: on one of the blackened and disintegrating scraps of what was the collar of a shirt, supposedly worn by one of the murderers, was a faint laundry mark in black ink – 'A-1 SBH'. The police could not have asked for a more promising lead. A laundry mark was almost like a fingerprint and could be used to trace a particular garment to its owner.

The first suspect on the police radar was Shantilal Bhanushanker Halwai, a convicted offender, but as he was in jail, the investigators quickly embarked on a laundry hunt. All laundry establishments in the city of Bombay had distinct laundry marks made in black ink, and these marks were always registered with the police. The first two letters indicated the laundry while the last two or three stood for the name of the person who owned the garment that had been sent for washing or ironing.

The police register revealed that A-1 was a quite a popular name for laundries and there were in fact four or five by that name. Now it was down to plain leg work, and the police finally zeroed in on the A-1 Laundry in Khetwadi, just a kilometre away from the scene of the crime. Yes, the proprietor confirmed, this was indeed his mark, and 'SBH' stood for Sayyed Bakar Hussain. He had given his shirt to be washed some days ago. The man had not been seen for a few days, but he came to the laundry regularly and so could be expected to make an appearance very soon.

The police were now almost certain that Hussain was the man they were after. More pieces of the jigsaw fell into place after Chunawala's cook (being unwell, he was not in the flat that day) said Sayyed Hussain had in fact been to Temple View thrice that day, the day before the murder. Inquiries revealed that Hussain had in fact been employed by

Chunawala at his automobile shop and had been dismissed sometime previously. Now, the motive was apparent. Hussain had sought to avenge his summary dismissal and had killed the Chunawalas. The unfortunate servant Annie had just happened to be in the wrong place at the wrong time.

It was now Tuesday evening, just a little over twenty-four hours since the murders. The police had moved remarkably fast, and now it only remained to grab the suspects. Hussain was known to be living in a building in Khetwadi with his cousin Sayyed Aziz, but neither had been seen since the previous day. Hussain was the main suspect, but Aziz's involvement could not be ruled out yet, and the police would need to get both the men. While a police team kept vigil at Khetwadi, another group of officers rushed off to an apartment at Peddar Road where Sayyed Hussain was said to have found employment as a driver, only to find that he'd left sometime earlier in the day. So back to Khetwadi they went, hoping their prime suspect would eventually show up there. The chase was now really on and the trap had been set. They'd done all the hard work, and with a little bit of luck they would be able lay their hands on the elusive SBH before the day was out. Hopefully, no one had tipped off the brothers that the police were on their trail.

However, fortune did smile on the police that evening. Around 6 p.m., Sayyed Aziz turned up at the Khetwadi building, inquiring about his cousin and was quickly taken into custody. An unsuspecting Sayyed Bakar Hussain also sauntered in an hour later and was swooped up. Both men confessed to the crime, police chief Rajadhyaksha told reporters later that night.

The men, the police revealed, were from Meerut in Uttar Pradesh. Sayyed Aziz was in fact a deserter from the army and had been employed as an orderly to an officer in Calcutta until a few weeks ago. They had planned to cross over the border to Pakistan after the murders and had been apprehended just as they were preparing to flee the city. The police recovered gold and pearl ornaments, wristwatches and currency notes worth around 11,000 rupees from the men. They also found several one-rupee notes wrapped around loose coins. These were apparently used by Chunawala to pay the watchman to buy the morning milk.

Given the notoriety of the Temple View murders, a huge crowd had assembled at the Esplanade Court when the suspects were produced before the presidency magistrate under heavy police guard. Everyone wanted to get a glimpse of the men who had perpetrated the foul deed. The suspects looked ordinary enough (as the photos in the *Times of India* edition of 26 October showed), with Sayyed Hussain dressed in his driver's uniform and Sayyed Aziz in cotton trousers and a bush shirt. They were not represented by any lawyer, and did not have anything to say either, the newspaper reported.[5]

The police were now the darlings of the press and the public. The 'arrest by laundry mark' was a yet another feather in the Bombay Police's cap. For Deputy Commissioner Sami, who was due to retire in three weeks, it was a fitting end to a remarkably successful career. The police officers who did the legwork also came in for well-deserved praise. The *Times* pointed out that ACP Basil Kane, Inspectors P.L. Mokashi and V.V. Vakatkar, DGSI B.S. Dalvi, Sub-inspectors T.E. Gaud, J.K. Mohite, G.S. Sawant, M.T. Gupte and R.K.

Dudhat, with a team of constables including Kazi Ahmed, had carried out the round-the-clock investigations under the guidance of Sami and Rajadhyaksha.

The plaudits were well deserved, for it isn't every day that a crime of such perversity is cracked in a little over a day. Rarer still it is (at least in our day) for junior police officers to find mention in the newspapers for their efforts in bringing criminals to book. A request was also made to the Mayor of Bombay by the Leader of the House in the Bombay Municipal Corporation to give a civic reception to the officers and men of the police who had worked to solve the case.

Criminal trials in those days were quick. Both Sayyed Hussain and Sayyed Aziz were tried in the Court of Sessions in Bombay and, as expected, sentenced to death. The testimony of the fingerprint expert, J.M. Daruwalla, proved conclusive in establishing the guilt of the two men, as did the laundry mark, which squarely placed Hussain at the scene of the crime. Their appeals to higher courts provided no relief, and Sayyed Hussain and Sayyed Aziz were duly executed within three months of their crime.

8

The Tragedy of Elokeshi*

Nobin Chunder Banerjee was a most unlikely murderer. That this affable young man, who obviously doted on his pretty young wife, would kill her in such brutal fashion was

*Geraldine Forbes, 'In Search of Elokeshi: the death of a young wife in Colonial India', *Readings in Bengal History: Identity Formation and Colonial Legacy*, Bengal History Association, 8 December 2017, https://www.academia.edu/37766411/Forbes_In_Search_of_Elokeshi_the_Death_of_a_Young_Wife_in_Colonial_Bengal_pdf, pp. 139–162; Tanika Sarkar, 'Talking about Scandals: Religion, Love and Law in Late Nineteen Century Bengal', *Studies in History*, Vol. 13, 1997, pp. 63–95; Soham Das, 'A Revisit to the 150-Year-Old Tarakeswar Affair', *People's Reflections*, 13 February 2023, https://reflections.live/articles/9482/a-revisit-to-the-150-year-old-tarakeswar-affair-an-article-by-soham-das-8276-le2invfc.html, accessed 22 February 2026; Chitrita Banerji, 'The Bengali Bonti', *Gastronomica*, 16 April 2013, https://gastronomica.org/2013/04/16/the-bengali-bonti/#comments, accessed 22 February 2026; Sanjoy Ghose, 'The Tarakeshwar case: When the "theatre" in the court room was more interesting than Shakespeare's Othello', *Bar and Bench*, 25 October 2020, https://www.barandbench.com/columns/when-the-theatre-in-the-court-room-was-more-interesting-than-shakespeares-othello, accessed 22 February 2026; 'Queen vs Nobin Chunder Banerjee', *Bengal Law Reports (1874)*, Vol. 13, pp. 20–22; Narasingha P. Sil, *Problem Child of Renascent Bengal: The Babu of Colonial Calcutta*, K.P. Bagchi & Co., Calcutta, 2017;

unthinkable. And yet that is what Nobin *babu* had done. On the afternoon of 27 May 1873, in an obscure village in rural Bengal, the devoted husband hacked his beloved Elokeshi to death, decapitating her with a *bonti* (a sickle-shaped implement used for cutting everything from vegetables to fish). He had then rushed out of the house in a frenzied state, screaming that he had killed her and promptly presented himself before the local *chowkidar*, demanding that he be arrested and punished for his crime.

The sleepy village of Kamrul in the Hooghly district of Bengal had never seen anything like this before. One can picture the tut-tutting and head-shaking among the village greybeards. Elokeshi brought it on herself, some would say. No, it was that scoundrel from Tarakeshwar who was responsible for this, others would counter. The real villain of the piece, most would agree, was Madhabchandra Giri, the head priest of the famous Taraknath shrine, which was thrust into the limelight when the case finally made it to court and the newspapers.

Sumanta Banerjee, *Dangerous Outcast: The Prostitute in Ninteenth Century Calcutta*, Seagull Books, 2019; Trinanjan Chakraborty, 'A Murder that scandalised 19-century Calcutta', *The Telegraph*, 23 September 2022, https://www.telegraphindia.com/my-kolkata/lifestyle/a-murder-that-scandalised-19th-century-calcutta/cid/1960837, accessed 22 February 2026; Indrajit Hazra, 'Elokeshi's sojourn: The woman is always at fault', *The Guardian*, https://sundayguardianlive.com/opinion/1462-elokeshi-s-sojourn-woman-always-fault, accessed 22 February 2026; Sir George Campbell, *Memoirs of my Indian Career*, MacMillian, London and New York, 1893. https://archive.org/details/memoirsmyindian00campgoog.

Nobin and Elokeshi, the two unfortunate protagonists of this tragic story, had not the slightest inkling of what fate had in store for them when they first met eight years ago. One doesn't know whether the young suitor, just into his teens, had been smitten with his pre-pubescent eight-year-old bride, but he grew to love her deeply during his fleeting visits over the years when they had to stay in their respective homes. This was all part of hoary tradition, with child-brides being sometimes betrothed to much older men, often with fraught consequences. Such alliances were not unknown in Bengal, as desperate fathers sought to wed their daughters into upper-caste homes.

This seems to have been the case with Elokeshi too, though fortunately, she found a husband who was devoted to her. Her life in her parental home could not have been easy. Her mother was dead, and her father, Nilkamal Mukhopadhyay, was a man of modest means who found it difficult to keep up with the aspirations of his second, and much younger wife, Mandakini. The stepmother, going by her subsequent conduct, seems not to have had Elokeshi's best interests in mind. Elokeshi's life would not have been different from that of any other girl in rural nineteenth-century Bengal. She would have attended to household chores, learning to cook and clean at any early age, hoping at some stage to attain a more comfortable life with her future husband.

By her standards, Elokeshi had married well: not everyone got a Kulin brahmin for a husband. And while Nobin was by no means rich, he had a job at the government printing press in Calcutta. This was promising enough. More importantly, he seemed to be a man of sober, temperate habits. Not for him the wining, dining and skirt-chasing that had caught on among the younger *bhadralok* in the fleshpots of the metropolis. Backed by the huge wealth they had amassed as traders, bankers and middlemen, the so-called *nabababus* (modern babus) of that era often lived ostentatious and profligate lives. One such worthy, Bhubanmohan Neogy of Bagbazar, was known to smoke cigarettes rolled up in banknotes and, on the occasion of Saraswati puja was said to have gifted a thousand Benarasi saris to the prostitutes of Chitpore Road.[1]

At sixteen, Elokeshi had matured enough to set up house with Nobin, but he probably wanted to wait a bit before he was able to live independently with her in the big city. The young girl therefore bided her time at her father's house, her somewhat dreary life relieved by occasional visits from her husband. The couple's married life, otherwise blissful, was said to have been marred by the want of a son. Nobin was apparently very keen on having a male heir to continue the family line. And it was this that led to the entry of a third person into their lives, which would soon forever be upended by tragic consequences.

Quite how Madhabchandra Giri got to know Elokeshi is a matter of dispute. The *mahant* of Tarakeshwar, one of the most revered Shaivaite shrines in Bengal, had an unsavoury reputation when it came to women. Some accounts suggest that he was consumed by lust after having spotted Elokeshi in her first flush of youthful beauty as she was bathing in a village tank. The more likely, if prosaic, explanation is that she was introduced to the mahant by her stepmother on the pretext of seeking the holy man's assistance for her to beget a son. Some accounts also have it that Mandakini acted more as a procuress, delivering her stepdaughter to satisfy the mahant's lascivious desires. Mandakini was known to be close to the mahant, who was said to have occasionally provided her with clothes and money – a fact that was known to her husband, who either would not, or could not, do much about it. Elokeshi was apparently taken by her stepmother one evening to the mahant's quarters for some kind of fertility treatment. What in fact happened was that the young girl was either seduced or – what seems more likely – raped by the mahant. The parents, most certainly the stepmother, were complicit in this and did not appear to have done anything to stop it. Moreover, they even seem to have connived at the abuse, and Elokeshi was often forced to stay with the priest to fulfil his sexual desires. If Nilkamal had any qualms about throwing his daughter to a wolf, there was not much he could do against the powerful Madhabchandra. Besides, he'd always been under the thumb of his dominant wife and would never venture to go against her wishes.

The good villagers of Kamrul were not blind to all this. Intrigues and liaisons of this kind, while not an everyday occurrence, are not very easy to conceal, especially in close-knit rural communities. Gossip and innuendo about the mahant's relationship with Elokeshi were soon a staple feature of conversation in the village – and inevitably Nobin soon got to know of it.

The unsuspecting husband arrived at Kamrul on 24 May, a Saturday. Weary of the trials and cares of Calcutta, he doubtless meant to while away the weekend in the caresses of his wife before returning to the drudgery of his job and the cramped room that he called home in the capital of Britain's

Indian empire. The pleasure trip would however turn into a nightmare very quickly. It may have been a pointed comment or a sly repartee at the village *choupal*, but Nobin soon got a hint of his wife's transgressions. He couldn't believe his ears. Surely, his Elokeshi could not have been cheating on him. Incandescent with rage, he stalked off to his in-laws' house and confronted his wife. Was there any truth in what he had just heard? Elokeshi would not lie to her husband. For all we know, she had probably been waiting to disclose the whole affair to him in some way without wounding his feelings, hoping that he would rescue her and take her away with him. She promptly confessed and told him the whole story. Being shown up as a cuckold would be terrible for any self-respecting man, but Nobin, to his credit, seemed to take it quite calmly. He understood the difficult position his wife found herself in, and probably blamed himself for not having taken her away to Calcutta earlier. But he poured out his fury on his in-laws. If anything, they were the ones who were really responsible for this. Declaring that he would no longer stay with them, he immediately moved with Elokeshi to her aunt's house nearby. The couple, in their shared grief, were now united. They would put this unsavoury episode behind and make a new life for themselves in Calcutta.

But here they were faced with an unexpected difficulty. Madhabchandra, who had heard of Nobin's arrival and his plans to take his wife away for good, would not consent to this. He sent a few of his goons to the village, threatening the couple with dire consequences if they attempted to leave. With no one in Kamrul willing to oppose the influential mahant, Nobin and Elokeshi were now trapped. Still, the couple did not lose hope. Given time, they would find a way to evade the mahant's men and make their escape. Nobin would have to think this through and find a way out.

But what he did next surprised everyone. On 27 May, after he had moved Elokeshi back to her father's house saying they would be leaving for Calcutta the next day, he picked up the heavy bonti and chopped off her head. Why he did this when he had seemingly reconciled with his wife is not clear. He may have been simply overwrought or frustrated by his impotence against Madhabchandra. Or it may be that, despite having forgiven his wife, he blamed her for the situation that he now found himself in and resented it. Maybe he had begun to have second thoughts about Elokeshi's fidelity. Had she really told him the entire truth? What if she had yearned for physical intimacy during his absence and willingly engaged in a liaison with the mahant? He had brought it up again with her and they quarrelled. Jealousy, suppressed rage, or the suspicion that he was being made a fool of, may have played a part. Whatever it was, Nobin saw red. The bonti was close at hand, and he struck hard, over and over again ...

The case of the *Queen vs Nobin Chunder Banerjee* or the Tarakeshwar Case, as it is more commonly known among the legal fraternity, was one of the celebrity trials of colonial India. It had all the elements of a modern potboiler: a beautiful young woman, a scheming stepmother, a lascivious godman, and a devoted husband who killed the only woman he had ever loved, in order to redeem his honour. And the murder weapon – a bonti! Surely, that was a first.

Nobin had surrendered immediately after his murder and had his statement taken down by the magistrate. He was duly arrested and charged with the murder of his wife. Meanwhile, the villain of the story had fled after Nobin charged him with adultery, an offence punishable by imprisonment in British India. Madhabchandra had quickly hopped across to the French-ruled enclave of Chandernagore, hoping to evade punishment. However, the authorities managed to quickly get him back with the help of an influential local zamindar (the French were probably glad to have him off their back) and the mahant was also made to stand on trial along with the man whose life he had wrecked.

The trial at the sessions court in Serampore quickly turned into a circus. The story was given huge play in the papers and crowds besieged the courtroom, often disrupting the proceedings. In fact, so large were the crowds trooping in every day that a ticketing system had to be introduced to regulate entry into the premises. There was probably less drama in the courtroom, where Nobin was defended by Wyomesh Chandra Bonnerjee, a very able lawyer who would later go on to become the first president of the Indian National Congress. While Nobin had confessed to the crime before the magistrate, his lawyer said his client had been under severe emotional stress. He also claimed that no one had actually seen Nobin in the act of killing his wife and that the prosecution's witnesses – Elokeshi's grandmother, Anandamoyee, her father Nilkamal and stepsister Muktokeshi – had lied to the court. If anything, his crime was far lesser than that of the mahant, who had seduced his wife and ruined his life.

Whatever the legal merits of the case, public opinion was solidly in favour of the wronged husband and Nobin had the benefit of a sympathetic jury. Legally speaking, this was a clear-cut case of murder, no matter what the provocation, but the jury was inclined to take a lenient view, declaring the defendant 'not guilty' on grounds of insanity. However, while Nobin's supporters and much of the public welcomed this verdict, the British judge presiding over the trial, Justice Charles Dickinson Field, would not agree. Public opinion was one thing, but the letter and spirit of the law could not be trampled upon. The jury's decision, to his mind, did not accord with the law as he saw it, and he promptly sent the case to the Calcutta High Court for review.

Justice Field's decision drew howls of protest from both the bhadralok and lesser mortals of Bengal. There was possibly an element of patriarchy and privilege involved too. A good man had been wronged by his wife (the blame, as always, lay with the woman) and had done what any self-respecting husband would have done. Surely, the judge could have shown some consideration for the poor man's state of mind. If a jury of locals had found it fit to acquit him, who was this British judge to rule otherwise? All eyes now turned to the high court where a two-judge bench would hear the appeal.

The mahant's case was far easier and less contentious. Everyone was out for Madhabchandra's blood. He would probably have received a sound thrashing from the mob gathered in the court premises if they could have got their hands on him. Justice Field was of the opinion that a clear case of adultery had been made out against the accused. The mahant had retained two notable British lawyers of the Calcutta Bar, G.H. Evans and W. Jackson, for his defence. The mahant's gatekeeper was a key witness for the prosecution, providing details of Elokeshi's assignations with the holy man, all of which were gleefully reported in the newspapers. The guilty verdict against the mahant with a fine of 3,000 rupees (some sources have the figure as 2,000 rupees) and three years' rigorous imprisonment went down well with the public, though there were demands from some quarters for a much harsher sentence. But Madhabchandra would not go down without a fight. He appealed against the verdict but could not obtain any relief from the High Court.

Upholding the lower court's ruling, Justice E.G. Birch was scathing in his remarks on the mahant's conduct: '(if he) is faithless to his trust, and if under the cloak of religion, and regardless of the decided prohibition of such conduct in the writings which he holds sacred, he employs his opportunities to debauch married women, he merits condign punishment'.[2]

Nobin's appeal, too, did not stand up to the High Court's scrutiny. The bench of Justice A.G. Macpherson and G.G. Morris found no merit in the case to support an acquittal on grounds of insanity. Disposing of the appeal, Justice Macpherson said:

It is clear that the murder was committed owing to the unhappy position in which the prisoner considered his wife and himself to be placed. He did the deed under the influence of anger, jealousy, and grief…But there is absolutely nothing on the facts before us from which any person can conclude that the prisoner was 'incapable of knowing the nature of the act', or he was incapable of knowing that he was doing what was wrong or contrary to law . . . On the whole we think the verdict of the jury so utterly wrong, and so utterly against the evidence . . . that it is our duty to convict the prisoner on the facts [of the case].[3]

Nobin was hence found guilty of culpable homicide amounting to murder and sentenced to transportation for life under Section 302 of the Indian Penal Code.

While Nobin was sent to the penal colony in the dreaded Andaman Islands to serve out his sentence, the mahant was locked up in the Presidency Jail at Alipore, where he was put to work on the oil-presses. But the masses did not forget Nobin. A signature drive was launched and mercy petitions were sent to both the governor-general and the lieutenant governor of Bengal, seeking a pardon for Nobin, who most people saw as the aggrieved party in the affair. These labours finally bore fruit and Nobin was granted a royal pardon on the occasion of Prince Edward VII's visit to India in 1876, after he had served just over two years in prison. Of his later whereabouts however, nothing is known. Incidentally, both Elokeshi's stepmother and father died while the trials were in progress. If the death of two prime witnesses during trial proceedings was deemed unusual, nothing seems to have been done about it.

And what of our villain? Madhabchandra Giri served out his three years and went back to Tarakeshwar. He was obviously a man of some resource, for he then ousted the incumbent mahant and, by some accounts, resumed his old philandering ways.

The Tarakeshwar temple received a lot of negative publicity during the course of the trial and after. The shrine had always been popular with infertile women who came there seeking cures and often fell into the clutches of the priests who exploited them for their own ends. Much before the Elokeshi affair, in 1824, the then mahant had been convicted of the murder of a man who was the lover of his mistress and subsequently hanged.

It was exactly a century later, in 1924, that a mass movement was launched against the misconduct of the mahants of Tarakeshwar, spearheaded by 'Deshbandhu' Chittaranjan Das and Subhas Chandra Bose. As public pressure mounted and the movement gained steam, the mahant at the time was replaced and a committee was set up to administer the affairs of the temple.

The Elokeshi case was by no means the first of its kind in colonial Bengal. Indeed, women indulging in extramarital affairs were victims in 20 per cent to 40 per cent of murder cases recorded between 1870 and 1875. However, what made the Tarakeshwar affair an egregious event was its impact on the Bengali society of the day. Its effect on the popular imagination was manifest not only in the plays, literary compositions and art of the period, but also in items of everyday use. Elokeshi-themed merchandise such as saris, betel-nut boxes, trays and (not surprisingly) bontis were soon on sale in the shops. A company selling a headache balm even claimed that the oil used in its product had been made by the mahant himself in the jail oil-press.

However, the most lasting legacy of the murder was the innumerable plays and songs that it spawned, with well over a dozen plays and farces being published between 1873 and 1876. Illustrated productions of these plays were also available for sale and were eagerly snapped up by the public.

However, among the most evocative works of art inspired by the Taraksehwar affair were the Kalighat paintings. A whole series of colourful paintings depicting various episodes of the Elokeshi story were produced, some of which now repose in the United Kingdom's Victoria and Albert Museum. The Elokeshi story was also told in the contemporary Batala woodcut prints of that period.

A disturbing, if not altogether surprising, aspect of the Elokeshi affair was the manner in which it was largely viewed by the public. Nobin was never really blamed for the murder, and indeed seems to have been applauded by much of Bengali society. For most people, Nobin had acted as any self-respecting man should have, and Elokeshi only got what she deserved. In that wise at least, the world hasn't changed much. The woman still takes the blame, and every age still has its Elokeshi.

9

The Jehangir Mansion Murders*

Late in the evening of 3 February 1971, a small but noisy crowd had gathered around the entrance to Jehangir Mansion, a six-storeyed apartment block standing next to the iconic Metro Cinema in Bombay. The locality, popularly known as Dhobi Talao, was always a bustling one – and would get livelier before that Wednesday night ended. No one really seemed to know what was happening, but a bunch of policemen had just gone into the building, so it was probably

---

* *The Times of India*, 3, 5 February 1971; R.S. Kulkarni, *Crimes, Criminals and Cops*, Vikas Publishing, New Delhi, 1989, p. 46; Mumbai Police, *Urbs Primus in Indis*, Commissioner of Police, Mumbai, 2006; R.S. Kulkarni, *Footprints on the Sand of Crime: A Crime-watcher's Reflective Autobiography*, Pan MacMillan, 2004; Benedict Costa, *Bombay: The Twilight Zone*, Hind Pocket Books, Delhi, 1972; F.D. Colabavala, *Indian Mafia in Action*, Orient Paperbacks, New Delhi, 1975; Meher Marfatia, *Once upon a City*, 49/50 Books, Mumbai, 2020; Berjis Desai, *Parsiana*, https://www.parsiana.com/news/news-you-can-use-details.aspx?id=YsXhBQNkhGo=&issue=291, accessed 22 February 2026; Berjis Desai, 'Even in Murder, Class Matters', *Bawa Musings, Parsiana*, 21 February 2016; https://www.parsiana.com/current-issue/articles.aspx?id=71%2FpCLa3fWw%3D&issue=294; Kulamarva Balakrishna, *A Portrait of Bombay's Underworld*, P.G. Manaktala & Sons, Bombay, 1966.

something serious. The milling crowd, waiting expectantly for a *tamasha* to unfold, would not go away disappointed that evening.

The cops from Azad Maidan police station arrived to find the fifth-floor corridor lined with animated residents, all helpfully pointing to a padlocked door. The inmates of Flat No. 1 had not been seen or heard from since the previous afternoon and an anxious relative had called the police. The lock was broken open and the police team, led by Deputy Inspector Joseph and Sub-inspector Kadam, stepped into the drawing room. There were no sounds from within, and since the curtains were drawn, nothing was visible in the evening gloom. After fumbling with the switchboard, one of cops switched on the light – to reveal a gruesome crime scene. Lying on an armchair, and long dead, was the body of Dorabsha Sethna, his full-sleeved shirt and dark trousers soaked crimson with blood. The eighty-two-year-old had probably been killed not long after he'd come home for lunch the previous afternoon, for he still had his shoes on. Hanging by the handle of a wooden cupboard nearby was his blood-stained coat, which also bore the marks of a sharp instrument that had pierced through the fabric. A jersey lying on an empty flower vase close by also bore similar marks. The old man had apparently been stabbed while he had his jersey and coat on and the killer had for some reason taken them off. On the blood-spattered floor were the remains of a small bonfire containing half-burnt scraps of cloth and charred papers.

In an adjoining bedroom were three more bodies – those of Nusserwanji Master (aged sixty-five) his wife Gaimai (aged seventy-two) and their long-time house help Bawla (aged fifty-five). The servant's body was lying under the cot, as if he had crawled in there to avoid or ward off his attacker. All the bodies bore multiple stab wounds and there were small pools of dried and congealed blood on the floor. Of the murder weapon there was no sign, but a long thin-bladed knife had obviously been used, or something like a stiletto, or possibly even a big screwdriver or similar instrument. The autopsy later revealed an eye-popping 147 stab wounds on the four corpses altogether. The discovery of the bodies set off a minor wave of panic among the building's residents. A few of them had followed the cops into the drawing room and those of a particularly nervous disposition had rushed out screaming. The news was out on the street in seconds and soon a growing throng of onlookers from the nearby apartments and business establishments gathered outside the building. The only time Dhobi Talao witnessed such scenes was when a box-office hit was playing at the Metro. A quadruple murder was breaking news indeed.

For the mostly elderly residents of Jehangir Mansion, the murders came as a shock, upending the routine of their usual sedate lives. To Sethna's neighbours, it was incomprehensible how four people could have been so brutally killed a few yards away from their doors without anyone hearing a thing. There had been no screams or cries, no sounds of a scuffle, they assured the police. But most of the residents in the building were in their sixties, and with these old folks, the police knew, one could never be sure. They may have been deep into their afternoon snooze while the incident occurred, and some of them were probably deaf as well. And what about a motive? The police could not say for sure. Sethna's wallet was still in his coat pocket and contained 52 rupees, and his gold watch was still on his wrist. But a cupboard in the flat had apparently been ransacked, and a couple of empty jewellery boxes had been left behind. So, robbery was probably the motive, if one could brush aside the brutality of the murders. The killer (or killers) seemed to have gone about their business in a frenzy. Was the murderer known to the victims? Was this an act of revenge? And if so, by whom? There were no immediate or obvious answers.

There was nothing at the scene of the crime that even faintly resembled a clue. A few pieces of paper and a scorched cloth bag were recovered from the ashes on the floor, as was an old one-paisa coin, now blackened. The burning seemed to have been at best a half-hearted attempt, and it was not clear what evidence was sought to be destroyed. Did the murderer panic after lighting the fire and quickly stamp it out thinking the smoke would attract attention? A few empty bottles of rum were also lying nearby. Had the killer downed a few stiff ones to steady his nerves after his murderous act? Had he got the bottles along when he entered the flat, intending to celebrate after the deed was done? Was this all preplanned? The men from the Fingerprint Bureau could not turn up any unknown prints either. The dog squad was pressed into service, but the canines could not pick up any trail. This was not surprising, given the number of people who had tramped up and down the stairs, and also the crowded locality in which the murders took place.

The police were, to put it mildly, quite baffled. The Bombay CID, which had taken over the case, went about its task methodically. An inquiry into the background of the victims and a reconstruction of the events of the 24 hours leading upto the crime were in order. All the residents of the building were interviewed, and an excited and motley collection of mostly old couples, bachelors and spinsters (Parsis for the most part, like the victims) assisted the police in painting a picture of the events leading up to the murders.

Old Dorabsha Sethna was a court clerk with Crawford Bailey & Co., a highly respected firm of solicitors, where he had served for over five decades. Among the oldest residents of Jehangir Mansion, he had been residing there for 35 years. His trusted manservant, Bawla, had been with him for well over two decades. The other two victims, Nusserwanji Master and his much older wife, Gaimai, had been staying in the flat for several years in what seemed to be a rather unusual arrangement. While the *Times of India*'s report on the murder referred to the Masters as Sethna's 'guests', it was no secret to anyone in the building that Gaimai was in fact his long-time sweetheart and had for many years played the role of housekeeper and confidant to the old man. She had been quite a head-turner in her youth and Dorabsha was still very fond of her. Indeed, as was revealed later, he had provided a lump sum of 15,000 rupees and a pension of 1,050 rupees per month for her in his will. The old lady had been a harmless, friendly soul who got on well with her neighbours.[1]

Nusserwanji Master, though, was an entirely different cup of tea. Not a very respectable chap, was the verdict in the neighbourhood. The company he kept could only be described as questionable. These included a woman named Bella Fernandes, a former cook-turned-dance teacher; Abdul Rehman, who ran a gambling den under the guise of a social club; and Babu, the bootlegger, who kept Master well supplied with illicit liquor. They were certainly not the most respectable of companions, and it was a source of no little wonder to the neighbours that Sethna allowed Nusserwanji Master to share his flat. Nusserwanji had no known source of regular income. He sometimes operated as a small-time estate agent and also claimed to be a private tutor to Bella's daughter. Master was also said to own (or had once owned) a flat in Acharya Building some distance away, but had apparently turned it over to Bella in exchange for a *pugree* (deposit) of 15,000 rupees. Bella's dancing school was also viewed as a rather shady joint, and during the subsequent trial she was asked some very pointed questions about the people who frequented it. Bella, however, refuted these charges, insisting that her school was a very respectable institution where young men were only taught to dance. Nusserwanji, she said, was like a father to her and only came to her house to give lessons to her daughter, and while prosecuting counsel were sceptical about these claims, they did not press the point.

While all these details ultimately had no real bearing on the case, they did expose Master as being not a very savoury character. He was also said to have defaulted on loans taken from some Pathan moneylenders. It was said in Bombay that to welch on a deal with the notorious Pathans was to forfeit your life. So, had the murder been a settling of old scores? Everyone had their own theory about the killings, but the most likely one was that whoever did it had come for Master, and the others were merely inconvenient witnesses who had been in the way.

There was certainly no reason why anyone would want to

kill the harmless Sethna. The police traced his movements on the day of the murders which, from the state of the bodies and the last-known sightings of the victims, were thought to have occurred between noon and 2.30 p.m. on 2 February. As was his wont, Sethna had left his office for lunch at about 1.10 p.m. that day. The lift was out of order and the old man – still remarkably fit in his eighties – had climbed the stairs to the fifth floor. He did, however, take a break on the third floor, where one of the residents, a Mrs Irani, had asked him to rest a bit and offered him a chair. He had gratefully accepted, and after 10 minutes or so, had taken her leave and walked up to the fifth floor, entering his flat at around 1.30 p.m. Whoever opened the door for him – either the other occupants or the murderer – was known to him, the police surmised. Had Sethna also been a target? And was the murderer waiting for him, having disposed of the other three earlier? The killer could well have come in immediately after Sethna. The table in the drawing room had been laid for four, and the inmates were clearly preparing to sit down for lunch. Had the murderer been invited? There was no way of knowing – not for the present at least. There were just too many intangibles, too many ifs and buts.

Still, the investigators managed to put together a fairly accurate timeline of some of the goings-on at the Sethna residence on the morning of 2 February in the hours preceding the murders. Around 9.30 a.m., Ramchandra, the liftman at Jehangir Mansion, had taken a young man in his early thirties, up to the fifth floor. The lift had been working then, and the visitor had come down in a little while, accompanied by Nusserwanji Master.

There had been other visitors that morning. Banoobai Driver, a poor old Parsi lady staying at Falkland Road, had come to see Gaimai sometime after 10.30 a.m. Sethna had apparently been of a charitable disposition, and a few people regularly called in at the house for help. Banoobai had chatted with Gaimai for a few minutes and had gone away with 50 rupees in cash and a bag of provisions. This was confirmed by Gangubai, the maid, who was then present in the house. Banoobai told the police that she had seen Master standing at the bus stop outside when she left the house around 11 a.m. The police were a little chary of taking Banoobai's word on the timing of her visit. The old lady's memory was patchy and it took hours of questioning to get even simple facts out of her. And even then, the police couldn't be sure if she'd got her facts right.

Mithubai Dalal, another supplicant, had visited the flat around 11.30 a.m. or 12 noon. The old spinster had chatted with Gaimai for a while and then left, taking with her some magazines and newspapers. While she was there, Pilcomai Choksi, one of Sethna's neighbours on the fifth floor, had also dropped in for a chat. Mithubai would later tell the police that a young man had been in the flat while she was there. He had been talking to the Masters in the bedroom, but moved out and sat in the living room once the ladies entered. The man was quite young and looked like a Parsi. Pilcomai had also noticed the young man but did not pay him much attention, and it was only much later that she remembered the young man and confirmed his presence in the flat. In all the excitement following the murders, she'd probably suffered a brief memory lapse and not mentioned the young stranger to the police.

The other piece of evidence regarding this mysterious Parsi-looking man was provided by Narmadabai, a tiffin-carrier or *dabbawali*, who rang Sethna's doorbell around 12.30 p.m. She had brought the Masters their lunch, as was her daily routine. A young man had taken the tiffin box from her and immediately shut the door. Narmadabai found this odd, for it was Gaimai or Bawla who usually answered the door. Also, she had to take back the empty tiffin box that she had delivered the previous day. So, she rang the bell again. The door was opened once more by the same man, the empty tiffin box handed out without a word and promptly shut again. Narmadabai was certain she had never seen him before, but recalled his features from the brief glimpse she had of him. He was thirtyish, tall and fair, wore glasses, and was dressed in a white shirt and dark trousers. Yes, probably a Parsi; and yes, she would probably recognize him if she were to see him again.

The young Parsi gent had been noticed by others too that day. Around 9.30 a.m., according to another witness, Master had been conversing with a young man at the nearby bus stop. The proprietor of a *bidi* shop near the bus stop recalled that Master had sought change for a 10-rupee note, and finding he had none, had asked a *gurkha* to get it from the Irani restaurant nearby. The necessary change was obtained and Master had given five rupees to the young man, who then left saying (in Parsi-Gujarati) he would be back in a couple of hours (*be kalak pachhi awaish*).

Did this as-yet-unknown Parsi come back around 11.30 p.m. and commit the foul deed? That seemed quite likely, and it would fit in with the sequence of events. The lift had conked out by then and he would have walked up the stairs, unnoticed by the liftman, who was probably not around. If he had indeed come back within a couple of hours, he would have been in the flat when Mithubai and Piloomai arrived. He had stayed on after the ladies left and had taken in the tiffin box from Narmadabai. What about the servant? He had not been in the house when Mithubai and Piloomai were present. Probably out on an errand. He too may have come in after the two ladies left, as did Sethna who came back home for lunch as usual around 1.30 p.m. The young man could have possibly killed all of them sometime between 12 noon and 2 p.m. (which more or less corroborated with the time of death) and then quietly left the flat unnoticed by anyone, after first locking the door behind him with a padlock.

So far, so good. The police were confident they'd got the sequence of events more or less right. Inquiries in the neighbourhood revealed yet another person who been seen going up the stairs of Jehangir Mansion that afternoon. This was Behram (or Bahira, as he was known in the neighbourhood), an old sponger who eked out a living doing odd jobs for Sethna. In return for the occasional cash handout he got to fund his drinking habit, Bahira would run errands such as paying electricity bills, getting medicines, etc. A little before 2 p.m., Bahira had rung the bell of Sethna's flat, but the door had remained shut. Thinking that the occupants were probably asleep, he had gone away, he told the police, but had returned at 4 p.m., only to find a padlock on the door. This was all solid witness material as far as the police were concerned, but they were also aware that statements and claims by the likes of Bahira could not be taken entirely at face value. Habitual drunkards and wastrels were bound to tell the police what they wanted to hear for fear of being victimized. Their memories and recollection of events varied with every telling and a good defence lawyer would rip their testimony to shreds in no time.

There was one fact that was now more or less undisputable. The padlock on the door appeared sometime after 2 p.m. So, the murderer had departed by then. He'd had plenty of time to ransack the flat, possibly clean himself up and wipe off any fingerprints (if he had stayed calm and kept his wits about him) from objects that he might have touched during his visit. He certainly made away with quite a haul. Interviews with relatives of the victims revealed that some very expensive pieces of jewellery were missing, including a pearl necklace that had a pendant studded with diamonds, a pearl brooch, and a bracelet studded with diamonds, pearls and emeralds. Sethna was also known to keep several cash-stuffed envelopes (apparently for his numerous supplicants) in his cupboard; of these, there was no sign. Gaimai's gold bangles and chain were missing as well. The murderer had been incredibly lucky to enter and depart from the building unnoticed. The street on which Jehangir Mansion stood was a busy one, always full of people, and groups of boys or men from the adjoining buildings and commercial establishments were always hanging around at the entrance to the building.

The lock on their neighbour's door was also noticed by Piloomai and her husband Jal later that afternoon. But Sethna had not been keeping well of late and the family may have gone off to see a doctor, the couple thought, and left it at that.

The lock was still there a few hours later, around 4 p.m. in the evening, when the maid Gangubai arrived. She wanted to return the keys, which she had taken from Gaimai in the morning, to Sethna's neighbour Dinshaw Tchakara's flat. Tchakara, a bachelor, always left his keys with Gaimai, who would open the flat for Gangu to clean. She had come there earlier too, around 2 p.m., she told the police, but found the flat locked. Thinking that Gaimai had probably gone out for some work and would soon be back, Gangubai decided to wait and sat down outside the door. She couldn't trudge up and down several times a day. A little later, Narmadabai walked up the stairs, this time with another tiffin box (for the evening meal). Seeing the lock on the door, the *dabbawali* handed over the tiffin box to the maid, asking her to give it to Gaimai when she returned, and went away. The maid waited for well over an hour, but it was now getting dark and she wanted to go home. But the tiffin box could not be left unattended, and so she knocked on the Choksis' door. Could they keep the tiffin box and give it to Gaimai on her return? The dabbawali had left it with her . . . Piloo was happy to oblige. A relieved Gangubai handed over the tiffin box and left the building.

A couple of hours later (it was well past dinner time now), with no sign of their neighbours showing up, and wanting to go to bed, the Choksis took the tiffin box to the Antia family next door. Would they mind keeping the *dabba* till their neighbours returned? Jaloo Antia, friendly soul that she was, certainly did not mind. Their task done, the Choksis turned in for the night. Where had Sethna and the Masters gone? It was quite unlike them to be away so late . . . well, they'd find out the next day.

The following morning the padlock was still on the door, and now the ladies in the building began to get a little nervous. They were all old-timers, quite attached to each other and fond of Gaimai. It had nearly been 24 hours since anyone from the Sethna household had been seen, and they were all a little uneasy. Someone suggested calling up the Parsee General Hospital to check if any of them had met with an accident and was admitted there. Jaloo Antia then took matters in hand and called up Gaimai's niece, a Mrs Vakil. Had Mrs Vakil heard from her aunt since yesterday, she asked. No? Well, Gaimai hadn't been seen outside the house since yesterday. Could she make some enquires among their relatives, or at least inform the police? Not surprisingly, the Vakils' inquiries turned up nothing and so, late in the evening, they had showed up at Sethna's door with the cops.

The events that followed put Jehangir Mansion squarely in the spotlight for the next few days. Not that the newspapers had been short of sensational stories, for the quadruple homicide was only one among many violent acts in what had been an unusually eventful week. On the day of the murders, 2 February, an Indian Airlines Fokker Friendship plane had been blown up in Pakistan by extremists from the National Liberation Front of Kashmir. The plane, en route to Jammu from Srinagar, had been forced to fly to Lahore by the hijackers who demanded the release of 36 people under detention in Kashmir. Thankfully, the 26 passengers and four crew members had been released unharmed a day earlier. In West Bengal, Communist leader Jyoti Basu was the target of an assassination attempt – the second in a week – when a bomb was thrown at his car by Naxalites at Barasat.[2]

While the plane hijacking and the attack on Basu made national headlines, the quadruple homicide got huge play in the city dailies over the following days. Press correspondents and photographers besieged Jehangir Mansion, and streams of gawkers and passersby hung about on the street outside. The arrival of the dog squad, a sure-fire attention grabber, had got everyone steamed up for a while, but that had turned out to be a damp squib as the canines failed to pick up any trail. The *Times of India* report on the murder also carried a photo of the building, with an arrow helpfully pointing at the fifth-floor flat.[3] Crime aficionados in the city pointed out the similarities in the case with those of the Temple View murders a couple of years ago when three members of the Chunawala family and their maid had been done to death. Then, too, the murderers had left behind a bonfire of their blood-stained clothes, but were detected by a laundry mark on one of the partly charred garments. There was nothing to help identify the culprits. The police had their hands full, interviewing the scores of people – maids, cooks, sweepers, newspaper boys – who habitually frequented the building, apart from the residents themselves. The owners and employees of the numerous establishments in the area – the sporting goods stores, restaurants, paan-bidi shops – were urged to rack their brains for anything they might recall about the events on that fateful day. Had any suspicious characters been hanging around in the locality? Had anyone at all, even casually, enquired or mentioned something about the deceased during the last couple of days? Did anything unusual or out of place occur that might serve as a clue to identify the perpetrators?

The Crime Branch team from the CID under Deputy

Commissioner Ramakant Kulkarni and Assistant Commissioner Basil Kane was kept on its toes as information about the victims and those associated with them trickled in, and many leads were followed, often with no results. For Inspectors V.V. Vakatkar, Suresh Pendse, Minoo Irani and the junior officers and constables, who did all the leg work, it was a busy and frustrating time.

In the meantime, a possible murder weapon had been located. Officers at the V.P. Road police station near Charni Road were informed that a *gupti* (a short sword-stick with a concealed blade) had been found by some boys playing in the compound of the Behramjee Jejeebhoy Parsee Charitable Institution on Queen's Road on 3 February, a day after the murder. The gupti had been wiped clean, but the police surgeon who examined it thought the injuries on the victims could have been inflicted by the sharp, thin-bladed weapon, which was sent to the forensic laboratory for closer examination. A routine alert on the police radio network to confirm if any offences had been committed over the last few days using such a weapon drew a blank. It was therefore quite probable that this was the murder weapon. Also, the place where it was found was only a couple of miles from Jehangir Mansion. Had the killer tossed it over the wall and caught a train at the nearby Charni Road station? That couldn't be ruled out, but the police had to find a suspect before they could confirm these hypotheses.

The only real suspect so far was the young Parsi seen by so many people. All the witnesses agreed on one fact: the elusive young man seemed a decent and harmless-looking fellow, not your typical street tough.

The police knew they had to find him to crack the case. The Parsis are a famously law-abiding race and never-do-wells in the community are rare. There was a Parsi bad egg about though, and with nothing to go on, the police initially latched on to him. Adi Cooper was the nephew of Dinshaw Tchakara, one of Sethna's neighbours. A drifter who lived by his wits, this disreputable young man kept company with a Mrs Grant, an old lady twice his age. He had a police record too. Over a decade ago, he had been a suspect in a double murder but was acquitted for lack of evidence. He'd also been involved in a robbery but had avoided jail by turning approver.

Establishing Adi Cooper's whereabouts was not easy. Tchakara confirmed that Adi visited him from time to time for financial aid, but he had always sent him away. His father, Shaviax, had also not seen him for a couple of years and had no idea where he was. Adi was a smart lad and good-looking too, but irredeemably crooked. After the robbery case, the family had tried to help him settle down and his uncle had offered him a job at his factory in Lalbaug, but Adi was lazy and had to be shown the door. No one had any idea where he stayed these days. The police contacted his known associates, mostly shady types, but Adi could not be traced. Then a Dr Pinto turned up at the CID office with a lead. Adi had apparently made off with his gold watch and 16,000 rupees and Pinto had now received a letter from Adi that gave his address as 'Pathikashram' at Anand, Gujarat. A police team was dispatched to Anand, where they found Adi on 13 February, now living with Mrs Grant in a bungalow attached to a church. Confronted by the police, Adi admitted to having taken Dr Pinto's money and gold watch but denied having been anywhere near Bombay on the day of the murder. He had not visited the city for months, he insisted. Moreover, he had a rock-solid alibi to prove it. The manager of Pathikashram stated very categorically that Adi had been staying there since August 1970 and had moved out only recently. Reverend Jerome, the pastor at the church (who knew Adi as R.B. Simpson), also confirmed that Adi had been at Anand on the afternoon of 2 February. In fact, Adi had given him an application seeking accommodation at around 1.30 p.m. that very day. He had come back with Mrs Grant the next day to collect his letter of admission and had moved into the bungalow on 4 February. The Reverend was quite certain about the dates and time, and he had the application submitted by Adi to prove it. For the Crime Branch sleuths who had entertained some hope that Adi might be the man they were looking for, this was indeed a crushing blow. There was no way Adi could have been at both Bombay and Anand on the afternoon the murders were committed. Another trail had gone cold. In fact, it had only been a time-consuming wild-goose chase!

It was now almost a fortnight since the crime and the police were nowhere near apprehending the murderer. Caustic barbs from the press and the public did not make the task any easier. For the men at CID headquarters, it was a frustrating time. Who was this young Parsi who was leading them such a dance? Surely, someone would know him or would have guessed his identity. Why hadn't the police received any tips? A sense of self-doubt was slowly creeping into the investigation. What had they missed? Had they overlooked a vital clue? There was only one way to find out. They would go by the book and question the old folks at Jehangir Mansion once again; get them to jog their memories a bit. Maybe, just maybe, someone would reveal something more this time.

So, the old-timers were interviewed a second time. Memory being what it is, some of them faltered a bit while recalling the events of two weeks ago, but the inconsistencies in their retelling were minor ones. The facts as they recalled them were still essentially the same. There was one exception, however. And as it turned out, it was vital. Piloomai Choksi had something more to add. She now recalled, somewhat sheepishly, that the young man she had seen in the Sethna's flat on the day of the murder had in fact come back the very next afternoon, well before the crime had been discovered. Why hadn't she revealed this earlier? She'd been distraught and overwrought when the police had first questioned her, Piloo said, and this very important detail had somehow slipped her mind. The young Parsi gentleman had rung her doorbell and enquired about Nusserwanji Master. Would she know where he had gone and when he would return? The young fellow had walked up five floors and was panting and so Piloo had invited him in and offered him a glass of water. There was a padlock on the door and the Masters seemed to have gone away since the previous afternoon; she had told him. The young stranger said he would come back later as he had to meet Nusserwanji, who had promised to secure him some accommodation nearby. As he rose to leave, Piloo's sister-in-law Perin, who was also present, asked if he would like to leave a message for Nusserwanji. Oh yes, the man replied, could they please tell him that Phiroze Daruwala from Andheri had called?

One can only imagine the relief and astonishment on the faces of the police officers when this revelation was made. This was a lucky bolt straight out of the blue. If only Piloo had remembered this earlier it would have saved them so much time and effort. But then, memory lapses were a common affliction with these old folks, and Piloomai was profusely apologetic and as one may imagine, a trifle embarrassed. To say that the police were thrilled would be an understatement. Admittedly, Phiroze was a very common Parsi name, but it was still something to go by. With a name and description, tracking down the young man would be so much easier. The police team that trooped out of Piloomai's flat was visibly energized.

It is said, and has frequently been noted, that some perverse logic draws murderers back to the scene of their crime. What drives them to take this foolish step is not known, but they do it often enough. It may simply be a child-like curiosity (or naïvety) to find out what's going on, to check if the police have made any headway in the investigation. Occasionally, the killer turns up, offering to help the police, or to make a belated attempt at setting up an alibi. For the devil-may-care types, it may be a way of cocking a snook at the cops. More often than not, this turns out to be their undoing. So too with Phiroze Daruwala.

A police dragnet was spread out over Andheri and inquiries were made at the Parsi colony there, but no one by the name Phiroze Daruwala was found. Lodging houses and hotels in the area were checked as well, to no avail. Friends and associates of Nusserwanji Master were asked if they knew anyone by that name, but could not (or would not) help. It was all very frustrating. The promising clue was not taking the police anywhere. In the end, a direct approach to the public was made. A police circular was issued to the city's Gujarati newspapers, seeking information about the young man, mentioning his name and providing a description. The police handout did not say Phiroze Daruwala was a suspect but only that they were seeking his assistance in the investigation. Could the young man come to the Crime Branch headquarters and speak to either DCP R.S. Kulkarni or ACP Basil Kane, or call either of them on the following telephone numbers?

The young man did not oblige. However, several others did, and the Crime Branch was soon receiving anonymous phone calls and unsigned letters about Phiroze Daruwalas from all over the city. Many of these tips were followed but failed to unearth the now-desperately-sought-after young man. Then, someone drew the attention of the investigators to a candidate for the upcoming Lok Sabha elections who matched the description given in the police handout. A newspaper report also carried a photograph of this man, who was in his early thirties and apparently a bullion merchant. The photograph was shown to Piloomai and Mithu Dalal, and both women immediately recognized him as the man who had visited the Sethna residence on 2 February. The police now had their man. Also, Phiroze Daruwala was staying at the Hotel Imperial Palace at Andheri (how had they missed him?) and when contacted by the police, readily agreed to come down to the Crime Branch office.

This he did promptly, looking smart and dapper in a neat blue suit. Daruwala seemed eager to help the police and was not at all nervous. He was a divorcé and had to move out of his parents' home at Hughes Road after marrying a Christian girl and was now living in a hotel at Andheri with his mother-in-law. He was a bullion trader and was standing for the parliamentary elections from the Bombay North-West constituency, he revealed. Yes, he knew Nusserwanji Master, whom he had met in the course of his social work and Master had agreed to help him find suitable premises to be used as an office for his election work.

He admitted to having been at Jehangir Mansion on the day of the murder and the next day as well. He had left the Sethna residence around 1 p.m., after the dabbawali had brought the tiffin. Two Parsi ladies had also been to see Gaimai while he was there. He remembered all that quite clearly. After leaving Jehangir Mansion, he'd gone to the bullion market to meet his business partners and then to the election office to organize some paperwork for his candidature. He'd been very busy all that day as he had to file his nomination by 3 February, the next day. News of the murders had come as a shock to him. He had learned about them from the newspapers on the evening of the fourth and actually meant to contact the police but had been incredibly busy. Did they have any idea why Master and the others had been murdered, he asked.

The investigators stayed tight-lipped and non-committal. Phiroze Daruwala was certainly a cool customer, but there was probably something about his manner, his eagerness to please, that told them he was probably not all that he seemed. They let him ramble on.

Daruwala then tried to make out that he had been aware

that Nusserwanji was not quite the respectable type. Had the police spoken to his friend Bella at Acharya Building? Nusserwanji was at her house almost every day; she might know something about the murder, he ventured. Also, he'd always suspected that Nusserwanji was involved in some kind of smuggling venture. Could he have fallen out with some smugglers and been killed because of that? Well, it was for the police to find out and he would always be glad to assist in any way he could.

He then stood up and took his leave. Could he please be excused? He had an appointment with the Chief Minister of Maharashtra to discuss the elections and could not afford to be late. Shaking hands with the officers, and with a smile on his face, Daruwalla walked out of the room.

While Daruwala's claims sounded convincing, the police knew they would have to be checked out, and in the meantime, he would be tailed. The plainclothesmen soon reported back. Daruwala did in fact go to Varsha, the chief minister's official bungalow on Malabar Hill, after he left the CID headquarters. He was also involved in a few rallies organized by his party over the next few days. However, the officers who visited the bullion market had a different tale to tell. Daruwala's partners confirmed that he had met them during the first week of the month, but that was on 3 February, not 2 February as he claimed. They were quite sure about the date, as he'd told them that it was the last day to file his nomination for the elections. Moreover, he'd been wearing a new suit for the occasion. They were positive about that. For the police, this discrepancy was a big break in an otherwise convincing alibi. Had Daruwala deliberately misled them or was it a genuine mistake?

Daruwala refused to accept his partners' version of events. And now he was combative. His partners were completely mistaken; he told the police. It was an understandable mistake, he agreed. It wasn't easy to remember what one did on a particular day a fortnight ago. But as he was the one involved, he was absolutely certain. He had been to the bullion market on 2 February, not the day after. It was simply his word against theirs. But he did have a point, so his partners were questioned again. This time they revealed that he was not officially a member of the bullion exchange and could not officially enter its premises and in fact did business on the pavement outside the exchange building. Such kerbside deals were quite common in the trade and sometime ago Daruwala had made a loss of 35,000 rupees on one such transaction; he was struggling to pay off his dues and was badly in need of money. He was then living at the Bombay International Hotel at Churchgate and the creditors who tracked him down there had found him staying with an infant (his daughter) and an *ayah*. He had paid them some money but was still deep in debt and needed more. So here, finally, was the motive.

Daruwala also tripped up on another front. A visit to the state election commission office confirmed that he had been there on 3 February. The returning officer and the officer on special duty were positive that he had been there on that day. When asked to explain this, Daruwala switched tracks. True, he had been there on the third, but he went there on the second as well, he insisted. The officials were making a mistake, as it was quite easy for anyone to be confused about dates and events from so long ago. He still stuck to his story; he was right and the election officials were wrong.

Now the investigators were truly stumped. Daruwala did have a point and the evidence against him was at best circumstantial, and a little flimsy at that. The police were not sure if it was good enough to merit a conviction in court. It was up to the higher-ups in the police department to make that call. The state law department and the legal remembrancer were consulted. The suspect was a candidate for elections. Without a watertight case, should they proceed against him? Would it vitiate the election process if he were charged and restrained from campaigning? If the magistrate threw out the case, the police department would have much to answer for. The choice was not an easy one. The legal remembrancer gave his considered opinion that an arrest would in no way vitiate the election process, but it was up to the police to prove their charges against the accused in court. Were they up to it?

The police, understandably, were still hesitant, but then fate played a hand. While the investigators debated their next steps, Daruwala unexpectedly walked into the CID office on 25 February and said he had withdrawn his candidature in favour of another contestant. This was an unforeseen stroke of luck. The police could now proceed against him, though they would still be riding their luck on securing a conviction. Late that evening, yet another bit of good news came their way. One of the plainclothesmen deputed to watch Daruwala said the suspect had regularly been visiting the Porchristy Guest House at Andheri, where he had lodged his daughter and mother-in-law, Mrs Dawson. He often visited them in the evening to see his daughter, to whom he seemed very much attached, but never stayed overnight. Mrs Dawson was then questioned and confirmed that this was true. Daruwala, she said, was now staying at a dharamshala near the Parsi Agiary at Charni Road. This piece of news was like a small ray of light at the end of what had so far seemed a very dark tunnel. The dharamshala was quite close to the place where the gupti had been found. The net was slowly closing in on Phiroze Daruwala.

From Mrs Dawson, the police also got to know that Daruwala's wife, Marie, was employed as a telephone operator at a five-star hotel. She was interviewed, and the sordid tale of Daruwala's life was laid bare. Marie Dawson had met Phiroze through a mutual acquaintance and he had married her in 1969 under false pretences, giving the impression that he had a steady job. Later, he had moved into her parents' bungalow at Bandra, where he had apparently tried to kill her mother by lacing her food with rat poison. The old lady had been rushed to Nair Hospital in time and had been incredibly lucky to survive. Marie was also certain that he was responsible for the untimely death of her father Henry, who had a stroke while he was sleeping. Phiroze, who had moved into his father-in-law's room claiming that his own bedroom was haunted, had done nothing to help. Instead of calling a doctor, he had given the old man a massage which, according to Marie, resulted in her father's death. Phiroze then called in his family doctor and convinced him to issue a death certificate saying the old man had died of heart failure. Moreover, he had also insisted on a cremation, saying that Henry had once told him that he wanted to be cremated like a Hindu. To the police, this sounded like an attempt to destroy evidence, of making sure there would be no body left to exhume if anyone raised a stink.

All this was news to the police. But there was more to come. One of the police officers recalled that it was this same Phiroze who, several years ago, had assaulted an old man from whom he had taken money to set up a fruit juice stall. The charming Parsi gentleman was turning out to be quite a rotter. And that was not all. Marie said he had sold off the bungalow at Bandra without informing her and had gambled away most of the money, putting the family in very dire straits. They had then moved to a seedy hotel in Marine Lines. Phiroze was apparently a compulsive gambler and always in need of money. While Marie spoke freely, it was obvious that she was scared of her husband and was holding something back. However, a little bit of gentle coaxing by the police revealed more about Daruwala's nefarious activities. He kept company with several shady characters, Marie revealed, and some of them had even threatened him as he owed them money.

Marie had another fantastic story to tell. One day, she had opened her husband's cupboard while he was away and was shocked to find two bottles of chloroform, a length of rope and some rubber hand gloves hidden there. When Marie demanded an explanation, Daruwala said he and his associates were planning to kidnap the city's notorious *matka* (gambling) don Ratan Khatri and extort money from him.[4] The terrified woman had somehow managed, with great difficulty, to dissuade him from executing this plan.

All this was certainly interesting, but could Marie possibly shed some light on her husband's activities on 2 February, the cops asked. It took her some time, but then she recalled that that was the day when Phiroze had bought a doll, a woollen shawl and a baba suit for their four-month-old daughter, Peggy. Phiroze had his faults, but even Marie had to admit that he was a doting father. He appeared loaded with cash that evening and had given her mother some money, besides paying off his outstanding bills with the tailor, paan-bidiwalla and the ayah's son. The paan-bidiwalla, Mahmood, was questioned, and he confirmed that Phiroze had given him a 100-rupee note on 2 February. He showed them his diary where there was an entry in Phiroze's own hand (he insisted on doing it himself) for the payment on that date. Mahmood recalled that the money had come from a fat wad of 100-rupee notes. For the police, this was a significant revelation. For the past week they had been tracking down and carefully questioning all of Daruwala's known associates. Their inquiries had revealed that Daruwala had been flat broke on the morning of 2 February and had in fact pawned his clothes at a shop in Grant Road earlier that day. So, how was he flush with cash by the evening? The answer was obvious: the proceeds from the robbery at the Sethna residence.

The police were now convinced of Daruwala's guilt and he was summoned for questioning. Characteristically, he tried to bluff his way out again. Yes, he admitted, he had been broke on the day of the murder and the money he had later in the evening came from some smugglers (didn't he tell them earlier that Master was involved in a smuggling racket?) who had approached him and sought his help to gain entry into Sethna's flat. He had quietly pocketed the key to the Yale lock on the front door on his first visit that morning and had handed it over to them. He had been given 7,000 rupees for this, he claimed. The smugglers had gone into the flat immediately after his second visit and he was not at first aware that they had killed all the occupants. He did not know these men personally, but could definitely identify them if the police were to produce them before him.

While his sang froid was admirable – and all this this was disclosed with quiet confidence – Daruwala must have known that he was now in the endgame. The police were not falling for his story of the mythical smugglers. We do not know if any strong-arm tactics were employed but the pressure was gently kept up. Did he get only cash from these smugglers or did they give him some of the stuff stolen from the flat as well, they asked. As he sat there quietly, a smile still playing on his face, the eyes of his interrogators boring into him, a flicker of doubt seemed to cross his mind. Had they located someone who knew he had sold some valuables on that day? The balloon had finally gone up for Phiroze Daruwala. He gave it all up. Yes, he admitted, he did sell some silverware and a few watches that day at a couple of shops in Khetwadi and Bapty Road. He seemed almost relieved to get it off his chest.

On 2 March, exactly a month to the day after he committed the foulest of crimes, Phiroze made a formal confession, unburdening himself before the Crime Branch officers. It was all a ghastly mess. He had not meant to kill anyone. All he wanted was money. His first visit on the morning of 2 February was a recce. Dorabsha Sethna was known to keep significant amounts of cash in the house and Daruwala intended to rob the place in the afternoon when only the Masters would be present in the flat. He arrived at the flat at 11.30 a.m., concealing the gupti (which he had obtained from Chor Bazaar) in a rolled-up newspaper. The unexpected arrival of the two Parsi women who stayed on to chat with Gaimai had upset his plans. Once they had left, he drew the gupti and, holding it to Gaimai's throat, demanded money. The old woman said all she could offer him was a measly 60 rupees! He could hardly believe his ears. 60 rupees? Was she trying to make a fool of him? Something snapped inside him, and in a fit of rage he had stabbed her. Nusserwanji, who had leaped to her defence, got the same treatment. Daruwala's blood was now up and he stabbed them repeatedly. He then proceeded to ransack the cupboard in the bedroom when he heard a sound behind him. Bawla the servant had unexpectedly turned up, letting himself in with a duplicate key. Killing Bawla was not part of the plan, but Daruwala was left with no choice. He attacked Bawla and the poor fellow had tried to get away and hide under the bed, but he had finished him off. By now his hands were soaked in blood, but he stayed calm. He cleaned up at the sink and methodically combed through the cupboard, where he found several envelopes filled with cash and also some pieces of jewellery. And then, unbelievably, someone rang the bell. He waited a few minutes, hoping whoever it was would go away, but the bell-ringer persisted. Looking through the keyhole, he saw that it was the dabbawali. He could handle that. Opening the door slightly, he took in the tiffin box and quickly shut the door. But the woman would not leave and demanded the empty tiffin box back. He then passed it out to her quickly and closed the door, hoping all the while that the wretched woman had not had a good look at him. Resuming his search, he found some more valuables and was preparing to leave when he heard a sound at the front door. Someone was trying to open the lock and get in. It was incredible (and would have been comical!) had it all not turned out to be so tragic. Could a chap not burgle a house in peace? This time it was Sethna, whom he stabbed after the old man had let himself in. There was blood all over the floor now and he tried cleaning it up a bit, without much success. He then made a small bonfire of the envelopes, some papers and the cloth bags that he found in the cupboard, and poured some rum over the fire for good measure, trying to lay a false trail. His shirt was now drenched in blood, so he changed into one of Sethna's, wrapping up his own in a newspaper to carry away. It would not do to leave a single clue behind. He then stuffed the cash and jewellery in a suitcase, cleaned the gupti and, wrapping it in a newspaper, prepared to leave. He had been about to open the door and let himself out when the bell rang yet again. Looking through the keyhole, he saw that it was an old man (Bahira), probably come to ask for some money. The man would soon go away, he decided, and stayed quiet. Sure enough, the old man left after a few more rings on the bell, and Daruwala made his exit, after putting a padlock on the door. That would keep away pesky callers for a while and buy him time. The cash and jewellery were in the suitcase and the paper parcels were tucked under his arm. Luckily, no one came up the stairs as he made his way down, and within minutes he was safely out of the building. He caught a taxi to the dharamshala at Charni Road where he was now staying and deposited his loot under the bed. After a quick wash-up, he hailed another taxi to take him to the Porchristy Guest House at Andheri. He took along a doll and a baby blanket that he had bought for his daughter. On the way he stopped at a Marwari shop to redeem his suit, which he had pawned for 100 rupees. He was back at the dharamshala late that night. Setting out early next morning, while it was still dark, he threw the gupti into the B.J. Compound and dumped his clothes at the Muslim cemetery at Marine Lines.

It was a straightforward and honest confession. All the loose ends were now tied up. The police subsequently recovered the jewellery and other items from the shops where Daruwala had sold them. All that remained was to secure a conviction in court.

Not surprisingly, when the case came up in the court of the additional sessions judge of Greater Bombay, Daruwala denied everything and was ably defended by the eminent B.M. Mistry. However, the prosecution led by Phiroze Vakil was equally brilliant, and on 22 December 1971, Daruwala was sentenced to death. Subsequent appeals to the high court and the Supreme Court failed, and his mercy petition to the President was also rejected. He was hanged at Pune's Yerwada Jail and the body was handed over to his father for the last rites. Interestingly, and perhaps fittingly, the symbol on which he stood for elections was the scales of justice.

Daruwala made quite a splash following his arrest and conviction for the quadruple murders. He made good copy, for several journalists who had interviewed him after he filed his election nomination had been impressed by his personality, and some sympathy and admiration for him seeped through in the press reports.

He apparently went to the gallows without any trace of bitterness. DCP R.S. Kulkarni recounts in his memoirs that

Daruwala had sent him a hand-written greeting card from Yerwada, wishing the policeman and his family a happy Diwali.[5]

———

I have always been very interested in what happens to the families of the victims and the condemned man after the law has administered its punishment. Sethna, the Masters and Bawla had no offspring. Of the colourful Adi Cooper, there was no trace. I doubt if he ever mended his ways, but not every wrong 'un comes to a sticky end. Inquiries among my Parsi friends and contacts in Mumbai about Daruwala's family, particularly his wife and child, yielded nothing. Someone, somewhere is bound to know, but I did not want to dig too deep. Some closets are best left unopened. Marie would be nearly eighty now, if she is alive. Their daughter Peggy, whose photo her father was said to be clutching in his hand as he stepped up to the gallows, would be in her fifties. I can only hope that the crimes of her star-crossed father who, with all his faults, loved her very much, did not cast a shadow on her later years and that she has been blessed with a quiet and happy life.

<h1 style="text-align:center">10</h1>

The Khambekar Street Poisoning Case*

Poisoning is one of the oldest and, in many ways, the easiest, means of getting rid of an enemy. When done skilfully, and by someone versed in the use of drugs, chemicals or poisons, detection is often very difficult, if not impossible. Before the advent of technology and the widespread use of scientific methods, getting a poisoner into the dock was not an easy task. It is not to be wondered, therefore, that poisoning cases repeatedly crop up in crime reports from the eighteenth century. One such case – and a notorious one at that – occurred in Bombay at the beginning of 1891.

The scene of the crime was Khambekar Street, a bustling thoroughfare in the Dongri locality, quite close to the Pydhonie police station. The street was said to be named

---

*S.M. Edwardes, *The Bombay City Police: A Historical Sketch 1672–1916*, Oxford University Press, 1923; *A Biographical Sketch of Sardar Mir Abdul Ali, Khan Bahadur, Head of the Detective Force, Bombay,* Bombay Gazette Steam Printing Works, 1896; *Gazetteer of the Bombay City and Island*, Vol. 2, The Times Press, Bombay, 1909.

after a local landlord, a Konkani Muslim by the name of Khambekar, but was also popularly known as Chas Street, after the several shops that sold buttermilk on that stretch of the road. It was here in January 1891 that a Muslim family of four and their servant died under mysterious circumstance within hours of one another after consuming their evening meal.

The facts are briefly these: Abdullah Noor Mahomed, a fifty-six-year-old retired Memon merchant, lived on the third floor of a large house on Khambekar Street. One of his sons, Bachoo, twenty-seven, and his wife also stayed with him. The fourth floor, which was also rented by Abdullah, was occupied by his seventy-year-old brother Molidina and his family – wife Halimabai, stepmother Karimabai and a nine-year-old grandson. Also residing on the third floor was a female servant, Fatimabai, and a young man named Dawood Abaji, who ran errands and assisted in the housework. Molidina, too, employed a female servant, Mariam, but she did not live with the family. The Memons hailed from Kutch in Gujarat and were part of the city's well-known and prosperous mercantile Muslim community.

On 21 January, a Wednesday, Abdullah stepped out of his house to meet his friend Haji Saboo Sidik, who lived nearby. Abdullah had left after taking his evening meal, along with his son Bachoo, at 7.30 p.m. This was a daily routine, and the two men were engaged in conversation when Molidina arrived in an excited state to inform him that Halimabai had taken seriously ill. The two brothers immediately went to the house of Pir Ahmed Shah, a native doctor or *hakim*, who then accompanied Molidina to his house, while Abdullah waited in the hakim's courtyard. In a little while, a messenger arrived at Molidina's house with more alarming news – Abdullah had been taken ill while sitting in the hakim's courtyard. Meanwhile, Saboo Sidik, being informed of his friend's sudden illness, also rushed to the doctor's house, but Abdullah died within a few moments of his arrival. Saboo Sidik and a few neighbours who had now gathered, carried the body to Abdullah's room and placed it on the bed. Molidina, hearing the commotion on the floor below, went there, and upon finding his brother dead, fell to the ground, gasping for breath. He was placed on a couch in the room but soon expired. By now Fatima, the servant girl, was also showing signs of distress and was taken by her brother and his daughter (who had been summoned) to their house, where she too died shortly afterwards. Karimabai, who was attending to Halimabai, on being told of the death of both her sons, rushed downstairs and seeing the bodies almost collapsed. With a great deal of difficulty, she was taken upstairs to her bed. Her ordeal, however, had still not ended. She was now told that Halimabai had also died. The inconsolable old woman, nearly maddened with grief, now sank to the floor. She was helped on to her bed, but passed away soon after.

The whole neighbourhood was in an uproar. It was known that all the victims had been taken ill after consuming the evening meal, and foul play was naturally suspected. The police soon arrived on the scene, and the five corpses were moved to the morgue at Kamathipura. A post-mortem duly conducted by Dr N.H. Choksi on behalf of Dr Sydney Smith, surgeon to the coroner, threw up some strange findings. Dr Choksi, who could detect no trace of poison in the bodies of any of the deceased, was of the opinion that all the five victims had suffered from heart disease.

The police were loath to accept this. Mir Abdul Ali, the head of the detective branch, and his officials were convinced that strychnine or some kind of vegetable poison had been administered to the victims. Getting rid of inconvenient family members by the use of poison, particularly the seed of the Datura plant, was not an infrequent occurrence in India. India was also home to bands of professional poisoners who often wandered from place to place, disguised as holy men or traders, befriending unsuspecting fellow travellers, whom they would rob after offering them sweets or a meal laced with poison. In fact, only a couple of years later, in 1893, had the Bombay City police succeeded in breaking up two gangs of Datura poisoners who had robbed a large number of people.[1]

It was suggested that the deaths at Khambekar Street might have occurred due to food poisoning, the evening meal having been cooked in utensils that were not very clean. Adulterated food or oil that had gone bad could also have been used in cooking the evening meal, and the deaths could just have been an unfortunate accident. The police, to their credit, were not won over by these arguments. They were certain that someone had plotted to kill the family. Further investigation being called for, viscera samples from the victims were then sent to Dr Barry, the chemical analyser to the government. His report was eagerly awaited and when it arrived the suspicions of the police were borne out – all five victims had died of strychnine poisoning.

It was now clear that someone had deliberately poisoned the Abdullah family. But the police had nothing else to go on and questioning of the surviving members – Bachoo and his wife – did not provide any further leads. There seemed to be no real motive for the crime, if that was what it was, as the victims seemed to have had no known enemies.

The investigation seemed to hit a dead end. Then, the police had a stroke of luck. Detective Mir Abdul Ali was told by a young man who had recently arrived in Bombay that a similar case had occurred in the same family a few months earlier. A woman by the name of Asubai, who had been related to Abdullah Noor Mohammad, had died under similar circumstances and was interred quietly in the Memon burial ground at Mangalwadi in Girgaum. She was the young man's aunt and he had always suspected that something was amiss in the manner of her death. He had been away from the city when the latest deaths occurred but was convinced that Bachoo was in some way, involved in the poisonings.

This was a serious charge, but one that the police could not ignore. They had to tread carefully though, as they couldn't accuse Bachoo of poisoning his entire family without solid proof. The first thing to do therefore was to conduct a post-mortem on Asubai's body. The necessary permissions were obtained and the corpse was exhumed. The contents of Asubai's stomach were extracted and a sample of the viscera was sent to the government chemical analyser. His report, eagerly awaited by the police, turned out to be the clincher: Asubai's viscera showed traces of strychnine. She, too, had undoubtedly been poisoned.

While the police were encouraged by the findings of the report, and Bachoo was now the prime suspect, convincing a jury to convict him of the killings would not be easy without further proof or a confession. Bachoo's first successful attempt at poisoning without being detected had probably given him the idea that he could repeat it with impunity, for some as yet unknown reason. Further questioning was called for and Bachoo was summoned by the police. His answers being not very satisfactory, the police formally arrested him on suspicion of murder – an action that led to a storm of protest from the local Memon community.[2]

The police, however, held a trump card. The family servant, Dawood, had agreed to turn Queen's Evidence and revealed his young master's nefarious plot. A week before the family was poisoned, Dawood had planned to go to his native village and had demanded from Bachoo some money that the latter owed him. Bachoo agreed, but asked him to delay his trip for a few days, during which time he wanted Dawood to do something on his behalf. Bachoo had then procured a white powder and asked Dawood to mix it in the food to be served to the five people in the family. The poison was to be administered to everyone at the same time, he said. On being asked by Dawood as to why he wanted to poison his family, Bachoo said he was heavily in debt and in need of money. The police found this to be true. Bachoo was a spendthrift and had cultivated extravagant habits. He had borrowed large sums from several moneylenders, whom he was unable to pay. They had apparently threatened to expose him to his father and file proceedings to recover their dues. The death of his father and others in the family would leave him the sole heir to the family property, which was considerable. Dawood, who did not seem to have had any qualms about poisoning five people, was to be paid 500 rupees for committing the despicable deed. The two conspirators had considered several ways by which the poison could best be administered – mixed into milk, tea or food – without raising suspicion. Finally, it was decided that Dawood would do as he thought best whenever a suitable opportunity presented itself. Elaborate plans had also been made to perform the necessary ceremonies and quickly take away the bodies for burial after the victims had died. Dawood had divided the powder into five parts and administered it to each of the victims by mixing it in their food, and Bachoo sat and watched them consume it without any guilt or remorse. Dawood had been ordered to make himself scarce once the deed was done, but the servant had lingered on for a while and was caught by the police just as he was preparing to leave the city.

The police now moved quickly to collect all possible evidence from the scene of the crime, before it could be destroyed. The packet of poison was found in the house on Khambekar Street and seized. The druggists who had supplied the poison were also traced to their shop in Pydhonie. Confronted by the police, they admitted to having sold 25 grains of strychnine to Bachoo. With Dawood's confession and the evidence now in hand, the police finally had a case that could stand up in court. All the loose ends had been tied up. Bachoo was committed for trial at the second criminal sessions of the Bombay High Court, presided over by Chief Justice Sir Charles Sergeant. The Memon community was solidly behind Bachoo and the best legal help that money could buy was made available to him. It was alleged that Bachoo had been framed and the evidence against him was concocted. The jury was not impressed and duly found him guilty of murder by a majority of seven to two, and he was sentenced to death. Bachoo's wife, who was also a suspect, was not charged, as there was not enough evidence to prove her guilt.

Bachoo appealed his sentence to the government of Bombay, which informed him that 'the offence which was brought home to him was of a diabolical character, and that any leniency in the case would be misplaced'.[3] He also made a final appeal to the government of India but found no relief. Bachoo was hanged for his crimes in Bombay on 6 June 1891.

11

The Parel Trunk Murder*

The news of a body being found in a box or trunk – headless, limbless or otherwise – has always held a morbid fascination for the newspaper-reading public. More so if the unfortunate victim happened to be possessed of feminine charms. No surprise, then, that the murder and the subsequent means of disposal of Sharifa Khatoon caused much excitement among the good citizens of Bombay in November 1887.

On the twenty-fifth of the month, a Friday, readers of the *Times of India* were alerted to a 'Mysterious Occurrence at Parel', where a wooden box tied up in a gunny bag had been found in a ditch near the Elphinstone Road railway station on the Bombay, Baroda and Central India (BB&CI) railway line. An old man had come across it early the previous morning and, revolted by the offensive smell emanating from within,

---

had concluded that the contents were of an 'extraordinary character'. The lowly police sepoy to whom the matter was reported decided that his superiors ought to be informed, and in a little while inspector Richard Raymond, in charge of the Mahim district, was on the scene.[1]

The lock on the box was broken, and inside, probably to no one's surprise, was the body of a young woman in her twenties. The corpse, which had been doubled up and thrust into the box, bore several marks of violence and was in an advanced stage of decomposition. On the abdomen was a large knife wound, with a smaller one below the right ear. The nose had been cut off and the face had been mutilated, evidently to prevent identification of the body. A handkerchief was found under the corpse, which had been dressed in '*trowsers and a cholee* (sic)', but there was nothing in the box that could provide any clue to the identity of the woman or her antecedents. A mattress was also found a few paces away from the box. A post-mortem on the body, which the police surgeon found crawling with maggots, revealed that the corpse was of a healthy woman, around twenty-five to twenty-eight years of age. She had been suffocated to death.

While the murder of a woman was not an uncommon occurrence in Bombay, it was not every day that the city police were faced with one stuffed into a box or trunk. Police inquiries in the nearby localities, the heart of the city's textile district, turned up nothing. The dead woman's clothes held no clues that could give the police any leads. The police also made a proclamation by drumbeat (known in local police parlance as 'beating bataki') all over town, hoping that someone might come forward with information about the woman, but they drew a blank. With none of the police stations in the city having received any complaint about a woman gone missing, it was quite likely that she had been murdered somewhere else and the body brought to Bombay to avoid detection. With nothing much to go on, the police set their informers to work and awaited developments.

In the meantime, acting on the theory that the murdered woman was most likely a stranger to the city, the police began making inquiries at the nearby rest-houses or *musafirkhanas*. Here, they had better luck. At the Ismail Habib musafirkhana, they learned that a Pathan named Syed Gul, who had been residing at Pakmodia Street, had a box similar to the one in which the body had been found. Nawab Khan, the keeper of the musafirkhana, told the police that Syed Gul, who was a carpenter, had arrived from Karachi in early September along with his nine-year-old daughter, carrying two wooden boxes containing his tools, clothes and other personal effects. A few days later, he was joined by his friend Nur Mohammad, who also stayed with him. On 24 October, a young woman by the name of Sharifa Khatoon had also come to stay at the musafirkhana. She said she was from Nashik and had quite a bit of jewellery on her person, including gold earrings, a necklace, silver bangles and anklets. Some days later, they had all moved out of the guest house and shifted to a house on the same street. Nawab Khan was told that the woman had married Syed Gul in a *nikaah* ceremony. Nawab Khan also identified the box in which the body was found as that of Syed Gul. The *qazi* who had performed the couple's nikaah ceremony was soon traced. Sharifa Khatoon was a widow, and he had conducted the marriage rites, for which Syed Gul had paid him four rupees, the qazi, Maksud Ali, told the police. He had obtained her signature on the memorandum of marriage, which he produced before the police.[2]

Now they finally had a suspect. But when the police knocked on the door of his lodgings at Pakmodia Street, Syed Gul was not in. He'd paid up his dues and left, the landlord told them. Further inquiries revealed that Syed Gul had suddenly gone off to Aden by the steamer SS *Wave* on 24 November, accompanied by his daughter and Nur Muhammad. Of Sharifa Khatoon, however, there was not a trace and no one knew where she had gone. The police also discovered that the clothes on the corpse were similar to the ones worn by Syed Gul's missing wife. While there was still no direct evidence against the Pathan, the police were now certain that the corpse in the box was that of Sharifa Khatoon. Syed Gul had done away with her for some reason and had fled.

Getting Syed Gul back would not be easy, and there were legal procedures to be followed. Aden, well beyond the shores of India, was part of the Bombay Presidency, but a valid case would have to be made out before the authorities in Aden to apprehend him there and bring him back to India. While the evidence against Syed Gul was not entirely conclusive, all the circumstances seemed to suggest that he was the guilty party. Police Commissioner Frank Souter was, however, confident that his men were on the right track, and accordingly, after informing the government of Bombay, sent a telegram to the British Resident in Aden to apprehend the suspects as soon as they landed there.

When the SS *Wave* docked at the port of Aden, a police party was waiting for Syed Gul and his companions. They were taken into custody and promptly shipped back under a guard provided by the Aden police, arriving back in Bombay on 10 December, where Inspector Framjee Bhicajee and other officers of the Bombay Police Detective Branch took them into custody.

At the police commissioner's office at Byculla, Syed Gul was interviewed by Mir Abdul Ali, Superintendent of the Detective Branch, and Inspector Dajee Gangajee, but proved a tough nut to crack. A few clothes similar to the ones worn by Sharifa had been found in Syed Gul's luggage, but his answers were evasive and he refused to admit that he had anything to do with her disappearance. The police were aware that without any direct evidence it would be difficult to convict him for the murder. They then went to work on Nur Muhammad, who, after a little persuasion, agreed to turn approver in return for a pardon. His confession laid bare the whole story.[3]

Nur Muhammad confirmed much of what the police already knew. Sharifa had been married to Syed Gul on 26 October and they had all moved to another house nearby. Here, he said, relations between the couple had soured. Syed Gul had apparently taken away and disposed of Sharifa's jewellery without her knowledge, and the couple frequently quarrelled about this. Fed up with Khatoon's intolerable temper, he had decided to do away with her and had sought Nur Muhammad's help. Syed Gul first attempted to kill Sharifa by putting arsenic in her paan-supari and food but was unsuccessful. In the end, deciding that strangulation was the best option available, he had obtained a pair of long blacksmith's tongs and had throttled her on the morning of 23 November. The body was stuffed into a wooden box, which was then wrapped in a gunny bag, tied up with coir rope and taken out in a hired bullock cart. The box had been unloaded outside Elphinstone Road railway station and placed on the roadside near the level crossing. For some reason, they also took along the mattress that Syed Gul had purchased at the time of his marriage and left it on the box. The two men then hired a man named Rama Sajan, who worked in the BB&CI railway workshops and stayed in a *chawl* near the station, to watch over the box, saying they would be back soon. But they never went back.

Rama was easily located and gave the police his part of the story. The two men had paid him an anna to watch over the box, Rama said, but when they failed to turn up after a few hours, he'd moved the box and mattress to his home nearby. However, a foul smell had begun to issue from the box after a few hours, and so, suspecting the worst, he'd dumped it along with the mattress in the ditch near the railway station that very night. The police had found the corpse the next morning. Rama had been watching from a distance as the box was opened but had been too scared to get involved and kept his mouth shut. That same day, Syed Gul and his companions left by steamer for Aden, having purchased tickets from the money obtained by selling off the ornaments of his newly wedded wife.

The last bits of the jigsaw had fallen into place and all the loose ends had been finally tied up. Though Syed Gul steadfastly refused to cooperate, there was now absolutely no doubt about his guilt. On 17 December, he was formally charged with causing the death of his wife Sharifa and remanded to police custody.[4]

During the five-day trial at the sessions court, as many as 24 witnesses, including the jewellers to whom Syed Gul had sold Sharifa's jewellery, were called by the prosecution to buttress its case against Syed Gul. The advocate general leading the prosecution said the police were to be complimented for their success in apprehending the culprits, and the presiding judge, Acting Chief Justice Bayley, in his address to the jury, said there was no reason to believe that undue influence had been brought to bear upon the witnesses by the police. The jury agreed, and unanimously found Syed Gul guilty.

Justice Bayley, while passing the sentence of death on the accused, said Syed Gul had been found guilty of:

> a most cruel and horrible murder, and no one who has heard the evidence can doubt for a moment that you took that woman's life as described by your accomplice. There is not the slightest reason to assume that the police have improperly dealt with the witnesses in the case and in the course of a long experience I have scarcely ever seen a case so clearly proved against a prisoner as this one.[5]

12

The DeGa Poisoning Case*

Pestonjee Dinshaw was a most unlikely criminal. As he stood in the dock on trial for his life in the sessions court of Bombay in February 1873, no one associated with this otherwise unassuming Parsi solicitor could imagine him resorting to black magic to meet his devious ends. For Pestonjee stood accused not only of an attempt to conspire to murder two people by the use of sorcery (a charge unprecedented in itself), but was also the alleged mastermind behind the fatal poisoning of four people a few months earlier in what was known as the Grant Road Poisoning Case.

---

*'Family of Eight Poisoned at Bombay', *The Maitland Mercury*, 2 January 1873, https://trove.nla.gov.au/newspaper/article/148333314, accessed 20 February 2025; 'The DeGa Conspiracy Case: The Trial of Pestonjee Dinshaw and Succaram Ragoba', *The Times of India*, 13–14 February 1873, https://www.google.co.in/books/edition/The_De_Ga_Conspiracy_Case_Trial_of_Pesto/uwcIgiH8LxgC?hl=en, accessed 20 February 2026; S.M. Edwardes, *The Bombay City Police: A Historical Sketch, 1672–1916*, Humphrey Milford, Oxford University Press, 1923; *A Biographical Sketch of Sardar Mir Abdul Ali, Khan Bahadur, Head of the Detective Police, Bombay*, Bombay Gazette Steam Printing Works, 1896; *Gazetteer of the Bombay City and Island*, Vol. 2, The Times Press, Bombay, 1909.

The poisoning, which occurred in November 1872, created a sensation in Bombay. The *Times of India* reported that the 'whole community was thrilled with horror'.[1] The venerable Old Lady of Boribunder was not exaggerating – it was not every day that the citizens of Bombay woke up to news of nearly 10 people, most of them related in some way to a single family, had been the target of an attempted poisoning.

The DeGas, the targets of Pestonjee's foul scheme, were a Portuguese family that had settled in Bombay for many years. Angela DeGa, the matriarch, had been widowed nearly a decade ago and lived with her four surviving children (out of a brood of 12) at Prospect Lodge on Grant Road. On the morning of 15 November, a box of cakes was sent to the house, purportedly by Dr Luis Rozario, a near relation. They were delivered in a box by a peon, or someone dressed as one, and no one took any particular notice of the man, who was never identified or seen again. The DeGas seem to have been generous and large-hearted folk, for they shared the cakes with relatives all over the city. Some were sent to the house of Angela's eldest son, Anthony DeGa in the suburb of Bandra, just across the Mahim causeway. Anthony in turn, sent a few to his neighbour and family friend, J.D. Pereira. A few cakes were also dispatched to the Mazgaon home of DeLima, one of Angela's daughters.

At dinner that evening, with the widow Angela presiding, were her sons Joseph and Michael and, daughters Angelica and Amelia. The cakes were called for and placed on the table by one of the servants. However, not everyone had them. Michael and Angelica declined, but forty-two-year-old Joseph tucked in well. The teenager Amelia only had a nibble and gave away the rest to one of the servants, who then shared it with three others in the kitchen. In a little while, all of them were taken violently sick with excruciating pains. Curiously, Dr Rozario, who was thought to have sent the cakes in the first place, was immediately summoned to treat them. Joseph purged a few times, but fell unconscious and passed away around midnight. Amelia and the servants went through repeated and painful bouts of vomiting but they survived the ordeal.

Across town, a similar scene took place. Anthony DeGa was seized with vomiting fits at his house in Bandra, and so was his friend, J.D. Pereira and his old mother, Domingo Pereira. Doctors were sent for, but despite their best efforts, which mostly involved purging the victims to get the poison out of their system, all three died within the span of a few hours. Anthony's wife and the DeLimas also became ill but recovered. The Pereira's ayah, who had also been given a piece of one of the cakes, was reported to be dangerously sick but survived.

An inquest of the bodies of all the deceased and, as poisoning was suspected, it was decided to send the stomach contents to the J.J. Hospital for analysis. Pereira and his mother were buried in the Bandra cemetery where, the *Times of India* reported, a large crowd had gathered to pay their last respects to the deceased, who were well-regarded members of the local community. Anthony DeGa was laid to rest at the Girgaum church, where again, a large number of mourners had assembled.

While the 'Grant Road Poisoning', as the press promptly dubbed the case, created quite a stir in the city, the police had nothing to go on. Dr Rosario was ruled out as a suspect. He said he had not sent the cakes and the DeGas were absolutely certain he had nothing to do with them. The servants at Prospect Lodge were questioned, but none of them could recall anything in particular about the mysterious peon who had delivered the box of cakes to the DeGa residence. On being told that it was a gift from Dr Rozario, one of the servants had accepted the box without giving it a thought and the peon had walked away. There was nothing by which to identify or trace him.

For the families involved, the whole affair was inexplicable. The widow DeGa, who had lost two of her children (from her large brood of 12), told the police that they had no enemies who could have possibly wanted to do away with the whole family or would have in any way benefitted from their deaths. They were middle-class folk who led quiet lives. Joseph DeGa had been employed as an accountant at the Bank of Bombay and his brother Anthony was an assistant at Forbes and Co., while J. D. Pereira was a managing clerk at Dallas and Co., a firm of solicitors. They had no known enemies. Michael DeGa came under suspicion, probably because he had declined to have the cakes, and was held at the local police *chowky* for a few days but was cleared of any complicity in the affair. Michael, however, suggested that the police keep an eye on Pestonjee Dinshaw, a solicitor known to the family, who he believed had something to do with the poisoning.

As it turned out, the cakes were actually meant for a newly wed couple in the family; Angela's fifth son Nicholas and his wife Rosemary Stevens, who had married a few months earlier, were away that fateful evening and so escaped unharmed. As the police inquiries continued, with no sign of a breakthrough, and the press kept up its clamour for the perpetrators to be brought to justice, the Bombay government announced a reward of 3,000 rupees for any information that could lead to the arrest of the culprit or culprits. The widow DeGa topped this up with a further award of 1,000 rupees from her own pocket.

The police, meanwhile, could do nothing but wait. Eventually, tongues were sure to wag and something would turn up. Soon enough, Superintendent Thomas Mills of the Bombay Police received an anonymous letter that claimed Pestonjee was behind the poisoning. Inquiries revealed that the solicitor was also the executor to the estate of Rosemary Stevens, the wife of Nicholas DeGa. The Parsi was, therefore, now a suspect and kept under watch.

The unsolved murders apart, there was another event that kept the city abuzz at this time. Lord Northbrook was on a visit to Bombay, and with the city administration pulling out all the stops to make the Viceregal tour a success, the police were accused of not having devoted the necessary resources to get to the bottom of the affair, a charge stoutly denied by Sir Frank Souter, the Commissioner of Police.

A few weeks on, the much-awaited breakthrough materialized. On 9 December, Khan Bahadur Mir Akbar Ali, the head of the Detective Branch, was informed that Pestonjee had been making inquiries about a certain fakir to help him get rid of some of his enemies. The informant, Ali Mohammad, was a jailbird and none too trustworthy. Pestonjee, he said, had sought his assistance through a man named Sakharam Raghoba to contact Kakishah, a fakir residing at Kamathipura who was said to employ black magic to help people get rid of their troubles. The solicitor apparently wanted a couple of people done away with.

The police were flabbergasted, to say the least. Resorting to the black arts to get rid of enemies was not unknown in India. In a land where superstition ran deep, large numbers of people rushed to babas and fakirs to get rid of afflictions, perceived or real. Superintendent Mills supported the claim during the trial when he claimed that belief in sorcery was common among the lower classes. He had known even educated 'natives' (referring to the elite class of Indians) resorting to sorcery and witchcraft, Mills told the court. More often than not, these supposedly holy men were frauds and charlatans, but rarely would a complaint be made to the authorities by their gullible victims. That a Bombay High Court lawyer, and particularly one who hailed from a community that was arguably the most educated and progressive in British India, would seek recourse through black magic was a hard pill to swallow. The informant came from the worst of Bombay's lowlife and could not be taken at his word. Still, the matter could not be ignored and Akbar Ali thought it was worth sounding out the police commissioner himself. Sir Frank Souter, always game for a daring venture, readily gave the go-ahead for a sting operation.

The plan was simple enough. A police team comprising Acting Deputy Commissioner R.H. Vincent, Khan Bahadur Mir Akbar Ali, his son Detective Inspector Mir Abdul Ali, Superintendent Thomas Mills and Inspector Ahmed Ali, would conceal themselves inside the fakir's house, where

Ali Mohammad would introduce Pestonjee and Raghoba to Kakishah. Whatever followed would be most interesting to watch, and with luck, the police might get some evidence to nail the crooked lawyer. The fakir, who was known to the police as a religious mendicant who sold amulets and charms (but not a sorcerer), was co-opted into the plot and agreed to play his part. It is doubtful that he had much choice in the matter!

On the evening of 11 December, the police team was in place in a makeshift room at the fakir's house situated in Third Lane, Kamathipura, the city's notorious red-light district. The tiny room had been partitioned off the first-floor landing by wooden boards. A few holes drilled into the boards would enable the police to see and hear all that went on in the landing, which was in itself a small room. The only light, a faint one, was provided by a small lamp on the floor of the landing. A little after 7 p.m., Sakharam Raghoba, Pestonjee and Ali Mohammad arrived. Kakishah was waiting and after the introductions and customary salutations, they got down to business. Raghoba informed the fakir that his seth (or master, referring to Pestonjee) was being troubled by two people – a man and his wife. He wanted to be rid of them. Could Kakishah help? He could, but first he wanted to know the caste of the intended victims. They were Christians, he was told. This was seemingly no obstacle for the fakir. Could they not be poisoned, he asked, but Pestonjee would not have it. He was categorically against the use of poison, or *zehr*. Instead, he wanted the fakir to use his '*illum*' – an Arabic word meaning science or art – to get rid of them. '*Zehr se mut mar dalo, tumhare illum se saaf karo,*' the police heard him say. Here the word *illum* was taken to mean sorcery or black magic. Pestonjee wanted it done quickly, within the next few days if possible. To avoid any suspicion, the victims must first fall ill and die within a few days of each other – not on the same day. Kakishah then asked for the names of the persons to be disposed of.

The solicitor was initially hesitant, but then gave their names as Nicholas DeGa and his wife Rosemary Stevens. Ali Mohammed then said the seth would pay 1,500 rupees on the day the couple fell sick and 3,500 rupees when they were dead. Pestonjee cut in here – he would not do that, but was willing to pay 500 rupees on the day Nicholas DeGa fell ill, followed by 2,000 rupees if he were to die in the next three days. The same terms would apply in the case of Rosemary DeGa too. The fakir then went into an adjoining room where he could be heard muttering something that was inaudible to the police, and came out holding a book. He then wrote down something in it with a pen and told the solicitor that the deed would be done ('*Kam hojayega*', according to the testimony of Mir Abdul Ali). The book, which was also described in some reports as a 'book of divination' and even as part of the Quran, came in for much discussion during the trial as none of the witnesses could get a clear view of it. On being asked why the solicitor wanted the couple killed, Raghoba said it was being done on behalf of a lady named Anne Pennell, a friend of Pestonjee's, against whom Nicholas DeGa had filed a suit in the high court. Kakishah wanted the victims to be pointed out to him as he did not know them by sight, and Ali Mohammad and Sakharam Raghoba agreed to do this the very next day.

Some desultory conversation then followed, after which the visitors left. The police had now heard all they wanted but refrained from making an immediate arrest. They would let the drama play out a few more days before moving in.

The next day, around noon, the fakir was taken by Ali Mohammad and Sakharam Raghoba to Elphinstone Circle Gardens (now Horniman Circle) where Nicholas DeGa, who was employed in a bank close to the Town Hall, was pointed out to him. The fakir was asked to look through a window of the bank at a man walking inside, whom Raghoba identified as Nicholas. Kakishah, who gave his full name in court as Kakishah bin Ibrahim, confirmed this in the witness stand and also identified Nicholas, who was then present in the court, as the man who was pointed out to him as the one to be eliminated.

It took another day for the police to make up their minds, and on 14 December the necessary warrants were produced. Pestonjee, who was taken into custody by inspector Mir Abdul Ali at Kalbadevi Road, did not protest or offer any resistance when he was shown the arrest warrant. Sakharam Raghoba was also arrested the same day from his residence at Gaiwadi in Girgaum. He too stayed silent when the charge against him was read out.

To say that the trial created a sensation would be an understatement. The singular and bizarre nature of Pestonjee's second attempt to get rid of Nicholas DeGa ensured that the sessions court was packed with gawkers waiting for a glimpse of the now notorious solicitor. The Parsi community had also turned out in full strength and seemed to take a lively interest in the proceedings, for it was not every day that one of them stood in the dock, accused of a conspiracy to murder.

Nicholas DeGa's testimony in the courtroom revealed the reason behind the multiple attempts on his life. Both Pestonjee and Anne Pennell were suspected of having embezzled large sums of money from Rosemary's father's estate, of which they were the executors. On 4 November, two weeks before the poisoning, a show-cause notice had been issued against them, seeking a proper account of the receipts and expenses of the estate, following which the two parties were in negotiations for a settlement. The DeGas had rejected an initial offer made by the solicitor and his lady friend, and this had probably prompted the latter to look for alternative means to bring the affair to a close.

The trial was conducted before Justice Bailey and a special jury was sworn in. The charge against the accused was that they had instigated Kakishah to murder Nicholas and Rosemary DeGa. Pestonjee was defended by Thomas Anstey and John Inverarity, both eminent members of the Bombay bar. According to the evidence from the police witnesses, Pestonjee had been quite specific in his instructions to the fakir that the DeGas were not be killed by poison, and the question of what the solicitor meant by the use of 'illum' gave rise to prolonged and excited debate, both within the courtroom and outside. According to James Flynn, the chief interpreter to the High Court, the word illum by itself signified science, knowledge, art or skill, and could be interpreted to mean sorcery only when used in conjunction with the subject itself. However, in popular usage it was generally understood to mean magic, sorcery or black art. As to what Pestonjee meant by '*saaf karo*', Flynn said it literally meant to polish off or get rid of, and was slang employed in the same sense as in English – meaning to kill. In the end, the jury seemed to have no doubts at all about the intentions of the accused and returned a guilty verdict. Pestonjee and Raghoba were each sentenced to seven years' rigorous imprisonment and though the verdict predictably went up for review before a full bench, no relief was granted to either.

Pestonjee served his term and walked out of jail, a free but disgraced man. Reputed for being a clever and competent lawyer, he was now effectively ruined as his name had been struck off the rolls of the Bombay bar following his conviction. He lingered on for a few years after his release and died in 1895. Sakharam Raghoba did not live out his sentence and died while serving time at the Thana Central Jail.

Interestingly, neither of the accused was charged in the Grant Road murders and stood trial only for having instigated Kakishah to murder Nicholas DeGa and his wife. The police could not have possibly convicted either Pestonjee or Raghoba in the poisoning case as there was nothing to directly link them with the crime. Neither had made any reference to it during their visit to Kakishah and the police who were watching and listening could not obtain any evidence to connect them directly to the poisonings. In the absence of the peon who delivered the cakes – the only person who could have provided damning evidence – there was nothing the law could do to bring a charge of murder against the accused. The police were also certain that the peon had been killed and his body disposed of, and there were unconfirmed reports that Sakharam had agreed to make a confession to that effect, but he passed away before the police got around to taking down his statement. The fate of the missing peon was never conclusively established.

13

The Umerkhadi Double Murder*

The murder of a woman by a jilted lover is not unusual in the annals of crime, but it is not often that one comes across a killer who quotes Persian couplets. A double homicide in the crowded, bustling locality of Oomercarry (now Umerkhadi), in central Bombay in June 1884 was remarkable in that it was the lovelorn murderer's command of Persian that allowed the police to get on his track and aided in sending him to the gallows.

The crime took place early on the first day of the Muslim holy month of Ramadan. Hajee Mohamed Shoostry, a prosperous Persian merchant residing in Umerkhadi, had returned home close to midnight on 24 June after a few cheerful hours in the company of friends. It was the evening before the day of fasting and huge crowds were out in the

---

The Times of India, 26 June, 1884; *The Times of India*, 30 June, 1884; S.M. Edwardes, *The Bombay City Police: A Historical Sketch 1672--1916*, Humphrey Milford, Oxford University Press, 1923; *A Biographical Sketch of Sardar Mir Abdul Ali, Khan Bahadur, Head of the Detective Force, Bombay*, Bombay Gazette Steam Printing Works, 1896.; *Gazetteer of the Bombay City and Island*, Vol. 2, The Times Press, Bombay, 1909.

narrow lanes of the Muslim quarter of the city of Bombay. Shoostry's house was situated in the middle of a fairly large compound in Munshi Ali Akbar Lane. Enclosed by walls nearly eight feet high, the house was a sizeable one with four rooms, the largest of which was the bedroom, while another was used as an office. Access to the property was possible only by means of a single large gate.

Shoostry's wife Haji Bibi had in fact been asleep when he arrived, and the couple had a late dinner before retiring to bed around 1 a.m. on 25 June. The door to their bedroom was, as always, left open for ventilation. The only light in the room was provided by a small kerosene lamp. An hour or so later, according to the *Times of India* report on the incident, Haji Bibi 'was aroused from her sleep by feeling the clammy touch of a man's hand on her person'.[1] Terrified, she cried out, 'thief! thief!' and was immediately stabbed with a knife. The kerosene lamp had gone out, and in the darkness, she heard sounds of a scuffle as the assailant attacked her husband. Someone then tumbled down from the bed – Shoostry, bleeding from numerous wounds, had collapsed on the bedroom floor. Then, according to the deposition Haji Bibi made before her death, the intruder came up to her (she was now out of her bed and presumably on her feet) and said in Persian: '*Pedri sookhta* [burnt father], you are the person who called "thief, thief".'[2]

By now the woman's screams had woken up the other inmates of the house, but by the time a couple of servants and the female cook arrived, the assailant had escaped. Fateh Ali, a servant employed by a solicitor living next door, told the police that he was woken up by the commotion. Upon rushing out into the street, he had seen a man running out of the gate of Shoostry's house. But Ali could not provide any further details. He hadn't paid much attention, as he thought it was one of Shoostry's servants.

The servants found the couple bleeding from multiple wounds. Shoostry was lying on the floor while his wife was sitting upright against the wall, her clothes drenched in blood. Both were still alive, however, and were rushed to the J.J. Hospital nearby. Their declarations were taken down by the second presidency magistrate, later in the morning, but neither Shoostry nor his wife could provide the police any clues to the identity of their assailant. The unfortunate couple clung on to life for four days after the murderous attack on them, but despite the best efforts of the doctors, succumbed on 29 June, dying within hours of each other.[3]

Incidentally, while the couple's assailant was yet to be caught, the law did come down hard on a particularly detestable crime against women that week. The *Times of India*, which carried a report about Haji Bibi's death, recorded that no less than three persons had been charged with 'nose-cutting' by the Bombay Sessions Court. Jetha Hurjee had cut off the nose and both ears of his wife on suspicion of infidelity, while Sonda Hameer and Shahboodin Haminoodin had cut off the noses of their respective mistresses. Trials in those days were not the long-drawn-out affairs they are now, and the juries in all three cases did not need much time in making up their minds. All three accused were found guilty.[4]

The police had no real clues to go on or leads to follow in the Shoostry case. The usual inquiries were made in the neighbourhood. Mohamed Shoostry (described by the *Times* as an 'unoffensive Mogul merchant') had arrived in Bombay from Basra a couple of years ago. A native of Shooster, he had a wife and four children in Iran. Haji Bibi, a native of Shiraz, was around twenty years old and was his second wife. They had been married for only a year and she was now pregnant. The couple had lived in Duncan Road in the Two Tanks area before moving to Umerkhadi over a month ago. They were quiet, homely folk, and no one in the locality seemed to have held a grouse against either of the deceased.

While there was seemingly no motive for the attack, it was clear that a deliberate attempt had been made to kill the couple. Nothing had been stolen from the house, so the assault was not the outcome of a burglary gone wrong. The assailant had climbed over the wall of the Shoostry residence with the sole intention of doing away with one or both of them. But strangely, he seemed to have arrived unarmed, as the knife used in the attack (and left behind) was identified by Haji Bibi as having come from her kitchen. The intruder had left behind a cloak and a skull cap, but these were commonplace items of clothing and there was nothing about them that could provide any clue to their owner.

The only intriguing part about the whole affair was the murderer's inexplicable remark made in Persian to Haji Bibi. Persian had been the official language and means of courtly discourse in Mughal India and continued to be so in the early years of British administration under the East India Company. Persian speakers could still be found among the native educated class in British India towards the closing decades of the nineteenth century, but not many spoke the language in Bombay. Whoever killed Haji Bibi seemed to have been fluent enough in the language to use idiomatic expressions. It was a slender clue at best, but something the police could work on. The officers in charge of the case were also convinced that the murderer was known to Haji Bibi. For reasons known only to herself, the woman had thought best to keep mum about the man who had attempted to kill her. Could it be a former lover, a jilted suitor? An inquiry into her past, the investigators reasoned, was called for.

Haji Bibi's friends and relatives were questioned again, this time a little more closely. It was then discovered that the deceased woman had had an admirer before her marriage. This was a gentleman by the name of Haji Mirza Aga who, by all accounts, was a polished speaker given to spouting Persian verses. Mirza had pursued the young woman ardently, and had been a frequent visitor to her mother's house. He had even sought her hand in marriage. Sadly, his passion was not reciprocated, or he may simply have been regarded by the family as a pest, and his advances were not welcome. In fact, Haji Bibi's brother had warned him against entering their house. The dejected suitor had then gone off on a pilgrimage to the holy city of Karbala, but had told his friends that he still entertained hopes of winning the lady's hand after his return. This was not to be, however, as Haji Bibi had been married off to Shoostry during Mirza's absence. The police now had a suspect and a possible motive. The disappointed lover was soon apprehended at a dharamsala in Null Bazar, not too far from the scene of the crime.

Inquiries at the dharamsala revealed that on the morning after the murder, Mirza had turned up there in a dishevelled state, some of his garments being torn and dirty. He had borrowed some clothes from another person, tied his own in a bundle and gone out again. It turned out that he had gone off to bury his clothes, which were later dug up and recovered by the police.

The police also managed to find a witness named Mohamed Tucki, a Persian who was an acquaintance of Haji Mirza's. Called in for questioning by the police, Tucki soon spilled the beans. According to him, Mirza had planned to rob the Shoostry residence and Tucki was to meet him there on 23 June but had decided against it. Undaunted, Mirza had decided to do it alone and attempted to scale the compound wall of the house that night but was unsuccessful and returned empty-handed. He then asked Tucki to be there the following night, on 24 June, to help him.

There was now no doubt about Mirza's guilt. When confronted with Tucki's statement, the disappointed lover confessed to having committed the murders. The clothes he changed into after the attack belonged to Tucki, and Mirza agreed to take the police to the place where they were buried. The clothes were dug up and recovered by the police in the presence of Deputy Commissioner Bell and other senior officials. Mohammed Tucki also identified the clothes and admitted to having lent them to Mirza at the dharamsala on the morning after the murders.

The case came up for trial before Justice Hart at the fourth criminal sessions of the Bombay High Court. A special jury was sworn in, and the prosecution was led and ably conducted by Charles Farran. Mirza, however, denied his guilt in court and retracted his earlier confession made to the police. But the evidence against him was overwhelming, and Justice Hart was convinced that the prosecution had made its case well. In his summing-up to the jury, he remarked that while the chief witness against the accused was an accomplice, there was enough corroborative evidence to convict Mirza.

The accused himself had provided material corroborative evidence by taking the police to the spot where his clothes were buried and by pointing them out and saying 'here are the bloody clothes'. The submission by the defence that the evidence had been concocted by the police could not be sustained, the judge said. The jury concurred and found Mirza guilty by a majority of eight to one. He was accordingly sentenced to death.

Mirza Aga retained his cheerful demeanour in the days leading up to his death. He ate well during his time in the condemned cell, and unlike most prisoners on death row, actually managed to gain weight – a rare occurrence for someone awaiting the noose. He is said to have maintained his sang froid till the very end, apparently helping the hangman adjust the rope around his neck with a smile on his face.

In the end, Mirza Aga went off in style. True to form, moments before he was launched into eternity, he recited a couplet from the Persian poet Saadi: 'Lovers are the slain ones of their beloved; from the slain ones no voice proceeds.'[5]

14

Jambulingam: South India's Robin Hood*

For those who grew up in India of the 1970s and 1980s on a diet of Hindi movies, the word *daku* [dacoit] conjures up images of hard-riding, rifle-wielding desperadoes, bandoliers

---

** History of the Madras Police: Centenary 1859–1959*, Police Department, Madras, 1959, pp. 355–7; 'From the Archives (October 5, 1921): Dacoit's Escape', *The Hindu*, 5 October 2021, https://www.thehindu.com/archives/from-the-archives-october-5-1921-dacoits-escape/article36827601.ece, accessed 3 March 2026; *The Straits Times*, 13 June 1923, p. 8, https://eresources.nlb.gov.sg/newspapers/digitised/page/straitstimes19230613-1.1.8, accessed 20 February 2026; K.N. Krishnaswami Ayyar, *Statistical Appendix, Together with a Supplement to the District Gazetteer (1917) for Tinnevelly District*, The Superintendent, Government Press, 1934, https://archive.org/stream/in.ernet.dli.2015.102731/2015.102731.Madras-District-Gazetteers-1917_djvu.txt, accessed 20 February 2026; 'Crimes That Rocked Madras', *The Times of India*, 10 September 2008, https://timesofindia.indiatimes.com/city/chennai/crimes-that-rocked-madras/articleshow/3465354.cms, accessed 20 February 2026; N. Sam Golden, 'Celebrating the Legendary Brigand: Memory of Jambulinga, in Folk Narratives', *LangLit*, https://www.researchgate.net/publication/384156596_celebrating_the_legendary_brigand_memory_of_jambulingam_in_folk_narratives, accessed 3 March 2026.

slung across their chests, swooping down on remote villages in the ravine-infested badlands of Madhya Pradesh and Uttar Pradesh. Looting the resident moneylender or *bania*, these always-mustachioed thugs also kidnapped women (when they didn't do worse) and shot up whoever got in their way, before riding off into the hills. There, in a suitably secluded cave, the gang made merry, with the leader (or *sardar*) sprawled on his charpoy, drinking himself silly and – when the script demanded it – ravishing a newly captured maiden. Occasionally, there was a police raid and the dacoits had to fight their way out, but in the end the law always won, with the bandit chief either being riddled with bullets or hauled off in chains, swearing eternal vengeance on his captors.

So much for Bollywood bandits! The reality was often more prosaic but no less deadly. The average bandit, after a usually brief career of freebooting, was tracked, hunted down and shot without mercy. He was often a merry rogue, living life on the edge, and sometimes admired by the very people he preyed upon. Often, he was hailed as a hero and tales of his Robin Hood-like exploits found their way into local folklore. But that was an exception. In the end, he was a criminal and treated as such. And, like most of his kind, he came to a bad end.

But the dacoit was not a staple of north Indian criminal lore alone. His writ ran across much of the country, both before and during the British Raj and continued even a few decades after Independence. The menace of dacoity was always hard to put down and the records of the Indian Police are rife with tales of encounters where quite a few policemen made the supreme sacrifice to bring these men to book.

Going by the tales of Sultana Daku in the 1920s to Gabbar Singh, Man Singh, Mohar Singh, Paan Singh Tomar and Phoolan Devi from the 1960s to the 1980s, the dacoit seems to have operated in north and central India alone. But this is not entirely true. The more settled and progressive south too saw its share of banditry (albeit on a smaller scale), as did the harsh desert terrain of western India.

The most famous bandit from the south of India was the elephant-poacher and sandalwood-smuggler, Veerappan. His life and times are too well-documented to merit further retelling but before him, there was another who was just as notorious in his heyday. Jambulingam Nadar is largely unknown today, but the police force of the Madras Presidency (much of which now comprises the state of Tamil Nadu) a merry dance during the 1920s, before he was finally eliminated in a police encounter.

As with all historical figures who find a place in popular folklore, it is sometimes difficult to sift fact from myth in the Jambulingam story. Born into a poor Nadar family in a small village in the Tinnevelly district (now Tirunelveli), Jambulingam is said to have been a small-time trader, dealing in *karupetti* [palm jaggery] who took to crime after being falsely implicated in a police case. The Madras District Gazetteer, however, claims that he began life as a poacher in the forests of the Panangudi Hills. With a gang of some 20 to 30 men, he operated along the borders of the Madras Presidency and the princely state of Travancore, straddling the Tinnevelly and Kanyakumari districts. Lying in wait in the dense thickets along the roadsides, the gang would waylay travellers and merchants on lonely stretches and rob them of their valuables. Their depredations went unchecked for quite a few years, with the police unable to bring them to book as Jambulingam had a good network of informers who warned him well before any police operation to nab him was underway. While policing the hilly and forested tracts where the gang operated, the police always faced a challenge: jurisdictional issues hampered cooperation between the Madras Presidency police and the Travancore police.

Emboldened by their success, Jambulingam's gang began expanding their operations in the early 1920s, venturing out of their forested lair to raid the smaller towns and villages in the area. They did not spare the police either and small patrol parties were sometimes ambushed and relieved of their guns and ammunition.

Jambulingam's fame soon spread beyond the Presidency and even overseas. A daring raid on a marriage party in Nambikiruchi, where the gang divested women of valuables worth 4,500 rupees, was even reported in the Straits Settlements, which had a substantial Tamil immigrant population.[1]

However, despite all his depredations, Jambulingam managed to cultivate a clean image as the Robin Hood of south India. He was said to have never troubled or molested women or the poor, who saw him as one of their own. Incredulous tales were told of his supposedly supernatural powers in evading the law. There was some truth in this, for the police did seem to have a tough time keeping Jambulingam behind bars whenever he was apprehended.

On one occasion in 1920, having fallen into a trap set by the Tinnevelly Police, he was captured along with his chief lieutenant Kasi and two others. The gang were lodged in the Nanguneri sub-jail awaiting trial but didn't stay there long. They broke out within a week, wrenching apart the window bars of the cell in which they were locked up.

The gang managed to dodge the police for several months before Jambulingam was again captured in June 1921. Soon, Kasi also surrendered to the police. As it turned out, he'd done this only to be by his master's side to help him escape. On 2 October 1921, when the two men were being escorted from the Palamcottah district jail to Nanguneri sub-jail, they overpowered their police escort and took off with their guns and ammunition.

A correspondent for *The Hindu* newspaper, quoting an eyewitness, described the escape:

Shortly after 3 p.m. on Sunday while Jambulingam and his friends were taken to Manjeri for a magisterial enquiry escorted by three constables, the party made a halt at Moontudappu for taking refreshments. Jambulingam sought the permission of the escort for the release of one hand from his handcuffs, which request was granted. Secure in the feeling that they had the key of the handcuffs in their possession, the constables left the *bandy* (*cart) temporarily for a drink. The prisoners held a hurried conference and quick as thought decided to make a bold bid for liberty. Jambulingam (sic) possessing himself of a carbine and a round of ammunition left the bandy and made a rush at a Mahomedan constable who stood nearest to him and felled him to the ground. The disposal of the other two men and freeing his comrades was the work of an instant.

The constables who were simply flabbergasted flew for their lives and the escaped prisoners marched triumphantly away. When my informant saw them Jambulingam (sic) was shouldering a gun while his associates had their handcuffs on and were not in the least perturbed. The escape of Jambulingam (sic) is the one topic discussed everywhere and though he is a terror his daring and coolness command attention.[2]

This daring escape was a slap in the face for the police. A manhunt for the convicts was soon underway. With the help of a couple of informers, the gang was quickly run to the ground, and Jambulingam and his associates were rearrested within a couple of weeks. Tried for robbery and dacoity, each of them was sentenced to five years of rigorous imprisonment.

But Jambulingam had no plans to serve out his full term. Within nine months he effected another escape from the district jail with two other convicts. Now on the run, Jambulingam made for the safety of the hills, where he had spent most of his younger days. The goodwill he had amassed there came to his aid. The locals in the area would not give him away, and for many months the police had no clue of his whereabouts despite a reward being offered for his capture. Also, two men who had ratted out the bandit earlier had been murdered – a sufficient disincentive for anyone inclined to help the police.

Jambulingam's time was running out, however. The police would not let up, and eventually their persistence paid off. Finally, on 20 March 1923, following a tip-off, they tracked him down to a house in Konoor where he was holed up with his ever-faithful Kasi. The place was surrounded, and soon a fierce gunbattle was in progress. With escape seeming impossible, one of the gang set fire to a neighbouring house, hoping to create a diversion that would allow Jambulingam to get away. As the bandits made a run for it, shooting their way out, Kasi toppled over, hit by a police bullet. Jambulingam survived the fusillade, finding shelter behind a large tamarind tree. But the end was inevitable. He kept the police at bay for some time but was ultimately shot dead. The pistol that he used in his last encounter is now displayed at the police museum in Vellore.

Jambulingam was a larger-than-life figure in his heyday, and tales of his daring and chivalry continued to be passed down the generations, losing nothing by repetition in the decades after his passing. Not until the rise of Veerappan in the 1980s, would another bandit capture the popular imagination in south India. An eponymously named Malayalam movie on the outlaw's life was made in 1982, with the hugely popular Prem Nazir in the lead role. The legend of Jambulingam lives on.

15

The Nanavati Case*

Deputy Commissioner of Police John Lobo would never forget the Monday afternoon of 27 April, 1959. It was not every day that a serving naval officer came into the Crime

---

*K.L. Gauba, *Famous Trials for Love and Murder*, Hind Pocketbooks, Delhi, 1967; Bachi Karkaria, *In Hot Blood: The Nanavati Case that shock India*, Juggernaut Books, New Delhi, 2017; Gyan Prakash, *Mumbai Fables*, Harper Collins India, New Delhi, 2011; S. Rajagopalan, *Famous Murder Trials*, N.M. Tripathi, Bombay, 1968; P.B. Vachha, *Famous Judges, Lawyers, and Cases of Bombay: A Judicial History of Bombay during the British Period*, N.M. Tripathi, 1962; Meenal Baghel, *Death in Mumbai*, Penguin Random House India, 2011; Susan Adelman, *The Rebel: A Biography of Ram Jethmalani*, Penguin Random House India, 2013; 'K.M. Nanavati vs State of Maharashtra', *Indian Kanoon*, 24 November 1961, https://indiankanoon.org/doc/1596139/, accessed 21 February 2026; Ashok H. Desai, 'On the Case of the state against Kawas Maneckshaw Nanavati', *Economic and Political Weekly*, Vol. 12, 23 April 1960, https://www.epw.in/journal/1960/17/special-articles/case-state-against-kawas-maneckshaw-nanavati.html, accessed 21 February 2026; 'The Nanavati Case', *Parsi Khabar*, 11 July 2011, https://parsikhabar.net/history/the-nanavati-case/3222/, accessed 21 February 2026; Berjis Desai, 'Even in murder, class matters', *Parsiana*, 21 February 2016, https://www.parsiana.com/current-issue/articles.aspx?id=7l%2FpCLa3fWw%3D&issue=294, https://www.parsiana.com/news/news-you-can-use-details.aspx?id=YsXhBQNkhGo=&issue=291, accessed 21 February 2026

Branch headquarters and confessed to having committed a murder. And Commander Kavas Nanavati, well turned out even in his civvies, was the most unlikely candidate for a homicide. The naval officer told the policeman that he'd shot the man who had seduced his wife. Lobo had been alerted to this fact some time ago by the navy's provost marshal, Commander Michael Samuel, whose advice Nanavati had sought before turning himself in to the police. But it did not make things any easier for Lobo. Minutes before Nanavati had walked in, the inspector at Gamdevi police station had called Lobo to say that a man named Ahuja had been shot dead in their jurisdiction a little while ago. Lobo figured this had to be the victim and the man who had pulled the trigger, an Indian Navy officer, was now seated before him. This affair, Lobo knew, would have to be handled very tactfully.

Nanavati was ashen-faced but composed. For a man who'd been cuckolded and had undertaken a very rash act to remedy it, he held himself up well. Offering him a glass of water, Lobo called in two of his officers. They would question Nanavati and conduct the investigation that had to follow. In the meantime, could he wait in the adjoining room? This was not a facility extended to commonplace criminals, but then, the man before him was in a different league altogether. Just how did this officer, who was so obviously a gentleman, get himself into such a pickle, Lobo wondered.

At thirty-seven, Commander Kawas Maneckshaw Nanavati had a solid naval career behind him and promising prospects ahead. Starting his career in 1942 as a gentleman cadet with the Royal Indian Navy (as it then was), he trained at the Royal Naval College at Dartmouth and saw service in World War 2. The well-spoken, good-looking six-footer's resume also boasted a spell as naval attaché to Indian High Commissioner V.K. Krishna Menon in London in the early 1950s. By 1956, he had risen to the rank of commander, and a year later was appointed as second-in-command of the battle cruiser INS *Mysore*. His dash and polish also made the young Parsi officer attractive to women. While in the UK on training, he'd met and dazzled Sylvia King, and the love-struck couple were soon married at a registry, fittingly enough, in the naval base of Portsmouth, in July 1949.

Kawas's English bride was a hit with the folks back home in Bombay, and his marriage to a non-Parsi, otherwise frowned upon and strongly discouraged by the community, did not meet with any displeasure. Sylvia was welcomed into the bosom of Kawas's large family, and soon the newly-weds set up home, moving frequently into naval flats in the Colaba area, but never really far from the family residence at Southlands. In due course, the couple were parents to three kids, Pheroze, Tannaz and Jamshed.

The Nanavatis enjoyed a happy family life – though, given his profession, Kawas was often called to sea and his absence must have been sorely felt. But Sylvia (Sylvie to the family) made up for it and kept the children entertained and occupied with birthday parties, visits to the grandparents and swimming sessions at the United Services Club.

But Sylvia's mind was on other things too. She had fallen for Prem Ahuja, a charming thirty-four-year-old bachelor who owned a United Motors car dealership at Peddar Road. The Nanavatis had been introduced to Prem at one of the many parties they were invited to, and it is said that Prem was attracted to Sylvia due to her striking resemblance to a girl he had loved in his younger days. Whatever the reason, they were both attracted to each other. Prem had a reputation for being a playboy and a ladies' man, something which drew even more women into his orbit. But to be fair, it seems that Prem was not really the monster and home-wrecker that he was later made out to be in the frenzied press reports of the affair. According to his friends and acquaintances, he was quite a nice chap, charming and well-mannered, who naturally attracted women. He did not necessarily have to chase them; often it was the women who did the chasing.

Prem Ahuja, a Sindhi, grew up in Karachi and was educated at Lahore. A regular at the clubs in Karachi, he was mostly seen with pretty women on his arm, often the daughters of servicemen. His seeming predilection for daughters and wives of men in uniform would one day bring him to a bad end, but he was not to know that then. His success with women continued when he moved to Bombay. The parties at Jeevan Jyot, the Nepean Sea Road apartment where he stayed with his unmarried sister Mamie, were well attended. There was booze, good food and music for the pretty women and eager young men who attended, and a good time was had by all.

Sylvia may simply have been lonely while her husband was away, and Prem was certainly very good company. He was also a known womanizer and would not have let go of easy pickings, but it would not be fair to blame him entirely for what transpired between them. It was mutual, and they were both consenting adults. Sylvia seems to have been certainly the more attached of the two and she may have even contemplated marrying him, but Prem did not seem the marrying kind. And then there were the kids. She was fond of them and could not possibly give them up and start a new life with someone else. And so, the affair rolled on . . .

If Kawas suspected that his wife did not love him anymore or had been unfaithful, the revelation was not very gradual. It was the beginning of the summer of 1959 and he had just come back from a two-month sailing tour. He had been home for over a week, but for some reason Sylvia had been cold and distant, almost aloof. On the afternoon of 27 April, as the couple sat in their living room waiting for lunch to be served, he asked Sylvia what the matter was. There was no reply. He pressed her a bit, but was again met with stony silence. He asked her if she had stopped loving him and if there was some else in her life. Silence again, but a silence that undoubtedly signified admission. Instinctively, he suspected it was Prem, but Sylvia would not confirm or deny that. But Nanavati had his answer, and was predictably furious. His wife had been having a dalliance with that scum of a playboy while he was away and had allowed herself to be seduced. But he still loved his wife, and thought he could repair the damage. He was also seeking an exit route out of all this. He would forgive her if she stopped seeing him again, could she do that? Sylvia stayed mum. There was nothing more to be said. Saying he would sort this out with that low-life Prem, Nanavati got up to leave. Sylvia probably read murder in his eyes and held him back, pleading that Prem might shoot him. Nanavati said he would probably kill himself anyway. A thoroughly alarmed Sylvia managed to hold him back, and the family then sat down for lunch.

But the food would have been mud in Nanavati's mouth.

He must have been raring for a confrontation with Prem, but the discipline ingrained by years of service in the navy kicked in and he stayed calm. In a crisis, an officer always stayed calm. But he knew how to take action as well. He would not be stopped. Lunch over, Nanavati dropped his wife and the kids off at the Metro Cinema to catch the afternoon show of *Tom Thumb*, as planned. He then drove to the naval dockyard where his ship, the INS *Mysore*, was berthed and spoke to the gunnery officer. Could he have a revolver and some cartridges from the armoury? He was driving with his family to Aurangabad that night and the road was lonely. He just wanted it as a measure of safety, he said. An unusual request by any means, for officers are not allowed to take their personal sidearm home when they are on leave. Nanavati could be very persuasive, and the gunnery officer may have felt that the commander indeed had a valid reason to ask for the weapon. Nanavati could undoubtedly be trusted to behave responsibly, and he would return the firearm in a couple of days. Within a few minutes, having signed the necessary papers, Nanavati walked down the gangway with a service-issue .38 Smith & Wesson revolver and six cartridges in a brown paper envelope, and drove off to his rendezvous with destiny. But first there was a brief stop at the Universal Motors office at Peddar Road to check if Prem was in. He wasn't. He'd gone home for lunch, the manager told Nanavati. The aggrieved husband headed off to Setalvad Lane, Nepean Sea Road. The moment of reckoning with his wife's paramour was only minutes away.

Rajpal, the servant who admitted him into Prem's second-floor flat, had no idea what the visitor wanted, but asked him to wait in the living room as the master was dressing. But Nanavati had not arrived to be kept waiting, and to the startled servant's surprise marched straight into Prem' bedroom, shutting the door behind him.

What transpired next has never been satisfactorily explained. According to Nanavati, he asked Prem whether he would do the honourable thing and marry Sylvia. The man was stepping out of his bathroom with a towel around his waist – not the best of circumstances for an interview with a cuckolded and visibly furious husband – and his retort was sharp and biting. He couldn't possibly marry every woman he slept with, Prem told the outraged husband. This was adding insult to injury. Threatening to give Prem a hiding, Nanavati moved to place the envelope containing the revolver on a nearby cabinet. Prem then lunged for the revolver, which Nanavati quickly whipped out, and ordered him to step back. The two men then grappled as Prem tried to wrest the revolver from the naval officer's grasp. And then the gun went off – not once, not twice, but thrice – and Prem slumped to the floor, dead. Nanavati later said he could recall only two shots, and could not account for the third. Prem's sister Mamie, woken up from her afternoon siesta as the shots went off, rushed out of her room. Nanavati was walking out of her brother's bedroom, revolver in hand, and she could see Prem's body on the bathroom floor through the open doorway. Pointing the gun at the terrified servant, Nanavati walked out of the flat and ran down the stairs. Waving aside the watchman who'd been startled by the shots and screams upstairs, he got into his car and drove off. The police arrived to find that three shots had been fired. One had missed Prem entirely, another had grazed his head and the third had caught him in the chest, killing him. Two of the bullets, flattened out, were found on the bathroom floor, having probably ricocheted.

The prosecution would not buy Nanavati's version of events when the case came up for trial. According to them, Prem's reply had so infuriated Nanavati that he had whipped out the revolver and shot him down where he stood. The gun had certainly not gone off by accident. And if the two men had fought, as Nanavati suggested, how come the towel did not fall off Prem's waist in that seemingly life-and-death struggle? The prosecution did have a point there.

For a man who had shot another in cold (or maybe a little hot) blood, Nanavati was treated with kid gloves right from the time he turned himself in to the police. The police were polite, if not deferential, and he was not severely inconvenienced in custody. The navy closed ranks behind their man and tried to get him out of the police lock-up. It was inconceivable that a naval officer could be made to share a cell with common felons.

Nanavati had been formally arrested on the evening of 27 April and the following day was produced at the court of the additional chief presidency magistrate. His lawyer did not seek bail but requested the court to allow Nanavati to sleep in the naval barracks, as the conditions in the police lockup were not conducive to his client's health. His client would present himself at the CID office religiously every day, he assured the court. The prosecution would not relent and wanted Nanavati either in judicial or police custody. The magistrate postponed the hearing to 5 May, but then the navy pulled out all the stops and the very next day the Flag Officer, Bombay, Rear

Admiral B.S. Soman himself applied for naval custody of Nanavati, to which the court agreed. Nanavati was driven by Provost Marshal Samuel himself, armed escort in tow, to the INS *Kunjali*, the naval jail.[1] The *Kunjali* had a separate cell for officers, and Nanavati's time there was spent in reasonable comfort, for the cell came equipped with a personal western-style toilet and bath. He also received regular visits from his lawyers, which might have been tiresome but were very essential if he had to get out of the mess he was in. A repentant Sylvia was also allowed to meet her husband regularly, and one assumes that in the two years Nanavati spent there, the couple managed to repair their strained relationship. Verily, there's nothing like a serious family crisis to make sundered hearts whole again!

While Nanavati would have breathed several signs of relief as the naval jeep ferried him to his new, temporary quarters, his struggles were only just beginning. The trial that would follow and the public outcry it triggered would take a huge toll on the now infamous naval officer and his family, driving him to eventually leave his country for a life of obscurity abroad.

It would not be an exaggeration to say that the Nanavati case split the city of Mumbai into two camps. The pro-Nanavati camp comprised the Parsi community, which thought their man had done the right thing, and others who were impressed by his naval background and service to the country and felt Nanavati was justified in shooting the man who had stolen his wife's affections. The other side, vociferous in their calls that justice be done to the slain Prem Ahuja, were the Sindhis. Incensed that the murder of one of their own was being effectively swept under the carpet and the culprit almost being allowed to get away with it, they banded together for what would turn out to be a bruising fight in the courts.

The Parsis, long excelling in the practice of jurisprudence, could be said to have been at a distinct advantage, for the community could boast of the cream of the legal profession among their number, a feature which continues till present day. Arrayed on Nanavati's side was a distinguished roll of legal talent, not the least his uncle Dhunjishaw Nanavati, a senior partner of Mulla & Mulla, one of Bombay's best law firms. The Sindhis, essentially a business community, had one big legal card up their sleeve though. Fighting from their corner was the redoubtable Ram Jethmalani, an up-and-coming lawyer who had made a name for himself fighting cases for refugees from his community. Jethmalani was nothing if not combative and his presence somewhat evened the odds for the Sindhi camp. The stage was set for a battle royale in the courts.

The newspapers would not be left behind. The first mention of the case in the venerable *Times of India* was on page 8 of its 29 April issue about Nanavati's appearance at the magistrate court. Very soon though, the story would make it to the front page and stay there often as the opposing sides battled it out.

While the Nanavati case was followed by all the news-sheets, there was one which literally went to town with the case and would in time come to be seen as being partisan to the Parsi point of view. This was the (now defunct) weekly *Blitz*, ably led into battle by the mercurial Russi Karanjia, who seemed to have made it his life's mission to set Nanavati free. The tabloid reported every little twist and turn of the case and its pages, awash with photos, were eagerly scrutinized by a voyeuristic citizenry that could never have enough of the oh-so-dashing Commander Nanavati.[2]

Fortunately for Nanavati, television had not invaded homes and minds then, so he (and everyone involved) was spared the relentless and breathless minute-by-minute media coverage that famous criminal cases are now subject to

While drama in the courtroom was a given, there was plenty of action outside as well when the trail opened at the sessions court. When the vehicle carrying Nanavati, escorted by Provost Samuel, rolled into the court premises on 23 September, an adoring crowd was awaiting. Nanavati got the optics right. As he strode in, tall and dignified, medals aglitter on his spotless white naval uniform, he was the veritable knight in shining armour. College boys and corporate executives, middle-aged housewives, teenage girls and twenty-something secretaries (who were blowing kisses), jobless gawkers and *taporis*, reporters, photographers, and most certainly pickpockets, pushed and shoved for a glimpse of their hero. This was repeated every day and was a sore trial for the police, who had to depute extra staff to rein in the crowds that would go 'Ka-was, Ka-was' every time Nanavati appeared. Needless to say, a Parsi contingent was out in force each day, cheering on their man. The trial was good for business too. The cutting chai and *sherbet-wallahs* on the pavements outside raked in the *moolah*, as did the hawkers selling 'Nanavati Pistols' and 'Ahuja Towels'. The sales pitch for the latter has probably never been bettered in Indian advertising – *Ahuja ka towliya! Marega to bhi nahi giregal* (Ahuja's towel! Won't fall off even if you drop dead!)

Inside the courtroom of Justice R.B. Mehta, Nanavati might have felt that he had things under control. He had been charged with murder under Section 302 of the Indian Penal Code, and also, alternatively, with culpable homicide not amounting to murder under Section 304, Part 1. To counter this and get him off the hook, he had a defence team comprising the cream of the Bombay bar, led by the eminent Karl Khandalawala, a lawyer from London's famed Inns of Court. Khandalawala was instructed by Shiavax Vakil, a veteran of Mulla & Mulla, and seconded by Rajni Patel, who would go on to make a greater splash in politics in the years ahead.

The prosecution, led by C.M. Trivedi, was almost colourless by comparison. However, it did benefit from the legal smarts of Ram Jethmalani who, while not appearing in court, had been retained by Mamie Ahuja to even the odds in what seemed like a decidedly unequal fight that was tilted heavily in favour of the defendant.

Knowing that they stood on shaky ground, defence counsel went for the 'grave and sudden provocation' theory. The murder, they said, was not premeditated as the prosecution claimed, but was done in a fit of rage. Prem's mocking reply – that he could not marry every woman he slept with – had provoked Nanavati, who had then attacked his wife's lover. A struggle had followed as both men tried to gain possession of the revolver, and Prem had been shot. It was nothing but an unfortunate accident.

The prosecution was having none of it. The commander had gone to Prem's flat with murder on his mind. He had obtained a gun under false pretences and intended to shoot the deceased from the outset when he set out from his ship. The defence's argument that Nanavati had obtained the revolver to kill himself could not stand, the prosecution maintained. Also, there was the towel. If indeed the two men had struggled, how was it that the towel did not fall off? When the police arrived at the scene, Prem's lifeless body was found with the towel securely tied around his waist. He had dropped dead right where he was shot. Also, another crucial point: there were blood stains on the bathroom wall and the door handle, but not a drop had spattered on Nanavati's clothes, which were spotless when he turned himself in to Lobo. If he had indeed grappled with Prem and the gun had gone off, would there not be at least some blood on Nanavati's clothes?

The defence tried to blacken the victim's character. Prem was nothing but a skirt-chasing scoundrel, a playboy businessman who lured women into his bed for his pleasure and then cast them aside. And another point: quite apart from the fact that he destroyed an otherwise happy family to satisfy his lust, the businessman had broken the prohibition laws. The police had found bottles whisky, rum and beer at his house. He was not a law-abiding citizen by any means, the defence claimed. Nanavati, on the other hand was an upright and honourable man. He had served his country faithfully for years and had been humiliated by an unscrupulous Lotharic. He was the wronged party in all this.

The defence also played the patriotic card. How were servicemen to attend to their duties if men like Prem were allowed to seduce their wives while they defended the nation's borders? Was this how the men in uniform were to be rewarded? In the eyes of the defence, the businessman who played fast and loose with soldiers' wives was (to use a term current in our times), nothing short of 'anti-national'. This was, strictly speaking, hitting below the belt and an emotional play to a very receptive and sympathetic jury.

The background of the two protagonists was also a factor in the case – and here Prem easily lost out to the Parsi. Nanavati came from a respectable family with a solid professional standing, and belonged to a community that played a big role in nation-building before and after Independence. The Parsis' role in establishing institutions that have contributed to India's economic growth and their penchant for founding educational and social institutions has always been praiseworthy. The community was also known for its philanthropy and generous donations to good causes. Most importantly, the Parsis had a reputation for being decent and law-abiding people. They were, in short, a model community, and India was proud of them. Prem, on the other hand, belonged to the Sindhi community, known for its sharp mercantile instincts and eagerness to make a quick buck. The smooth-talking, hustling Sindhi was not very much admired, especially after hordes of them moved to India from Pakistan, following Partition in 1947. Viewed as interlopers, they were good businessmen who drove a hard bargain – traits admired in today's go-getting devil-take-the-hindmost culture – but did not sit well with most Indians in the still-idealistic decades after Independence. It was not fair to the Sindhis, but that unfortunately, was how things stood, and Nanavati benefitted in this battle of perceptions.

Sylvia, the other protagonist in the love triangle, did not fare very well either. At her first appearance in court on 13

October, clad in a white sari, the harassed woman had to run the gauntlet of the hostile crowd outside the courtroom. She was booed, cat-called, hissed and (apparently) spat at. This was the unfaithful wife who had cheated on her noble husband. Her English origins did not help. What could one expect from a *gori memsaab*, after all?

Sylvia, however, was fortunate in that the Nanavati family stood behind her like a rock. Shocked and grieving (after that unbelievable evening when a friend of the family picked her up from the Metro Cinema), and being a foreigner in a country that seemed to have suddenly turned hostile towards her, Sylvia had to draw on all her reserves of strength to get through the next few years. She was fortunate in her in-laws. Her brother-in-law would physically shield her as she walked into the courtroom with the jeers of the crowd ringing in her ears. Inside, she had to tell her story to the whole world, and it was not easy. She said she had been 'infatuated' with Ahuja, but her letters found in Ahuja's flat in fact showed that her feelings for him ran much deeper, even hoping for the unlikely possibility of marriage with Ahuja. Though there was not much in her testimony that differed from Nanavati's version of events before he left her to settle scores with her paramour, her every word and emotion was scrutinized and commented on by a voyeuristic public in the days that followed. There was talk that the couple would divorce, but this did not materialize – to the disappointment of many of Nanavati's female fans.

Nanavati was, without question, the people's favourite. As far as the man in the street (unburdened by legal niceties) was concerned, he had done the right thing and Prem Ahuja had got what he deserved. The women were smitten by the dashing naval officer. 'Numerous college girls are said to have lost their heads to the handsome Commander. Some have swooned after seeing him. Others have reportedly sent him 100-rupee notes marked with lipstick. A few love-lorn nymphets have even made him offers of marriage, anticipating a divorce,' the *Blitz* reported.[3]

All this tamasha did not really make for a good trial. The atmosphere both outside the courtroom and within was charged, much to the displeasure of the presiding judge. Justice Mehta had his work cut out to ensure that the proceedings did not take on the aspect of a farce. Partisan supporters of Nanavati who packed the courtroom often cheered for him or tried to shout down the prosecution witnesses, and had to be frequently admonished by the bench. There was also a silent, if somewhat sinister, spectator at the trial – a dummy skull (which many thought was the real thing) fitted with Ajuha's so-called skull cap, one of the exhibits in the case, which was kept on a table near the press benches. The *Blitz*, which claimed to be 'Asia's Foremost Newsmagazine', carried a photo of the 'skull cap' in its issue dated 24 October 1959.

Finally, after all the examining and cross-examining of witnesses, it all came down to the nine-member jury. Except for a lone dissenter, they were all solidly behind Nanavati and he was held not guilty.[4]

The sole dissenter, incidentally, was Reginald Pierce, who later said that had the crowd outside known it, he would have been lynched. An Anglo-Indian who came to India in 1925, aged seventeen, he had worked as a weaver for much of his life at the David Sassoon Mills, Phoenix Mills and

Bombay Dyeing. His name was picked from a hat, after he had responded to a *Times of India* advertisement for people for jury duty. 'He was a fine fellow,' he said about Nanavati later. 'I think he was an honourable murderer, but a murderer all the same.'[5]

The verdict was greeted with applause in the courtroom, and the crowd outside cheered itself hoarse. But Justice Mehta would not have it. He did what judges are meant to do – ensure that a trial is fair and the ends of justice are met. The law, Justice Mehta decided, could not be made an ass of. Describing the verdict as 'perverse', he refused to accept it and referred the case to the high court.

The verdict predictably divided opinion around the country, and not within the legal fraternity alone. The press expended reams of paper in dissecting the jury's decision and the judge's refusal to countenance it. The case then went up to the Bombay High Court, but Nanavati could get no relief there. A two-judge division bench of Justices J.M. Shelat and V.A. Naik found him guilty of murder under Section 302 and sentenced him to rigorous imprisonment for life. Justice Shelat also observed that the jury had been misdirected, and agreed that the verdict was perverse.

Nanavati should now have gone to a proper prison, but the saga did not end there. His supporters did not give up; telephone calls went out to people in high places and, inexplicably, within hours of the high court ruling, Sri Prakasa, the Governor of erstwhile Bombay State, suspended the sentence, allowing Nanavati to stay at *Kunjali* till his appeal to the Supreme Court was disposed of.

This unprecedented move by the governor caused a furore. The legality of the order was questioned, but was later upheld by the high court. Nanavati could enjoy his comfortable quarters at the naval detention centre for some more time yet. The minor scandal resulting from the governor's order singed Prime Minister Nehru himself. Navy Chief Admiral R.D. Katari and Defence Minister V.K. Krishna Menon had apparently pleaded on Nanavati's behalf and prevailed on the prime minister to intervene. Menon, no stranger to controversy, and never one to shy away from it, admitted to the *New York Times* correspondent that the central government had intervened at his request so that the 'stain of turpitude should not destroy the career of a promising young officer'. Nanavati, it must be remembered, had served as naval attaché during Menon's time in London. The much-reviled defence minister's faults and foibles were many and legendary, but for all that he was a man who stood by his men when they were in peril.

Finally, and inevitably, the Nanavati case came to the highest court of the land. But the Supreme Court would not consider the appeal until Nanavati had first surrendered to the civil power, and on 8 September 1960, Nanavati had to give up his stay at INS *Kunjali* and move to a civilian prison. In the end though, it was all to naught and the apex court upheld the verdict of the high court. Commander Nanavati, it seemed, would have to spend fifteen years of his life behind bars.

Life at Arthur Road Jail would not have been easy for Nanavati after the sojourn at *Kunjali*, but it couldn't have been very tough either. He was kept in a special cell and allowed privileges such as home food. His family, meanwhile, was not having an easy time. His elder boy was made the butt of vicious jokes and taunts at school, which left him scarred for years. The younger kids were packed off to boarding school to keep them out of the relentless media glare. Through all this, Sylvia remained calm and composed, braving the storm that had engulfed her life. Her parents asked her to move back to England, but she refused. She would stick with her husband and fight it out, waiting for the tide to turn.

And turn it did, slowly but surely. In October 1963, Nanavati's lawyers managed to secure him parole on the grounds of ill health, and Nanavati left his prison cell for a comfortable bungalow in the more salubrious environs of the hill station of Lonavala for the remainder of his sentence. But that was not the end of the affair.

The Nanavati saga is nothing if not an unending chain of unexpected events and surprises. The Parsis had not given up the fight for their man, and Russi Karanjia tried everything to get Nanavati out of jail. Petitions were drafted and signature campaigns launched, and every legal avenue was explored to set Nanavati free. One such route was a governor's pardon. And that was the means Nanavati's backers employed to finally get him out for good. It was actually very crudely done, and certainly could not have been done today. Nanavati was, all said and done, a very lucky man, and a fortuitous set of circumstances helped him clear the final hurdle to freedom.

It so happened that in March 1964, Bhai Pratap, a Sindhi philanthropist who had done much work to help refugees from the community, was languishing in jail on a charge of cheating. The Sindhis backed him to man, and a petition seeking a pardon for their benefactor was now pending the governor's approval. The person holding that high office at the time was none other than Vijaya Lakshmi Pandit, a former president of the United Nation's General Assembly and (more importantly) the prime minister's sister. As Bhai Pratap's plea landed on Pandit's table, Nanavati's lawyers saw an opening and went for it. Rajni Patel, with Sylvia in tow, approached Ram Jethmalani with a proposal. Could he possibly secure Mamie Ahuja's no-objection to a pardon for Nanavati, if the Parsis on their part did not oppose Bhai Pratap's release? The Sindhi lawyer was surprised, but agreed to give it a shot. Mamie took some convincing but Jethmalani managed to persuade her that her stock would rise considerably if she were to play her part in getting the man who had done so much for their community out of the cooler. It would be a win-win for both camps, and they could leave all this behind and get on with their lives. Nanavati had already spent three years behind bars, and now maybe it was time to let bygones be bygones and bring some closure to this whole affair.

Mamie, to her credit, agreed. A deal was struck, the pardon came through and Commander Nanavati left the Lonavala bungalow, a free man. In the end, it was as simple as all that. The otherwise sordid Nanavati saga had ended on a rather tame note.

Not that the 'pardon' was well-received. Questions about entitlement and privilege were raised and debated endlessly, and while Nanavati's backers and the pretty young things were ecstatic, there was also some bit of tut-tutting, not least in the legal fraternity.

The Nanavati case did change legal history in one way though. It brought the curtain down on the trial-by-jury system in India. Sympathy for Nanavati notwithstanding, the blatant partisanship of the jury had not gone down well in many quarters. A vital and valid question was now raised: could a bunch of men and women, untrained and unaware of the law, who are quite likely to be swayed by passion and unconscious biases, be trusted with a matter of life and death in a courtroom, or indeed with any legal question, for that matter? The answer had to be a resounding 'no', and jury trials were therefore abolished by the government. The nine jurors (or, more correctly, eight) in the Nanavati trial had unwittingly sounded the death knell for a system which, while giving the accused the privilege of being tried by their peers, was inherently flawed.

And what of the Nanavatis? Kawas was a free man, but even after the brouhaha over the trial had died down it was apparent that the family would never be able to lead a normal life in India, at least in the foreseeable future. The only realistic option was for them to move abroad. In 1968, the Nanavatis emigrated to Canada, and by all accounts the now firmly reconciled couple put their past behind and lived a happy life. Kawas passed away in 2003, without ever having spoken his mind about the most distressing event of his life. Some fifty years after he shot Prem Ahuja, an Indian newspaper is said to have contacted Kawas for an interview, but he politely declined. He had, hopefully, buried the ghosts of his past.

And what of Sylvia? Like most modern grannies, she has a Facebook profile. Her photos reveal the face of a woman who (aside from the dark days of the 1960s) has led a happy life.

Nanavati was undoubtedly the Indian Navy's most famous officer, if not for all the right reasons. The navy would not have wanted any of its officers to be involved in another murder trial, and there was none for many decades after the Nanavati affair. Then, almost fifty years later, in 2008, another naval officer found himself in circumstances almost similar to that of Nanavati. Lieutenant Emil Jerome Mathew hit the headlines for having murdered television executive Neeraj Grover in a fit of rage after finding him in his (Mathew's) girlfriend Maria Susairaj's bedroom. Mathew was awarded a ten-year jail term while Maria drew a lesser sentence for destruction of evidence and was released after three years in prison.

The Nanavati case 'inspired' (for want of a better word) many movies based on the love-triangle theme, notably *Yeh Rastey Hain Pyaar Ke* (1963), *Achanak* (1973) and, most recently, the Akshay Kumar-starrer *Rustom* in 2016. The public, it seems, can never have enough of the life and times of Commander Kawas Nanavati.

16

Raman Raghav: The Terror of Bombay*

The terror that was Raman Raghav, gripped India's commercial capital only for a brief while in the mid-to-late 1960s. Known by several aliases, he kept the city in thrall during the monsoon months of 1968 when nearly a score of people, mostly pavement and slum-dwellers in the western suburbs, were brutally attacked, some, fatally. His blood-drenched reign came to an abrupt end

* R.S. Kulkarni, *Crimes, Criminals and Cops*, Vikas Publishing, New Delhi, 1989; Khushwant Singh, *Portrait of a Serial Killer: Uncollected Writings*, Aleph Book Company, New Delhi, 2015; Anirban Bhattacharya, *The Deadly Dozen: India's Most Notorious Serial Killers*, Penguin Random House, Gurugram, 2019. BBC News Desk, 'Raman Raghav: When India's "Jack the Ripper" terrorised Mumbai', *BBC News*, 5 November 2015, https://www.bbc.com/news/world-asia-india-34719646, accessed 21 February 2026; Divyadeep Singh, 'Raman Raghav: Unmasking Serial Killer's Reign of Terror in the City of Dreams', *ABP News*, 8 June 2023, https://news.abplive.com/news/india/raman-raghav-unmasking-serial killer-s-reign-of-terror-in-city-of-dreams-mumbai-crime-1606473, accessed 21 February 2026; TNN, 'Retired Cop who arrested serial killer Raman Raghav Dies', *The Times of India*, 15 November 2020, https://timesofindia.indiatimes.com/city/mumbai/mumbai-retired-cop-who-arrested-serial killer-raman-raghav-dies/articleshow/79228472.cms, accessed 21 February 2026.

when he was spotted by an observant Crime Branch officer and quickly apprehended before he could perpetrate further crimes. Raghav's trial took several years and tested the best legal and medical brains in the country, for the man was obviously deranged and securing a firm conviction was not an easy task. In the end, charges were brought against him for only a single attack when he had killed two labourers in the last week of August 1968. In hindsight, Raman Raghav's second spell of killings could arguably have been thwarted, for the police had actually hauled him in as a suspect in a series of murders that had occurred between 1965 and 66. However, he had been let off for lack of concrete evidence, free to unleash a second round of mayhem. While it is difficult to arrive at an accurate count of his victims, he seems to have been responsible for at least forty murders, meriting the sobriquet that the press was quick to confer on him – 'India's Jack the Ripper'. This his story . . .

———

Bombay in the late 1960s was slowly becoming a crowded metropolis. As the country's commercial hub, it drew in a never-receding tide of migrants for whom housing was an obvious problem. The city therefore expanded out into the suburbs, where a housing boom was steadily underway, as the newly emerging middle-classes gradually left their teeming chawls for the apartment blocks coming up in the suburbs. But for the city's poor there was no relief, and they perforce congregated in the sprawling slums that now became an essential backdrop of suburban life. It was here that Raman Raghav found most of his victims.

The first round of killings occurred in 1965 in the slums around a municipal water line, known as the duct line, which ran through the suburbs on the city's Central Railway route, where too a string of shanty towns had sprung up over the decades. It was among the residents of the tin-shacks and decrepit huts along the pipeline that Raman Raghav found his first victims. The targets had been chosen at random and there was nothing in the murders that suggested a trend or a motive, except perhaps robbery. But they were all brutal, and all the victims had been bludgeoned on their heads with a heavy, blunt instrument. The killings always took place at night.

While most of these unfortunates succumbed to their injuries, the few that did survive Raghav's murderous assaults had no recollection of the incident nor could identify their attacker. He had crept into their flimsy dwellings, most of which lacked sturdy doors, and attacked them as they lay on the ground or on their charpoys after a day of toil. Since the residents were in a state of terror, the police set up a round-the-clock watch but the killer managed to give them the slip every time. But as is often the case with police work, it is routine that more often than not leads to a breakthrough. The night patrol finally picked up a man who had been seen prowling around the area for no ostensible reason.

The man gave his name as Raman Raghav, but was found to have had several aliases – Sindhi Dalwai, Talwai, Anna, Tambi, Veluswami – for he had a police record. His fingerprints were on file and he had been convicted for nine offences earlier, most of them related to property. More seriously, he had been charged with murder in 1951 in the course of a dacoity, but was convicted only of the lesser charge of robbery, drawing a five-year jail term. Crime Branch Homicide Squad chief V.V. Vakatar, who had been in charge of Mulund police station when these crimes were committed, would later recall that he'd found Raghav a hard nut to crack. The only curious thing that the police found in Raghav's possession was a diary in which he had penned in words like *'khallas'* and *'khatam'* (meaning finished in colloquial Hindi) and had also added some figures alongside. This was all Greek to the police, and Raghav firmly refused to explain their meaning. In the end, with nothing concrete to pin on him and no concrete evidence to link him to the pipeline murders, the police had no choice but to set him free. He was, however, interned from the Bombay city limits for a period of two years. Later, when he was caught a second time, the police realized that the murders had ceased during the time that Raghav had been away from the city.

The second series of murders commenced in mid-1968 in the western and northern parts of the city, mostly in the Malad, Oshivara, Kandivali, Borivali, Dahisar belt. Among the first victims was a *bhaiyya* (as natives from Uttar Pradesh are called in Mumbai) from Oshivara. Dwaraka bhaiyya, as he was known, was a rent collector staying near one of the buffalo-sheds in the locality. The area was home to several such sheds, which were a source of the city's milk supply and were populated by migrants from Uttar Pradesh who made a living selling milk. In those days, the *doodhwaala* bhaiyya was a well-known fixture of the city.

Dwaraka had once run his own milk business, but having suffered losses, had given it up and become a rent-collector for

Fakruddin Bori, a stable owner. He occupied a small dwelling close to the stables, where he lived alone. One rainy day in July, a small boy waiting on the veranda outside happened to peep in through the open door of Dwaraka's room – and he had the fright of his life. The old man was lying on his charpoy with his head battered in while a pool of blood had collected on the floor below. The boy raised the alarm and soon a crowd had collected, to be followed shortly by the police. Dwaraka's head had been bashed in, probably with a heavy object while he lay asleep, for there were no signs of any struggle in the tiny room. Nothing of value seemed to have been taken from the sparsely furnished room except, strangely, an old stove and an umbrella. Surely, robbery did not seem to be the motive for this murder. The man had no known enemies, and though he had fallen out with some business partners, there was nothing to indicate they were in any way involved in this crime. The Goregaon Police registered a case of murder, but could not make any headway in the investigation.

A few days later the killer struck again, this time at Pathanwadi in Malad. Again, the victim was a man staying all by himself in a little hut on the edge of a marsh. Abdul Hafiz, or 'Master' as he was known, was a teacher at the nearby municipal school. His little tin-roofed hut, which he had constructed himself, had two exits. A few planks nailed together made up the front door, while a tin sheet fixed to a wooden frame served as the rear entrance. There was no furniture to speak of except the charpoy on which Master slept. The only light in the room was provided by a kerosene lamp, which was apparently kept burning all night. Hafiz Master's only valuable possessions seemed to be the half-a-dozen fowls kept in a wire-mesh-fronted box outside. And yet, he had been brutally beaten to death, seemingly only for his old wristwatch, which was missing when the body was found. He had relatives living elsewhere in the city, but no enemies, and led a quiet life. The Malad Police registered a murder case, but could find no suspects to pin it on.

The Malad Police were kept busy by Raman Raghav. He next struck at Dhanjiwadi, close to the Bombay–Ahmedabad highway. A young couple and their two-week-old child were the next victims. The family had been sleeping in their hut when Raghav forced open the door (it had been tied to the doorpost with only a string) and attacked them, leaving the charpoy and the floor awash in blood. Miraculously, they all survived the assault for a short while but the woman succumbed en route to the hospital and the infant died a few hours later. The man lived to tell the tale, but could recall nothing. He had flopped on to his charpoy after a day of hard labour and had woken up in hospital the next morning. However, the police did find something that Raghav had left behind. Some 20 feet from the hut, concealed in the grass, was an old umbrella and the murder weapon – a heavy iron rod, shaped like the number 7, with the lower ending tapering to a point. It was a fearsome-looking thing that had obviously been fashioned out of some other instrument. A purpose-built murder weapon.

This attack was followed by others, and on a couple of occasions Raghav was lucky to get away. On the night of 21–22 August, he attacked a couple staying in a chawl at Kajoopada in Borivali. Ramchandra Pawar was awakened by the sound of falling utensils, and going into the kitchen saw a man standing near the window, the bars of which had been wrenched apart. Before he could raise an alarm, the man struck him with a crow bar and also delivered a couple of blows to his wife Sushma who had woken up on hearing his cries. Their son, too, was now up and began to cry. As the night was rent by his victims' screams, Raghav panicked and quickly jumped out of the window. By the time the neighbours arrived and launched a search, he had vanished into the night. The attack had been deliberate and well-planned, for the doors of all the neighbouring houses had been latched from the outside and tied with string. Forcing the doors open took some time, helping Raghav make his escape. The attacked couple, who escaped serious injury, had managed to get a good look at him by the light of a kerosene lamp and were able to give the police a description of their assailant. The man was in his thirties, short and dark-complexioned, and was wearing khaki shorts and a bush shirt. He had hit them with odd-shaped iron rod, some two feet in length, Pawar and his wife told the police.

Raman Raghav was now well into his stride and the tally of his victims was mounting, with murders being reported every few days. Devram, a milk-seller from Raywalpada in Dahisar, was killed while he slept in his dilapidated hut where his goats were tethered for the night. His wife Ramai, who slept with their child in another hut close by, found him dead early one morning. His head had been beaten to a pulp. While there was really nothing worth stealing in the hut, Ramai's only valuable possessions, a pair of silver toe-rings and a silver ring, kept in a cloth bag hanging by a nail on the wall, were missing.

A few days later, a so-called bhagat, a holy man, was found murdered in Parekh Nagar in Kandivali. The victim, of whom not much was known, lived in a hut made of palm fronds and eked out a living by cutting and selling grass. He had apparently given up worldly affairs and gave religious discourses to people who came to him with their troubles. He had nothing worth stealing, and his only possessions – a string of beads, a picture of Lord Shiva in a wooden frame and a copy of the Ramayana – were found in a pool of blood below his charpoy. The only thing missing was a pair of spectacles. Fortunately for the police, the picture frame yielded some fingerprints which did not match the victim's, and the police entertained the flimsy hope that the prints might have belonged to the killer.

The police had now realized that a serial killer, quite possibly deranged, was now on the loose. For Deputy Commissioner Ramakant Kulkarni, who had only recently taken over as head of the Crime Branch, it must have been a nightmarish time. Kulkarni was the youngest officer to have ever held that prestigious and coveted post, but, as he puts it in his memoirs, he enjoyed the confidence of Commissioner E.S. Modak, who suggested he personally take over the investigation. All the police had so far were a description, a possible set of fingerprints and one of the killer's murder weapons. Significant in themselves, they were not of much help at the moment. But a pattern was emerging: the killer was striking with disturbing regularity, only by night, and picking his victims regardless of gender from the lower strata of society, in the shanty towns and slum colonies. Patrolling was intensified and extra staff were posted to the suburbs where the killer was known to be operating.

Around midnight on 25–26 August 1968, Babu Shinde, a watchman employed at a buffalo shed at Chinchavli in Malad, was alerted by his thirteen-year-old son about a man lurking in the nalla that ran behind the shed. Father and son went to have a look, but the stranger had vanished by then into the grass- and scrub-covered wasteland around the shed. A few minutes later, they were disturbed by the sound of vessels falling in a hut close by. The make-shift dwelling, put together with planks and divided by gunny bags into two rooms for privacy, was shared by two labourers from Benares, Lalchand Yadav and Dular Yadav. Flashlights in hand, the father and son quickly ran out, just in time to see someone running out of the hut. As they gave chase, crying *'chor, chor'*, the intruder jumped into the *nalla* and waded across to the adjoining school compound, where he disappeared. Shinde and his son then ran back to the labourers' hut, where a gory sight greeted them. Lalchand and Dular lay on their *charpoys* with their heads smashed and blood all over the floor. The killer had struck again!

The police duly arrived, and while it was clear that the hut had been ransacked, they could not know what, if anything, had been stolen from among the victims' meagre possessions. Shinde recalled noticing that the killer had been clutching something under his arm, but could not say what it was. The fingerprint experts picked up a few prints from a stain-less-steel box lying on the floor. If they did not match those of the victims', they were likely to be those of the killer who had probably thrown down the box after a hasty examination of its contents.

These killings bought out the press in full cry. The city, particularly the western and northern suburbs, was rattled. Panic had set in and there were now fewer people out in the streets at night. Hutment dwellers locked their flimsy doors a little more securely, and neighbourhood watches were set up. The public, in a display of zeal and responsible citizenship, hauled a few 'suspects' to the nearest police station, and occasionally a vagabond who could not account for his presence in a certain locality was thrashed before being handed over to the police. The killer seemed to be operating only in a certain area, but there was no telling when he would 'expand' his operations. Fantastic rumours about the killer's ability to change his appearance were floated. Vigilante groups armed with cricket bats and hockey sticks patrolled the deserted lanes and bylines of the city slums by night, on the lookout for the murderer. Everywhere, nerves were on edge.

The press, which had been reporting the murders with great abandon and growing alarm, did its bit to help. Reporters on the crime beat recalled similarities in the recent killings with the murders in the eastern suburbs a few years earlier. At least nine people had been killed and ten injured in those attacks, but the police had never managed to get their hands on the culprit. Had the killer returned? The modus operandi was much the same, even if the area of operations had changed. The police, too, were thinking along similar lines. Officers who had investigated the Duct Line killings were roped in for inputs – and Raman Raghav's file was reopened. What had he been up to in the years that he had been externed from the Bombay City limits? More importantly, where was he now?

The Crime Branch sleuths moved fast. Details of Raghav's previous run of alleged killings were scoured through and police officers fanned out across the city to interview all those who had earlier been acquainted with him. A look-out notice for the suspect was issued, and the hunt was officially on. Soon, plainclothes officers got their first lead from Manjulabai Dalvi, a maid servant staying at Kajoopada. She had been staying some months earlier in the same chawl as Raghav some months earlier, whom she knew as 'Sindhi Dalvai'. He was also called *Anna* (a commonly used term meaning elder brother in south India). He lived alone and she did not know what he did for a living, but she had seen him on 24 August in a lane near her house. She'd stopped him and casually asked what he had been up to, and Raghav had not been very responsive. He had come to meet somebody, he said, and walked away. Manjulabai recalled that Raghav had been dressed in khaki shorts, a blue shirt and old brown canvas shoes, and was carrying an umbrella. Shown Raghav's photo from the police files, she immediately confirmed that he was indeed the man known to her as 'Anna' or 'Sindhi Dalvai'.

The police now had more to go on. The Fingerprint Bureau confirmed that the prints lifted from the picture frame and the steel box matched those on record in Raghav's file. There was no doubt now that Raman Raghav was the man they were looking for. It would be no easy task to search for a man with no known address in the country's most crowded metropolis.

But Lady Luck favoured the police, and they did not have to wait too long to apprehend the killer. Early on the morning of 27 August, Alex Fialho, a sub-inspector attached to the Dongri police station, spotted a man answering to the description given in the police notice near Bhindi Bazar. The thoroughly professional and competent Fialho, who had joined the police in 1948, was carrying a photo of the suspect in his pocket. The suspect's clothes were as described – khaki shorts, blue shirt and old canvas shoes. But what had in fact caught Fialho's attention was the umbrella that the man was carrying. It had not rained in the Dongri area overnight; so why was he moving around with an umbrella?

Wanting to see how Raghav would react on seeing a policeman, Fialho went near him, but Raghav coolly walked past, betraying no sign of panic. The sub-inspector followed him for a while and then, tapping Raghav on the shoulder, asked him accompany him to the Dongri police station for questioning. Fialho had observed that the umbrella was wet, and a quick call revealed that it had rained in Malad the previous night. The man he had detained had therefore come from the place where the killer had last been seen.

Raghav was searched and his pockets were found to be stuffed with an odd assortment of articles – a pair of scissors, spectacles, a couple of combs and a plastic bag containing a bar of soap, garlic, tea powder and an incense stand. Also stuffed into his pocket were two scraps of paper with some mathematical marks scrawled on them. There were also stains of dried blood on his shirt and shoes. His fingerprints were taken and found to match those of Raman Raghav alias Sindhi Dalvai in the police files. Finally, it seemed, the police had got their man.

One can imagine the joy and relief at Bombay Police headquarters when the Dongri cops called in. It had taken a bit of luck, but the city's first known serial killer had at last been caught. The news quickly spread around the city and crowds gathered outside the police commissioner's office, where the Crime Branch office too is located. Hordes of journalists and photographers laid siege to the place, badgering their contacts in the department for details about Raman Raghav. The evening papers carried news of the arrest and photos of the short, stocky, very ordinary-looking serial killer, his hair neatly combed back and a permanent scowl on his face, were splashed across the front pages the next day. For the fearful Bombay-wallahs, particularly those residing in the western suburbs, Raghav's arrest must have come as a big relief.

Alex Fialho, who would forever be known as the man who caught Raman Raghav, was the hero of the hour. Congratulations poured in from all quarters, and Police Commissioner Modak sanctioned an immediate cash award for 1,000 rupees for the sharp-eyed officer. Fialho was recommended for, and received, the President's Police Medal for apprehending the country's first known serial killer since Independence.[1]

While the killer was now under lock and key, the real work of investigation had only begun. The team of officers interrogating Raghav found him quite a handful, and as Inspector Vakatkar had discovered during their earlier encounter at Mulund some years ago, he was indeed a tough cookie. He refused to cooperate and would not admit to anything. That he was not 'normal' was apparent, and so handling him was not easy. Usually, a couple of slaps would loosen the tongues of even hardened criminals, but Raman

Raghav was a different cup of tea altogether. Then, suddenly, he seemed to change his mind. The police had decided to adopt a soft approach and asked him if there was anything he would particularly like. '*Murgi*,' he said instantly. To humour him, he was served chicken with a generous helping of gravy, something he seemed to relish. Then, with a full belly, he was suddenly a changed man and became more responsive, and a little cocky. He asked the officers if he could have a prostitute – obviously, a demand which could not be fulfilled. He then sought a comb and a mirror, and when these were produced proceeded to comb his hair, peering very intently into the mirror. The dreaded serial killer it seemed, was something of a dandy. His vanity satisfied, Raghav got down to business. 'Now, tell me, what do you want?'[2] The police said they wanted to talk about the murders. Raghav agreed with alacrity. He would take them to all the places where he had committed the murders and tell them everything.

The Crime Branch officers were kept busy over the next few days driving all over the western suburbs as Raghav pointed out the places where he'd attacked his victims, some of whom the police had no knowledge about. At a certain spot on the Western Express Highway near Jogeshwari, he asked the driver to pull over. Crawling into a dense thicket on the wayside, he came out with an iron jimmy, or crowbar, in his hand. This had been used to clobber his victims after he had discarded the 7-shaped iron rod. It had been fashioned for him by a blacksmith at Jogeshwari, he revealed. The weapon he had left behind at Dhanjiwadi in Malad had also been made to order by another blacksmith, Lalchand Vishwakarma. It had been hammered out of a broken axle, probably from a truck, which Raghav had given the blacksmith in June, he told the police. Vishwakarma, who had known Raghav for a few months as Sindhi Talwai, had asked him why he needed such an odd-looking tool and was told that as he stayed in a jungle, he needed it for digging and also to tether animals. Raghav had come back some time later, the blacksmith revealed, this time with an iron rod, and had asked him to fabricate yet another instrument like the previous one (discarded in Malad). The earlier one had been very heavy, Raghav said, and he now wanted one that was lighter. He left the iron rod behind in the smithy but never came back for it.

Raghav also took the police team to several locations in the suburbs, often in marshy spots, where he had hidden the numerous low-value items stolen from his victims. As he gradually disclosed details of all the murders he had committed, the police were convinced that Raghav was telling the truth. By his own admission, he had been involved in some forty murders since 1965, but the police could never be sure if that was all. They did, however, piece together the story of his life, as narrated by him, with some details confirmed by people he had been associated with.

Raman Raghav was born in a village in the Tirunelveli district of Tamil Nadu. One of six siblings, including four sisters, he said he was deeply attached to his elder brother. From an early age he had taken to petty crime, into which he had been introduced by his father, a convicted criminal. He said he was not very attached to his mother, and his formative years, when he received no formal schooling, probably laid the pattern for his future career. Lacking employable skills, he moved to Bombay in the 1950s and worked as a millhand for a few years, supplementing his income by committing robberies, sometimes employing violence. He had been arrested a few times and sent to jail for a few months on each of these occasions. After being externed from Bombay in 1966, he shifted to Pune and committed thefts in Wadgaon, Dehu and Talegaon. He had come back to Bombay in early 1968 when he set out on his second killing spree, beginning in June.

Raghav expressed no remorse or regret for his actions. When asked by the magistrate before whom he made a formal confession (under Indian law, confessions made to the police have no legal standing) as to why he had committed these murders, he said he had received 'orders from above'. Interestingly, he gave his name to the magistrate as Sindhi Dalvai, which was also how he was known to most of his acquaintances in Bombay. The name in itself was unusual for a south Indian, and one wonders why he used that particular alias, for the other names he went by – Anna, Tambi, Veluswami – were typically south Indian names.

Psychiatric examination revealed that Raghav was a misogynist, with a long-festering grievance against women. He did not trust the opposite sex at all, for his earlier encounters with women had only led to what in his warped mind was a betrayal of trust. According to Khushwant's Singh's account of Raman Raghav's character, written in 1969 after meeting doctors who had examined him at great length, his first wife had become pregnant by another man while he was in jail. A second alliance arranged by the family also got nowhere as the woman was found to have been abandoned by another man and had had a child with him. With such unpromising matrimonial starts, it is not surprising that

Raghav found an outlet for his sexual urges with prostitutes. He got into trouble over a woman yet again when he was accused by a friend's wife of having made advances to her, which got him thrown out of the chawl he was residing in. Little wonder then that he came to despise the fairer sex, though he craved their company to meet his physical needs.[3]

Raghav's hatred for women also manifested in the most revolting sexual perversion. He confessed to the police that he had been tempted to have sex with one of his female victims after killing her, but had been scared away. But on one occasion he had killed a woman who was sleeping next to her two children, and by his own admission, he had sucked her breasts and had sex with the corpse.[4]

He was also obsessed with sex and prostitutes. He suggested to the jail administration that they let him out on bail for a year and provide him with a woman under the age of thirty (a prostitute would do!) just to satisfy his urges. He assured them that he would not commit any crimes during this period.

While the doctors found him to be otherwise intelligent and quite 'normal', he was not quite right in the head. His mind was somewhat unhinged, but he seemed to be aware that his actions were unlawful and also understood the consequences of his actions. In the end he was charged only for the double murder of the two Yadavs at Malad.

At his trial in the sessions court, which began in June 1969, his defence counsel argued that Raghav was of unsound mind and therefore incapable of defending himself. However, Dr C.A. Franklin, the police surgeon for Greater Bombay, under whose observation Raghav had been for nearly a month, contended that the killer did not suffer from psychosis and had all along been aware of what he was doing. Raghav also understood the nature of his crime and the proceedings now underway against him. He could, therefore, not be certified as insane.

The trial proceeded and further medical opinion was called for. Dr Patkar, a psychiatrist who had interviewed Raghav at Arthur Road Jail on 5 August 1959, concluded that the accused was suffering from chronic paranoid schizophrenia, which had developed over a number of years.[5]

Various points of law and psychiatry were finely parsed during the course of the trial, and in the end, the additional sessions judge held Raghav guilty of the charge of murder and sentenced him to death. Raghav did not appeal the verdict, but under the law, a death sentence has to be confirmed by a higher court. The Bombay High Court ordered that a special medical board of three psychiatrists be set up to determine if Raghav was of unsound mind and therefore incapable of making his defence.

The members of the specially constituted board interviewed Raghav on five occasions for about two hours each. In their opinion, the accused was clearly of unsound mind and had exhibited delusions of persecution and grandeur. The degree of unsoundness was such that he was incapable of cooperating with and instructing his counsel in the conduct of his trial. The judge agreed, and proceedings in the confirmation case were postponed. Meanwhile, Raghav was to be held at Yerwada Central Jail in Pune.

There were more legal twists and turns as the state preferred an appeal in the Supreme Court, and Raghav underwent further medical examinations and treatment until, finally, in August 1987, a two-judge bench of the Bombay High Court set aside the death penalty and sentenced Raghav to imprisonment for life.

Raman Raghav was now sixty and had been under solitary confinement in the death cell for eighteen years. He had only a few more years to live, though, and died of kidney failure at Pune's Sassoon Hospital in 1995.

Mumbai's first-known serial killer lived, at least partly, in a delusional universe. The psychiatrists who examined him and the policeman who interviewed him were occasionally allowed glimpses into his strange world – the world of '*kanoon*', as he put it. People had at various times tried to change his sex, he said, but were unsuccessful because he was a representative of '*kanoon*'. Homosexual temptations had been put in his path, but he had avoided them as he believed they would convert him into a woman. Raghav also laboured under the delusion that there were three governments in the country: 'the Akbar government, the British government and the Congress government', all of whom were trying to persecute him and put temptations before him. He was also convinced that he was a '101 per cent man', something he repeated often.

The secrets from the innermost recesses of Raghav's diseased mind went away with him, but his story has been kept alive in popular culture. DCP Kulkarni, who went on to become director general of police, Maharashtra, devoted a lengthy chapter to Raman Raghav in his memoirs. Film director Sriram Raghavan made a documentary film titled *Raman Raghav – A City, A Killer*, starring Raghuvir Yadav as the notorious serial killer. In 2016, Bollywood biggie Anurag

Kashyap directed *Raman Raghav 2.0*, a film about a fictional serial killer starring Nawazuddin Siddiqui.

After Raman Raghav, Mumbai had only one serial killer, but he was never apprehended. This was the so-called 'Stoneman' who bludgeoned twelve people to death between 1985 and 1987. Each of the victims, all pavement dwellers and beggars, was found with his head crushed with a heavy stone. The attacks stopped in mid-1987 and the killer was never found. However, a similar series of attacks occurred in Calcutta, beginning in June 1989. Again, the victims were all poor people sleeping on the streets. In a four-month spell, the Calcutta Stoneman killed seven people, and was never heard of again. Were the attacks in the two cities carried out by the same person? No one knows.

17

The Simla Train Hold-Up*

For the scores of tourists who ride the Kalka–Simla toy train every year, the 95-kilometre journey is an absolute delight. An outstanding example of Victorian railway construction, the narrow-gauge route offers magnificent views of the Shivalik ranges, winding its way past charming hillside villages, deep valleys and fearful gorges before terminating at the erstwhile summer capital of the British Raj. Boasting over 100 tunnels, 864 bridges and 919 curves, it is also an engineering marvel that draws rail aficionados from around the world.

The line, which was opened in June 1903, has had its

---

*B.M.S. Bisht, 'Robbery on the Kalka–Simla Line (1942)', *Railways of the Raj*, October 2008, https://railwaysofraj.blogspot.com/2009/10/robbery-on-kalka-simla-line-1942-sad.html, accessed 21 February 2026; Raaja Bhasin, *Simla: The Summer Capital of British India*, Rupa Publications Pvt. Ltd, New Delhi, 2011, pp. 137–38; Edward J. Buck, *Simla Past and Present*, 2nd ed., The Times Press, Bombay, 1925; Papua Rao Naidu, *The History of the Railway Thieves in India: With Illustrations and Hints on Detection*, Vintage Books, Delhi, 1996, p. 149; Roger Perkins, *Punjab Mail Murder: Story of an Indian Army Officer*, Picton Publishing, 1986; Sunil Nair, *Tales of Crimes Past: A Casebook of Crimes in Colonial India*, Hachette India, New Delhi, 2022.

fair share of history, tall tales and ghost stories. The most famous of these is undoubtedly that of Colonel Barog, the chief engineer of the railway, who messed up the alignment of one of the tunnels, for which he was fined the princely sum of one rupee. Unable to live down the embarrassment, the colonel committed suicide and was buried near the tunnel. In recognition for his services (and to assuage a guilty conscience?), the railway company later named the tunnel (No. 33) and the nearby station after him. However, this doesn't seem to have mollified the old soldier's ghost, who is still said to make an occasional appearance near the tunnel.

While the unfortunate colonel's story is familiar to most Indian railway fans, a lesser-known tale is that of the attack on the Rail Motor Car that occurred just a few years before the British left Simla and India for good.

Introduced around 1910 to ferry the viceroy and his staff to the hills, the Rail Motor Car was akin to a semi-luxury coach on rails, seating around fifteen passengers and equipped with a driver's cab and engine out front that gave it the appearance of large, though slightly ungainly, motor lorry. The service seems to have been popular with British officials and their memsahibs, and the Rail Motor Car soon became a regular feature of the Kalka-Simla Railway (KSR). A contemporary advertisement of the North Western Railway (NWR), which operated the service, shows a white-painted Rail Motor Car with six presumably satisfied passengers (with Wolseley helmets, peaked caps or other headgear, also white, on) looking out of the windows. The highlighted features of the service were: speed, comfort, cleanliness and safety. The last would be called into question at least once.

Riding a train in the hills may seem quite adventurous for a first-timer, but for some there's often little excitement other than an animal straying on to the tracks or a minor landslip during the rains. After a few rides, the journey can become quite dull, and a chore to get through. Not so, however, for the twelve passengers who boarded Rail Motor Car No. 14 on the evening of 20 June 1942. As they settled into their seats for the long ride down to the plains, not one of them would have imagined that they were riding into a nightmare.

For railway driver Wahiuddin, the 4 Down run was a regular affair, but he still had to keep his eyes peeled on the numerous curves and bends in the track. One could never be too careful in the hills – one little slip and you could have a disaster on your hands. Presumably, he saw the huge boulders on the track well in time, but couldn't avoid hitting them. There was a curve a little ahead and the brake had to be applied gently. But Wahiuddin didn't get to do much else. Barely had the Rail Motor Car come to a halt than a fusillade of shots crashed out from the surrounding hills and the driver slumped forward in his seat, dead.

The stunned passengers in the back were too shocked to react. Had the car been derailed? However, one of them with rather more presence of mind had quickly sized up the situation. 'Get down,' he yelled, as more bullets smashed through the windows. Sam Wheeler, an assistant mechanical engineer of the North Western Railway, was one of the passengers. He dived to the floor, which was soon awash in blood as more people were hit. One of the passengers at the rear of the coach shouted to the driver to turn out the lights.

There were a few army officers on board too, but they were unarmed and could offer no resistance.

The shooting stopped after a few minutes and one of the robbers, the lower half of his face masked by a cloth, stepped into the coach with a rifle and ordered the passengers to step down and hand over their valuables. Lieutenant Getley, an employee of the NWR and the first man to get down, was shot in the back of his neck, apparently as he had failed to keep his hands up as ordered. Fortunately, the wound was not fatal and Getley survived. Two other passengers were not so lucky, and two more were injured. Having looted the passengers, the robbers vanished into the night.

News of the attack soon reached Kalka and a relief train with armed police, mechanics and a driver were dispatched within an hour. The injured were given first aid by the local railway doctor and sent off by the first available train to the Railway Hospital at Ambala. The two deceased passengers were later buried at the Sanjauli cemetery in Simla, with senior British officials, including the lieutenant governor of the Punjab, attending the funeral. The Rail Motor Car, among the latest and most modern in the KSR fleet, was not much damaged, having got away with only nine bullet holes and five broken window panes. As an immediate measure though, the running of Rail Motor Cars was suspended during the night and armed escorts were provided on all night-time trains operating in the area.

While the railways were by far the safest and quickest means of transport in British India, they weren't immune to crime. Indeed, within a few decades of the introduction of railways into the country, a new class of criminals, categorized by officialdom as 'railway thieves', had sprung up. Their depredations ranged from petty theft to organized looting of railway property, but violent crime was not unusual, and by the turn of the twentieth century had become more frequent. Among the most notorious of these was the murder of George Hext, a British officer of the 8th Punjab Regiment, in a first-class compartment of the Punjab Mail in 1931. Hext and a fellow officer, Eric Sheehan, were stabbed after they put up a fight during the course of a night-time robbery. Hext died of his wounds but Sheehan survived. Their attackers managed to jump off the train but were eventually tracked down and brought to justice.[1] Occasionally, women were also attacked, and in at least two cases ladies travelling unescorted had been thrown out of the windows of running trains after being robbed.[2]

The Punjab government announced a reward of 10,000 rupees and a plot of land to anyone providing information leading to the arrest of the criminals. The attack certainly had the authorities worried. Since the beginning of the Ghadar movement during World War 1, the Punjab had been a restive province. The Lahore Conspiracy Case was still part of recent memory, as were the revolutionary activities of Bhagat Singh and his comrades, which had set off a firestorm of protest across the province and indeed the whole of British India. Was the Simla incident carried out by a criminal gang or was its part of a larger conspiracy to foment trouble across the country? The authorities were both clueless and worried. With World War 2 having gotten well into its stride by 1942, the security of Britain's Indian dominion was paramount to the supremacy of the Empire in South Asia, where Japan had already entered Burma and was threating the borders of India. The Cripps Mission earlier that year had been a failure and the Congress was whipping up resistance across the country, which would soon culminate in the Quit India Movement in August.

The police did not have much to go on. For a start, they weren't even sure how many men had been involved in the raid. None of the witnesses could be sure of the number. They'd kept their hands up and heads down and had been probably praying for their lives. According to Sam Wheeler, the only words uttered in English by the man who had opened the door were 'Hands up!' – not much of a clue. He was the only person seen by the passengers, but there were sure to have been others in the gang, keeping watch in the darkness. The bullets retrieved from the scene were of non-standard size, but strangely enough, there were no empty cartridges lying around even though many rounds had been fired during the attack.

It was well over a year-and-a-half before the first clue surfaced. Three men had been shot at during a robbery in Bhatinda. One of the victims was killed, while the other two were injured, and probably escaped a worse fate by playing dead. A forensic examination of the bullets used in the attack showed they were of the same non-standard calibre as those used in the Kalka robbery. The police, however, had more luck with the Bhatinda case and traced the prime suspect – a Pathan named Abdul Karim – to his quarters in the railway colony. Upon being challenged, Karim fired at the police party, shooting down the sub-inspector leading the raid. A regular shoot-out then commenced, and when the police finally broke through the door and entered the house, they found Karim lying dead. He'd killed himself with the last bullet in his revolver. His wife, who was injured during the shooting, lay nearby, while his eight-year-old son had survived unscathed.

Abdul Karim, the police learned, came from Bannu in the North-West Frontier Province (NWFP) and had earlier been employed as a leading fitter-in-charge at the Kalka railway workshop. He had been a very skilled craftsman and, as the police found, had planned the railway hold-up and had also fashioned the guns used in the attack. The police recovered an ingeniously made revolver and a Tommy gun that had been repurposed so that the cartridges would not be ejected when the weapons were fired. Further searches at the railway quarters in Kalka where Karim had stayed also turned up another revolver, a tin of black powder and a few other ingredients used to produce guns and ammunition.

Inquiries at Kalka also revealed that Abdul Karim had a brother, Abdul Rahim, who was a skilled gunsmith. When the latter's house at Dera Ismail Khan in the NWFP was raided, the police found bullet moulds which had been used to produce the bullets used in the attack at Kalka. A gold-tipped Ever Sharp pencil that had been taken from one of the passengers was also found in the house. Abdul Rahim soon confessed to his part in the attack, which he said had been planned by his brother. He too had fired on the Rail Motor Car from the hillside and had kept watch while his brother went down to relieve the passengers of their valuables. They needed the money, he said, to pay off a few debts that the brothers had incurred.

The attack of the Rail Motor Car was soon forgotten and the service continued to be popular, having another brief tryst with history when it carried Mahatma Gandhi to Simla for his famous conference with the Viceroy, Lord Reading, in 1945. The KSR kept up the service for several years after Independence, before it was stopped in 2012. However, it is now back in service with an upgraded coach and a more modern look, and continues to delight passengers as it did a century ago.

18

The Shakereh Murder Case*

It is around 10 a.m. on 30 March, 1994, and a huge crowd has gathered on Richmond Road, a fairly upmarket area in the heart of old Bangalore. Jeeploads of policemen have arrived at a bungalow standing on Plot No. 81, a large piece of very prime property belonging to the family of Sir Mirza Ismail, the former diwan of the erstwhile princely state of Mysore. A few labourers have been called in and are now

---

*'Swami Shraddhananda vs. State of Karnataka', *B&B Associates LLP*, 2006, https://bnblegal.com/landmark/swami-shraddhananda-v-s-state-of-karnataka/, accessed 21 February 2026; Rediff Specials, 'My Mother was alive when she was buried', *Rediff*, https://www.rediff.com/news/1998/sep/21bang.htm, accessed 21 February 2026; Bala Chauhan, 'Swami Shraddhanand: The pathological liar who buried his wife alive', *The New Indian Express*, 27 November 2022, https://www.newindianexpress.com/thesundaystandard/2022/Nov/27/swami-shraddhanand-the-pathological-liar-who-buried-his-wife-alive-2522507.html, accessed 21 February 2026; Geeta Pandey, 'Dancing on the grave: The decades-old murder that shook India', *BBC News*, 23 May 2023, https://www.bbc.com/news/world-asia-india-65397222, accessed 21 February 2026; Monika Monalisa, 'Murder He Wrote', *The New Indian Express*, 20 April 2023, https://www.newindianexpress.com/cities/bengaluru/2023/Apr/20/murderhe-wrote-2567548.html, accessed 21 February 2026.

digging up the ground just outside one of the bedrooms. A short, heavy-set man, handcuffs on his wrists, is calmly watching the proceedings. He is Murli Manohar Mishra, alias Swami Shraddhananda, husband of the lady who owns the property. Despite a long night of interrogation by sleuths of the Bangalore City Crime Branch (CCB), he looks composed and unruffled, occasionally exchanging a few words with the cops standing around him. He knows what's buried under the ground just a few feet away, but seems to be waiting as expectantly as any other onlooker at the scene. The labourers have prised away a layer of heavy flagstones and are now digging into the bare, brown earth. It is heavy work, but they keep at it, and soon their picks hit a wooden board. A sigh goes up among the assembled crowd. Ah! Nearly there! A few more shovels full of dirt are tossed aside, revealing a large wooden box lying slightly on its side. The top of the box – which the fanciful would say resembles a coffin – is prised open with a crowbar. Everyone now steps back as a foul stench emanates from within the box. Inside, as everyone peering into the pit can now see, is a mattress, concealing the skeletal remains of a woman, a tuft of hair still adhering to the skull. Sticking out and curling around the mattress are the remains of a human hand, as if the victim, in a last, desperate lunge at life, had attempted to claw her way out of the darkness that enveloped her.

———

After a slow and desultory three-year investigation by the police, the mystery behind the disappearance of Shakereh

Khaleeli, grand-daughter of Sir Mizra Ismail, had finally been solved.

Shakereh Khaleeli had led a star-crossed life. Born to wealth, elegance and power in an aristocratic family, her grisly and untimely end was perhaps fated. The daughter of Gauhar Taj, one of Sir Mirza's four children, she had always attracted attention. Beauty, grace and charm, combined with her royal connections, meant that she was always something of a head-turner. Born in August 1947 in Madras, she had finished her schooling in Singapore where her father, Ghulam Hussain Namazie, had business interests. Her marriage to her cousin Akbar Khaleeli, the son of her aunt Shah Taj, when she was just eighteen, must have come as something of a surprise to her many suitors, but the match had apparently been decided on by her grandfather Sir Mirza when she was just a twelve-year-old. The suave Akbar and the lissome Shakereh made a good pair. Akbar had been born and brought up in Bangalore, where he attended Bishop Cotton Boys' School, and later read law at Madras Law College. However, he decided against taking up the legal profession, instead joining the Indian Foreign Service, where he had a distinguished career as India's ambassador to Iran and Italy and, later, as high commissioner to Australia. Shakereh was the perfect wife for the up-and-coming diplomat, and the early years of their marriage passed peacefully. The debonair Akbar and his beautiful, intelligent wife were just the kind of couple that sparkled at diplomatic parties. The high life was something both partners were used to and enjoyed, and the couple were soon blessed with four daughters. Life for this lovely couple seemed to be very good indeed.

However, in a few years, as their kids grew up, the cracks were beginning to show. Shakereh had tired of her role of hostess to the suave diplomat. The life of a Foreign Service officer's wife is no piece of cake. She's always expected to be on her best behaviour, smiling and mingling with guests at endless embassy soirees and events – essentially a prop to her husband's career. It can wear down the most patient of women, and after a few years Shakereh had had enough. She wanted to go home. Akbar, a kind and thoughtful husband, agreed, and so Shakereh moved to Bangalore with her four daughters.

Shakereh had always had an independent streak, and now she was determined to make a life for herself, unaided and unsupervised by her husband. She began to dabble in the construction business, which in a sense was a family trait. Her grandfather Sir Mirza Ismail was, after all, the grandson of Agha Aly Asker, a Persian horse trader who made Bangalore his home in the early eighteenth century and was responsible for constructing the governor's residence and Balabrooie, the state guest house, besides many other fine buildings across the city. The family had much land in Bangalore, and making the most of her family connections, Shakereh set about establishing herself as a property developer. This move was to have fatal consequences for the Khaleeli family, for it was to further her business prospects that she invited Murli Manohar Mishra, aka Swami Shraddhananda, into her home.

Nobody seems to know how a man like Shraddhananda managed to worm himself into Shakereh's confidence. The two were poles apart. Shakereh was beautiful, charismatic, and carried herself well. He, on the other hand, was short and paunchy, nothing great to look at, with no real occupation or prospects. How anyone with Shakereh's looks, background and talents could be taken in by Shraddhananda was a wonder to all who knew her.

Mishra hailed from the Sagar district of Madhya Pradesh. A school dropout, he had shifted to Delhi in his late teens and had found employment with the family of the Nawab of Rampur, whose properties he helped to manage. Somewhere along the way he also dabbled in spirituality, donning the white robes of a godman and calling himself Swami Shraddhananda. Shakereh was introduced to him during a visit to the Nawab's family in 1983. He was very good at handling property matters, she was told. This seemed like a godsend to Shakereh, and she quickly invited him to visit her in Bangalore and help her sort out some troubling issues in her construction business.

The swami was only too happy to oblige and soon landed up at the family home at Sankey Road. He was initially a welcome guest, and even Shakereh's daughters seemed to have had no objection to his visits. Well-spoken and unfailingly polite, he charmed everyone who came into his circle, though there were a few who found him smug and over-nice.

In time though, Sharddhananda became an almost permanent fixture at the Khaleeli residence. He would stay there for long periods, ostensibly at Shakereh's request, as she did not want him travelling up and down, to and from Delhi every time she needed his assistance. She was also now living alone with her daughters in Bangalore, Akbar having been posted as ambassador to Iran. Doubtless, this led to some tongue-wagging in the city's conservative Shia community to which the family belonged, but Shakereh shrugged it all off.

Shraddhananda was helping her sort out her vexed property matters, and that was all that mattered to her.

No one knew quite why Shakereh decided to marry Shraddhananda. It might have been love, or maybe she was just lonely and vulnerable. The swami was a smooth-talker, and in the absence of her husband the lonely woman had simply turned to him for advice and comfort, which probably blossomed into love. In any case, she dropped a bombshell on her family and friends when she asked Akbar for a divorce in October 1985. Barely six months later, in April 1986, she married Shraddhananda under the Special Marriages Act. The family was horrified, but they rallied around the father and a distraught Akbar took off to Italy, where he was now posted, with his four daughters. The Shia community, for its part, was unforgiving, and Shakereh was promptly ostracized. But she seemed not to care, and now began living with Shraddhananda in the bungalow at 81, Richmond Road. The couple did not have many visitors, the only other occupants of the house being their helper Raju and his wife, the maid Josephine.

Freed of family constraints, Shakereh now began paying more attention to her construction business. Apart from the huge 38,000-sq. feet Richmond Road plot, which had been bequeathed to her by her parents, she also held plots of land elsewhere, which she now tried to develop and sell. Shakereh also made a will in Shraddhananda's favour, besides executing a general power of attorney appointing him as her agent and attorney. The couple also started a private company called S.S. Housing Pvt. Ltd and opened joint bank accounts. S.S. Mansion, a three-storeyed apartment block that the couple built, stands just a 100 yards away from the site where Shakereh's corpse was interred.

During this time, Shakereh also became pregnant, and delivered a stillborn son. After four daughters, she had always wanted a boy and, according to Shraddhananda's detractors, this was the reason why she had married him. The swami had apparently convinced her that he could help her conceive a male child with his supposedly occult powers, and this was what had drawn the unhappy woman to him.

But Shakereh's second marriage too was not destined to be a happy one. The couple began to quarrel, and Shakereh could be very vocal in her displeasure. She wasn't happy with the manner in which Shraddhananda had sold off some of her valuable properties, abusing her trust and the power of attorney she had given him. It may be that she had finally seen through the charlatan that she had invited into her life, or she may have simply missed the pleasurable whirlwind of her former social life or her estranged daughters. Whatever the reason, she was feeling lonely again and tried to get back in touch with her children.

It was now 1990 and her daughters were back in India and settled into their own lives. Sabah, her second daughter, who was now working as a model in Mumbai, had always kept in touch with her, and it was to her that Shakereh now turned, probably in a belated attempt to pull together the pieces of her life.

Shakereh had chanced to meet her daughter at Delhi airport, and thereafter the two had been in constant touch over the phone. Sabah also promised to come to Bangalore soon to spend time with her mother. Shakereh's new-found closeness with her daughter rang alarm bells for Shraddhananda. His hold on Shakereh was now slipping, and it might have occurred to him that she might even divorce him and go back to her family – a disturbing circumstance, which he would have realized he had to forestall. The godman then tried to stop Sabah's access to her mother. Her calls to Richmond Road were met with vague responses from the swami. Other members of the family who enquired about Shakereh's whereabouts were also fobbed off by the swami, with vague and unconvincing replies.

All this looked very fishy, yet no one from Shakereh's immediate family or friends ventured to confront the swami or question his motives. Shraddhananda, for his part, seemed to be working to a plan. Early in May 1991, he had a large wooden box made to order and delivered to the house, where it was kept in the guest room. The curious thing about this box was that it had wheels attached to the bottom (to facilitate easy transportation, Shraddhananda said). Nobody knows if Shakereh ever saw the box or inquired as to why it had been ordered. The swami later told the police that he needed the box to export handicraft items, some of which were quite heavy.

But that was not what the box was meant for, according to the police. Shraddhananda, according to them, had by now made up his mind to do away with this wife, and the box was part of an elaborate plan to get away with cold-blooded murder. But a few more props still needed to be in place. Soon a few labourers were called in and were digging up the ground a few feet outside the couple's bedroom wall. A rectangular pit, ostensibly for a new sump, was soon ready.

At around 8 a.m. on 28 May 1991, the police claimed, the maid Josephine made tea for Shraddhananda and his wife and left the cups on the table in the dining room. Shraddhananda, who offered to take the tea to his wife, then put a handful of sleeping pills into Shakereh's cup and took it to her bedroom. A little later, he told Josephine and Raju that Shakereh was feeling unwell and should not be disturbed.

Around 10 a.m., having received a telegram stating that a close relative staying in Gudisuvarapally, Andhra Pradesh, was unwell, the couple sought Shraddhananda's permission to leave for their native village and also asked for some money in advance. This was granted, but Raju was ordered to move the wooden box from the guest room to Shakereh's bedroom before they left. Raju did as he was told (he had to call in a few men to help with this) and was paid 1,200 rupees for his trouble, besides 500 rupees for travelling expenses. The couple then left the house.

With the servants out of the way, Shraddhananda rolled up the mattress around Shakereh's insensible body, pushed it into the box and nailed down the lid. He now had to get the box out of the room and into the pit, but this would be almost impossible without anyone noticing. Besides, Shakereh had put on a lot of weight and the box was consequently heavy. Shraddhananda had, under some pretext, already knocked down some part of the lower portion of the bedroom wall. The box was pushed out through this hole and into the pit. The swami then shovelled in some loose earth, just enough to conceal the box. The next day, a few labourers were called in and the pit was completely filled in and cemented over with Kadappa slabs.

When the servant couple came back a few days later, their mistress was missing. While their culpability can always be a matter of debate, it does seem incredulous that they bought Shraddhananda's story that their mistress had gone abroad and never wondered why she didn't turn up for the next three years.

While the servants didn't seem to be unduly perturbed by Shakereh's disappearance, her daughter Sabah was certainly concerned. She repeatedly called up the house, only to be told that Shakereh was out of town or not available. Shraddhananda would keep fobbing her off with vague and often bizarre replies about her mother's whereabouts – she was in Hyderabad for a wedding one week; the next week she'd just flown out to Kutch, in Gujarat, for yet another wedding; she was upset about some issues with the income-tax department and did not want to see any one. On one occasion he told her that her mother was at the Roosevelt Hospital in New York. Convinced that Shakereh would have never left the country without telling her, Sabah then had a friend in the United States contact the hospital, only to be told that no such person had ever been admitted there. When a furious Sabah confronted Shraddhananda with this, he just laughed it off saying he had done it at Shakereh's behest!

Nothing daunted, Sabah landed up in Bangalore demanding to see her mother, only to be once again frustrated by Shraddhananda's evasive replies. Determined to find out what had happened to her mother – and perhaps with an uneasy sense of foreboding – Sabah filed a 'missing person' complaint at the Ashok Nagar police station. The cops, however, did not seem to pursue the matter very seriously.

They did speak to Shraddhananda, but let him off after routine questioning. Shakereh was away overseas, he said, and he did not know why she was staying away from everyone, but that had nothing to do with him. By this time though, her disappearance had become a talking point among her friends and the wider community, and the family is said to have even met soothsayers and fortune tellers in a desperate bid to locate the missing woman.

But if Shraddhananda thought he would get away with his horrible secret, he hadn't bargained on Sabah's persistence. While the case was put into cold storage for all practical purposes, Sabah did not let up on the search for her mother and kept pestering the police to do more. Finally, one day she created a big fuss at the office of the then Additional Director General of Police P. Kodandaramiah, complaining that his officers were not doing anything to find her mother. The officer was sympathetic, and assured her that he would personally look into the case. It was then that things finally began to get moving. B. Azmatullah, assistant commissioner of police, Central Crime Branch (CCB), was directed to take a fresh look into the case and see if any new leads could be found.

Having familiarized himself with the details of the case, Azmatullah decided to approach it from a different angle. The CCB team, realizing that Shraddhananda was a tough nut to crack (he had already obtained anticipatory bail to secure himself against arrest), decided instead to concentrate on the suspect's servants. It was inconceivable, they thought, that the mistress of a household could vanish so completely without her servants being aware of it. They had to get the servants to talk, but it had to be done without arousing any suspicion. Bringing them in for questioning would only give the game away, and so it was decided to keep a watch on the couple and await developments.

As any experienced policeman will tell you, much of police investigation involves routine inquiry and waiting for things to happen. Running around looking for clues does not always lead to results. And so it was in this case, too. The sleuths tailing Raju soon observed that he had a weakness for country liquor and that many of his evenings were spent at a toddy shop imbibing the heady stuff. As everyone knows, there's nothing like liquor to loosen tongues, and soon Head Constable Mahadeva had befriended the servant while he was in his cups. All it took was some gentle prodding and a few glasses of arrack down his throat for Raju to sing like a canary. He didn't know what had happened to his memsaab, he said, but on the last day that he saw her the swamiji had asked him to move a huge wooden box into her bedroom. What was the box for? Well, he had no idea, but the swamiji had got it made to order at the *lakda bazar* a few weeks before madam vanished. It was quite large and he had got four men to unload it from the truck and get it into the house. It had been kept in the guest room until the day he had been asked to push it into madam's bedroom. He had no idea what happened to the box after that; he had never seen it again. If Raju's lack of curiosity surprised Mahadeva, he didn't let on. He'd got what he wanted. The CCB sleuths could make a pretty good guess as to what had gone into that box. But they had to locate it first.

Azmatullah now decided to tackle Shraddhananda directly. He was brought to the Crime Branch office for questioning, the swami initially refused to answer any questions. Raju was a drunkard and didn't know what he was talking about, he said. More questioning – and possibly a few slaps – seemed to refresh his memory. He admitted to having ordered the box. He had used it to store some handicrafts which he had dispatched to a client. Who was the client? Could he provide an address? More evasive answers. The swami kept on hedging, but his interrogators were not buying any more of his stories. Finally, after many weary hours of questioning, Shraddhananda finally broke down and made a clean breast of it. And yes, he'd show them where he had put that box.

The police now moved quickly. An exhumation order was obtained, and after Shraddhananda had pointed out where exactly he'd buried his wife, the digging began. The whole process was also videographed, the first time this was ever done anywhere in India.

A forensic examination of the box's contents revealed that the skeletal remains were indeed those of Shakereh. Her mother Gauhar Taj also identified a few rings found in the box as belonging to her daughter – they had probably slipped from the fingers after the flesh had rotted away. The remains of a nightgown around the bones were also identified by the maid Josephine. It was the very garment that Shakereh had been seen in on the day she disappeared.

The investigation also unearthed other damning evidence that suggested a motive for the murder. The swami had been disposing of bits of Shakereh's property after getting rid of her. In fact, just two days after he had buried her, he sold thirty-four plots carved out of Shakereh's properties to various people using the power of attorney executed by her in his favour. The joint bank accounts were used to deposit the sale proceeds, and these amounts were withdrawn as soon as they were credited. He had also emptied out the bank lockers that Shakereh had opened in their joint names. To keep up the fiction that she was still alive, he had also forged her signature on income-tax documents.

The police now had a watertight case for a murder charge against Shraddhananda. While it was almost entirely based on circumstantial evidence, the prosecution, led by eminent lawyer C.V. Nagesh, was hopeful of securing a conviction.

The trial at the Sessions Court was a hard-fought one, with the prosecution lining up nearly forty witnesses to bolster its case. It made headlines across the country and was avidly followed in Bangalore, which in the early 1990s was yet to fully come into its own as the country's technology capital. The idea that a descendant of one of the city's most illustrious sons had probably been buried alive was unthinkable, to say the least. The most disturbing aspect of the case was the likelihood that the victim had probably been buried alive. Sabah, for one, has always claimed that her mother was not dead when she was put into the box. For her distraught daughter, the bones of Shakereh's hand sticking out of the mattress could only mean that her mother had regained consciousness after the effects of the sleeping pills had worn off, and that the unfortunate woman had tried to somehow claw her way out of the grave.

On 21 May 2000, the Sessions Court awarded Shraddhananda the death penalty, which was upheld by the Karnataka High Court in 2005. However, after an appeal in the Supreme Court, the sentence was modified to one of life imprisonment, but without the possibility of remission – meaning Shraddhananda would have to spend the remainder of his life in prison. The swami was lodged at the central prison in Bangalore, but on his own request was transferred in 2011 to the Central Jail at Sagar in his home state of Madhya Pradesh. He is still there, having spent over thirty years behind bars.

A couple of years ago, a documentary on this infamous case, titled *Dancing on the Grave*, was aired on Amazon Prime Video, which led Shraddhananda to send a legal notice to the makers, claiming that the four-part series would prejudice his case in the Supreme Court.[1] The documentary is remarkable in that the filmmakers managed to get access to Shraddhananda and interview him at the prison. The swami, now eighty-plus, still looks very fit despite the long years of incarceration. He shuffles along slowly, slightly hunched, but is still quite active for a man of his age. His mental faculties haven't dulled either, and he comes across as a very effective and persuasive speaker. Hearing him put forward his view on the case, one is almost tempted to believe his version of events. Shraddhananda says he did not kill his wife. He claims he had panicked after finding Shakereh lying senseless on the bed after he returned home that fateful afternoon. Not knowing what to do and having no one to turn to for help, he then decided to put her into the box and bury her in the pit – and after that there was no going back. He says he was sure that no one would have believed his story as Shakereh's family and friends were dead against him, and he had no choice but to do what he did. And so, he had to keep on lying to her daughter and to anyone else who inquired about Shakereh. According to the swami, he is merely a victim of circumstances over which he had no control. He also believes that there was a conspiracy against him as Sharekeh's family, according to him, did not want him to have all the prime property that would rightfully have been his after his wife's death.

Even as he was undergoing his sentence, he made an unsuccessful claim to the property on Richmond Road in a civil suit. He then appealed to the High Court, which found that there was nothing in law to specifically bar a criminal from inheriting the property of someone he had murdered. However, citing a Privy Council judgment (*Kenchavva Kom Sanyellappa Hosamani vs Girimallappa Channappa Somsagar*) dating back to 1924, which disqualified a murderer from inheriting property from his victim, the appeal was rejected.[2]

Shraddhananda had also appealed to the Supreme Court in 2023, seeking parole on grounds of good behaviour. He is, by all accounts, a 'model' prisoner, having given the jail authorities no trouble during his lengthy prison spell. He is also said to have conducted yoga and spiritual classes for his fellow inmates. The apex court, however, was not convinced and his plea was rejected.

In December 2023, he filed a mercy petition with the President of India, the highest constitutional authority in the country. The petition is still under consideration. With no action being taken, Shraddhananda appealed to the Supreme Court in January 2025 seeking a direction from the authorities to act on his plea. However, the apex court rejected his plea in December 2025, asking him instead to approach the Karnataka government with his grievances.[3] And so Shraddhananda continues stay behind bars. Some would say the swami is only getting a taste of his own medicine. Thirty years in jail is as good as being locked up alive in a box.

19

The Mystery of the Rajabai Tower Deaths*

For generations of cricket-lovers practising their craft on the wide expanse of Mumbai's Oval Maidan, the Rajabai Tower across the road has always been a benign, if imposing, presence. Flanked by the magisterial splendour of the Bombay High Court and the old Secretariat, the 280-foot-high clock tower is one of the defining features of the University Library – in itself an architectural marvel. Designed by Sir George Gilbert Scott and named after the mother of the pioneering industrialist Premchand Roychand who funded its construction, the clock tower is also known as Mumbai's Big Ben, by which it is said to have been inspired. But never

---

* *The Times of India*, 27, 28, 30 April 1891; *The Times of India*, 9, 11, 13 July 1891; Aditi Sen, 'The Mystery of the Clock Tower Deaths', *Parsi Khabar*, https://parsikhabar.net/bombay/the-mystery-of-the-clock-tower-deaths/14604/; Bakhtiar Dadabhoy, *Sugar in Milk: Life of Eminent Parsis*, Rupa Publications Pvt. Ltd, New Delhi, 2008; B.K. Karanjia, *Godrej: A 100 Years, 1897–1997*, Vol. 1, Viking Penguin India, 1997; B.M. Murzban, *The Parsis in India*, Vol. 2, Danai Mangasmriti, 1997; *Life of Sorabjee Bengallee*, Times of India Press, 1893, pp. 65–67.

since its completion in 1878 had the yellow Porbunder-stone building figured in the history of the country's premier metropolis – until the Saturday afternoon of 25 April 1891, when two young Parsi women fell (or were thrown) to their deaths from its looming height.

The two bodies hit the ground within a minute of one another.

Dadabhoy Pestonjee was waiting outside the Bombay High Court in his *shigram* (bullock cart) around 3.45 p.m. when he heard a dull thud, followed by another a few moments later. Something heavy, it seemed, had fallen in the University gardens a little distance away. He then heard a boy cry out that two Parsi ladies had fallen from the library's clock tower. Jumping down from his cart, Pestonjee ran towards the roadway under the north side of the Rajabai Tower. Two young women lay on their backs in a pool of blood on the gravel-studded path. Pestonjee, by his own account, was first on the spot. Looking up, he observed that the telephone wire overhead was broken. Three other men, also Parsis, had arrived by now, and together they gently dragged the bodies under the shade of the library porch, even as a couple of policemen came running. The saree of one of the ladies being in disarray, Pestonjee tied a knot in it to cover up her body.

A crowd soon gathered, and as the younger of the two ladies showed faint signs of life, a buggy was summoned to take her to the nearby Goculdas Tejpal Hospital. It was too late for the unfortunate woman, however, and the doctors pronounced her dead on arrival. The body was then sent back, and on the orders of Deputy Commissioner of Police G.H. Gell, both corpses were placed in the entrance hall of the University Library.

In the meantime, some sightseers who were up in the tower while the tragedy occurred, and also those in the library, were detained for questioning. It was clear that the ladies had either jumped or had been pushed, and foul play was immediately suspected. An ugly rumour began circulating: the women had been decoyed to the tower by some men who had tried to molest them, and had either jumped from one of the windows on the third floor (where a window was found open) to save their honour, or had been thrown down by their assailants.

While it was obvious from their fair complexion and distinctive apparel that both the deceased were Parsis, none among the scores of people from the community who had by now descended on the library seemed to know who the women were. The suspicion of foul play was strengthened when an examination of the bodies by two Parsi doctors revealed scratch marks, possibly made by fingernails, on the thighs and breasts of the women. There was also a long tear in the trousers of the younger woman, and it was noted that her *kushti* (sacred thread) was missing. The elder lady's *mathabana* (a thin white linen headscarf) was also missing.

It took well over an hour for the city coroner, Dr Thomas Blaney, to arrive and examine the bodies. Finding that a positive identification was yet to be made, he ordered that the corpses be transferred to the morgue. Finally, even as stretchers were being organized, the dead women were identified as Bachoobai and Phirojbai, both of the Godrej family. With Dr Blaney's permission, the bodies were then moved to the family residence at Frere Road, where they were kept overnight under a police guard.

Some startling facts were revealed at the inquest next morning. The two ladies had left their house the previous afternoon to visit Bachoobai's aunt at Chira Bazar, a few kilometres away. They hadn't told anyone that they were going to the Rajabai Tower, a revelation which came as a big surprise, if not a complete shock, to the family. The elder of the two, twenty-year-old Bachoobai, was the wife of Ardeshir Godrej, a student at Elphinstone College. Phirojbai, Ardeshir's younger sister, only sixteen and a pupil at the Alexandra Girls' School, was also married. The Godrej matriarch, Dosibai, revealed a curious, if somewhat prurient, fact during the inquiry: while both the girls had been married for some years, they were still virgins. Ardeshir, a modern and progressive husband (and two years younger than his wife) had resolved to wait till he completed his education before consummating his marriage. Phirojbai's husband was a student at the J.J. Institution, and as they were both very young the couple did not live together as man and wife.

The two women had never been to the Rajabai Tower before, and neither had ever spoken about wanting to go there. The teenage Phirojbai never went out alone and was always accompanied by a servant on her way to school. Bachoobai did go out by herself occasionally, but only as far as her mother's house at Dhobi Talao. No one could account for their presence at the tower that afternoon. Did they change their minds at the last minute and go there just for a lark, or had they deliberately lied, having set up a rendezvous with someone at the tower? Tongues started to wag and nasty, suggestive rumours began doing the rounds . . .

The question of suicide was also brought up, but did not seem very plausible. Ardeshir's mother Dosibai said both girls had been very happy when they set out. They were also on the friendliest of terms with their husbands, and there was certainly no domestic distress to compel them to end their lives. The theory of an accidental fall was also mooted. Did one or both of the girls, while looking over the parapet, slip and fall? And did one of them, attempting to hold on to the other, also plunge to her death? The inquest, which was only meant to formally identify the bodies, and try and determine the circumstances under which the ladies met their deaths, did not take long. The coroner's jury were then taken to the tower to examine the various rooms on each floor to ascertain if the ladies had fallen out of the third-floor window, or whether they had toppled over the veranda below the clock, or from the viewing gallery at the top. There were no conclusive answers to any of these questions, and the inquest was adjourned to 29 April, when it would be held at the morgue, after the post-mortem was conducted.[1]

Frere Road had been besieged by a large crowd while the inquest was in progress, and a number of mounted policemen had to be deployed to clear the road to the Godrej residence. While there was nothing as yet to suggest conclusively that the ladies had been assaulted, the impression that they had been victims of foul play seemed to have captured the public imagination and was hard to dispel. Solving the mystery would not be easy, and as the *Times of India* informed its readers the next day, whether the Rajabai Clock Tower case 'will turn out to be suicide, accident or murder is at the moment problematical'. The prognosis would turn out to be prophetic.[2]

The post-mortem examination, conducted by Dr Sidney Smith, the coroner's surgeon, was a matter of the great public interest. He alone could pronounce – officially, as it were – whether or not one or both ladies had been violated (as was feared by many), or if they had been molested or assaulted in any manner. Dr Smith examined both the bodies carefully and took down notes for the report that he would later prepare. He concluded that their deaths had occurred due to injuries sustained by their fall from the tower. The marks on the thigh and breasts of one of the deceased had, in his opinion, resulted from her falling on the rough gravel path. The injuries were caused by contact with a rough and hard surface. He did not think the marks were caused by fingernails. He detected traces of dust in all the marks on the bodies, except those on the breasts. There was a slight rupture of the hymen of the younger woman, but this could have happened after death, he opined. According to Dr Smith, there was nothing on the bodies that pointed to an assault or attempted rape.

Meanwhile, the police had been quite active, and several people had either been detained at the university or called for questioning later that evening. Two peons working at the university had been detained, along with the clock peon at Lund & Blockley (who designed the clock and maintained it), as also a young Parsi named Maneckjee Aslajee, the sole suspect in the case. A host of visitors had been at the clock tower around the time the two ladies were there. Their initial statements to the police and their recollection of events later at the sessions trial differed occasionally and, when faced by a battery of lawyers, did not stand up to cross-examination. While not entirely inept, the police investigation left much to be desired. And if well begun was half done, the beginning was far from propitious.

Atmaram Babaji, the *havildar* in charge of the university peons, had been seized by the police within minutes of the bodies falling down. He'd been spotted walking away quickly from the scene, and Pestonjee, finding his behaviour suspicious, asked the police to detain him. Atmaram said the two ladies had come to him earlier in the day, wanting to go up to the viewing gallery. He had accompanied them, along with Dowlat Luxmon, a peon from the accountant general's office, who too wanted to see the clock room. He had refused to take the two annas the ladies had initially offered him, but this amount was later given to him by the peon and he believed it came from the two women. He had taken them to the library hall and unlocked the door to the balcony which connects to the winding staircase of the tower. The two women had then gone up, along with the peon, while he went to fetch the key to the clock room from Lund & Blockley's peon. Some Muslim women had also gone down the stairs before the Parsi girls went up. There was quite a crowd at the top when he went up with the key – the peon with three of his friends who had come up via the spiral staircase from the ground floor, the two Parsi girls, two other men, a Muslim man and two boys. He had offered to show the ladies the clock room on the floor below, but they refused, saying they would stay on the veranda (or viewing gallery) for half an hour before going down. Having shown the peon and his friends the clock room, he accompanied them downstairs, when they met a Bengali babu and a boy heading up. He then sat down in the Senate room downstairs when, at about a quarter to four, one of the library peons informed him that two ladies had fallen from the tower. On hearing this, he had immediately locked the library door leading to the balcony and went downstairs to have a look, when he was nabbed by the police.

Atmaram's statement to the police did not make any mention of a young Parsi gentleman coming down the stairway. However, the *Times of India* report the next day said Atmaram had met a Parsi gentleman descending from the tower as he made his way up. This could well have been an error on the part of the correspondent, as Police Superintendent MacDermott later testified in court that Atmaram's statement did not say anything about seeing a Parsi or any other young man on his way down from the tower.

The Bengali babu, Surut Chandur Chowdry, turned out to be an assistant stock verifier from the Calcutta office of the East Bengal Railway. He'd been sight seeing in Bombay and wanted to get an aerial view of the city from the top of the clock tower. He was at the top landing at about a quarter to four along with his nineteen-year-old son, but had not seen anyone on the way up. This was at variance with Atmaram's statement and was to become a recurrent motif during the trial, with most witnesses disagreeing with each other's recollection of events, casting doubts on their sworn testimonies and confounding the case altogether. Chowdry said he saw three people at the top: an old Muslim gentleman with a small boy (his twelve-year-old nephew), and a Hindu youth, aged about eighteen. He had stayed there till 4 p.m. as he wanted to hear the bells chime at the hour. He had not seen the ladies at all, nor did he hear any screams. When he was about to descend, two policemen had come up and asked him to wait as there had been a robbery. Later, he was questioned, along with others who had been on the tower, by an English police officer (Beaufort) about the Parsi ladies. Surut Chowdry's son corroborated his father's account, and both were allowed to leave.

Dowlat Luxmon, the accountant general's peon, largely agreed with Atmaram's version of events, but said that in addition to his three friends and the two ladies there was also a Parsi man, aged about twenty, an eight- or nine-year-old Parsi girl and two Hindu men at the top-most landing. His three friends and the young Parsi had climbed up by the tower staircase, while the ladies had made their way through the library. All except the two young ladies had then gone with Atmaram to the clock room, after which they all went downstairs. The havildar had told him that the ladies did not want to see the clock room (they'd apparently been there before) and would enjoy the view from the gallery a little while longer. Later, they had all seen the dead bodies on the porch. He also recalled seeing a man who looked like a Bengali babu going up the stairs as he was descending. The Bengali had inquired if there was anyone up at the top, and he had replied in the affirmative. Luxmon's statement, again, differed slightly from that of Atmaram's in that in his recollection of events put four more people at the top landing, making a total of 10. The picture would get even more confusing as time passed.[3]

Maneckjee Aslajee, the young Parsi who had been at the

top of the tower while the ladies were there, was the prime suspect from the outset. Having gone to the High Court to collect some papers regarding a case, he thought he would go up to the tower to see the view, purely on a whim, he told the police. He had paid a few annas to the peon (whom he called a coolie) at the ground-floor entrance, who then unlocked the door to the spiral stairway. He had observed the view from the top for a few minutes and had then descended, when he saw the havilidar (Atmaram) going up. He had seen the two ladies but hadn't spoken to them at all. He had seen three or four women and two or three men in the tower. Sometime later, when he heard that two ladies had fallen from the tower, he went to the university grounds to have a look. A Parsi gentleman had pointed him out to Superintendent MacDermott, who then took him aside to ask him a few questions. The officer had asked him to open his coat, and finding that the waistcoat inside was torn, demanded an explanation. Aslajee said it had been caused by a 'slut belonging to Merwanjee Daruwalla' who had 'rushed' at him a month and a half ago. It was torn further after it was sent to the washerman. MacDermott, who naturally thought the waistcoat could have been torn in the course of a struggle with either of the two ladies, detained him immediately for further questioning. However, he was allowed to leave very late that night (at 3 a.m. the next morning, in fact) after his statement had been taken down. MacDermott had asked him to be present at the inquest the next day, and he had complied. The other witnesses at the tower were also allowed to go after their statements had been taken down. As the *Times* very succinctly put it, the police were now faced with 'the arduous task of solving the problem as to whether this terrible tragedy occurring in one of the most frequented quarters of Bombay in broad daylight was the result of suicide, accident or the perpetration of one of the foulest crimes on record'.[4]

There was, however, another version of what had transpired at the tower when Aslajee was being questioned by the police in the university compound. Jamsetji Enty, a clerk at M/s Conroy and Brown, solicitors, claimed to have seen Superintendent MacDermott holding Aslajee by the neck and leading him away. He had asked MacDermott to inquire why Aslajee's jacket was torn and his pantaloons soiled, and had put the same question to the suspect in Gujarati. Aslajee's reply was that he had seen two Khojas (men from the Muslim mercantile community) scuffling with the two ladies in the tower and had intervened to help them. Enty said he was not sure if MacDermott understood Gujarati as the policeman had then taken Aslajee away.

The two Khoja men, if they ever existed, were never discovered by the police. Given the vaunted efficiency of the Bombay City police, considered second to none in the country even at that time, it was odd that these two men whose evidence would have been vital to the investigation could not be found. Aslajee also claimed to have never spoken to Enty. He had spoken to a bearded man in the university grounds, he said, but Enty was not that man.

By Monday morning, some thirty-six hours after the incident, the police had not made any headway in the investigation and Superintendent MacDermott reported to the Commissioner, Colonel W.H. Wilson, that though several witnesses had been questioned, no one had been taken into custody as yet. Wilson was now under enormous pressure from the influential and vocal Parsi community. One of their leading lights, the industrialist Sir Dinshaw Maneckjee Petit, Bart., wrote to Wilson the same day offering a reward to anyone who might come forward with evidence that would help clear up the mystery behind the deaths of the two girls. The commissioner is said to have asked the baronet to wait at least till the coroner's inquiry was complete before taking such a step.[5]

The public, meanwhile, had its own theories and suspicions, which they expressed in letters to the editor of the *Times of India*.[6] A gentleman styling himself as 'Surmise' claimed to have 'bestowed some thought upon this lamentable occurrence' and arrived at the conclusion that the two ladies, 'discontented with their domestic life' had in a moment of weakness entered into a suicide pact and decided to end their lives together. Another correspondent, Jal B. Vakil, ruled out the suicide angle. There was not the slightest reason to infer that the two women were unhappy, he wrote. Indeed, it had been established that they were in a 'merry mood' when they set out from their house, and had gone to the Bai Bhicaji Kavyashala to attend a lecture, but finding it was to begin only much later in the evening, decided to go to the clock tower to while away the time. Given this fact, a 'mere child would refuse to bring itself up to the belief that they committed suicide'. It would be better, Vakil felt, 'to withhold pronouncing our own opinion' while the matter was being investigated and to await the jury's verdict. Yet another reader suggested that the *Times* had given out the impression that most Parsis were leaning towards the suicide theory. This was a 'revelation' which he and others of his community regarded as 'simply preposterous'.

While the police investigation was getting nowhere, Aslajee was not out of trouble yet. On 1 May, the three Parsi children (two boys and a girl, all aged around ten and twelve) who were believed (by some) to be at the tower that day, gave a signed statement implying that Aslajee had something to do with the women's deaths. For the three minors, Ardeshir, Cowasjee and Nawazbai, it must have been something of an ordeal, giving statements and testifying on four separate occasions: first before a lawyer, followed by one at the coroner's court, then with a magistrate, and then at the sessions trial. Not surprisingly, the fact that they were accompanied by elders and their recollection of the events of that day were largely uniform and unvarying gave rise to the suspicion that the children had been tutored. According to Nawaz, Aslajee was at the tower that afternoon and she had seen him talking to two men, who appeared to be Khojas. Aslajee had followed the women when they came up, and something had transpired at the tower that left the women agitated and scared. The girl had seen Aslajee going away with his clothes in disarray, though she could not say what exactly he had done to the two women.

A damning statement indeed, and one (if a jury chose to believe it) that could cost Aslajee his neck. As things stood, he had little if any support from his own people. The Parsis are a close-knit bunch and its members can usually be counted on to back each other in times of trouble. Not so for Aslajee. A majority of the community seemed to have made up their minds that he had attempted to rape or at least molest the women. The Gujarati-language newspaper *Jam-e-Jamshed*, determined to see that justice was done to the deceased, led the chorus against Aslajee. A few weeks after the tragedy, Jehangir B. Murzban, editor of the *Jam-e-Jamshed*, informed the police that Aslajee's servant Bala had found a note in his master's coat that day asking two men to meet him at the Rajabai Tower at 3 p.m. This seemed to be the real thing, but the police were slow in following up on it, and when they finally located the merchant to whom the servant had sold the clothes (presumably in an attempt to save his master), they had vanished – and so had the note. Bala was taken into custody and questioned, and on the basis of his statement Aslajee was arrested and committed to take his trial at the sessions court on 8 July.

'The Trial of Mancekjee Aslajee' was assiduously followed in the press, with the *Times of India* devoting several lengthy columns to it each day, updating its readers on what was probably the most sensational news story of the year.

Aslajee was charged on five separate counts: (1) with having committed murder by causing the death of Bachoobai (2) with having committed murder by causing the death of Phirojbai (3) with having committed murder, either by causing the death of Bachoobai, or causing the death of Phirojbai. (4) that, Bachoobai having committed suicide, with abetting the commission of such suicide; (5) that, Phirojbai having committed suicide, with abetting the commission of such suicide. The prosecution was led by acting Advocate General Basil Lang, assisted by his nephew (and later advocate general) Basil Scott. Aslajee was represented by Chitnis, Motilal & Malvi, with Mr J. Jardine leading the defence. The formidable

John Duncan Inverarity, one of Bombay's most eminent barristers, was given a 'watching brief' (as an observer) by the relatives of the deceased women.

The public gallery at the sessions court was packed with Parsis, most of whom were determined to see Aslajee swinging at the end of a rope. To an impartial observer, it seemed more likely a case of the *Parsees of Bombay vs Maneckjee Aslajee* than *Empress vs. Maneckjee Aslajee*. A nine-member special jury, composed entirely of Englishmen, was sworn in for the trial. As the proceedings got underway, the foreman of the jury complained that they could not hear what was being said by the witnesses. Justice Charles Farran then ordered that the witnesses be placed near the jury box. His Lordship also said he would 'endeavour to make the witnesses speak up' so that the reporters in the press box could clearly hear the evidence.[7] Translators were also at hand, as most of the witnesses spoke only local languages (Gujarati, Hindi or Marathi). As was not uncommon in such trials, crucial bits of evidence were probably lost in translation. The jury, for its part, would have other concerns as time went by.

The main difficulty faced by the prosecution in making the charges stick to the accused arose from the testimonies of the witnesses not agreeing on the essential details. The number of people who visited the tower on that day could not be ascertained with certainty. Nor could the witnesses entirely agree on the timing of the tragedy (anywhere between 3.30 p.m. and 4.00 p.m.), the sequence of events or who else was around during that crucial half-hour. Their recollections were often contradictory, and any prompting by the lawyers to refresh their memory only befuddled them further.

Among the first to testify was Malikbhai Maniklal, who had gone to see the tower that day accompanied by a boy named Syed Lal. He did not remember the time, but said the 'sun had gone towards the west'. For someone who described himself as a cultivator, Malikbhai did not seem accustomed to physical exertion. He was breathless half-way up and lay down on the first landing, he told the court. He could not see the sky from where he lay. He had walked around the tower, but saw only a bania boy up there and no one else. A good many people had gone up while he was climbing but he could not recognize any of them, although he did remember the Bengali babu. Later, some policemen had come up and asked him not to leave the tower. Syed Lal's testimony largely mirrored that of his elder companion. The schoolboy had gone up with Malikbhai, and when the latter felt giddy and lay down, he had fanned him. A few people went past during that time, but he could not be sure who or how many. He remembered the Bengali babu, and when he was going down the police came up and asked him to stay put. He could not be sure if they had been up at the tower for a quarter of an hour before descending. Cross-examined by Jardine, he said he did not hear any screams while he was up there. He had heard the bells chime, but did not hear them strike either three or four.

Eleven-year-old Hemachand Cutchra was also at the tower that afternoon. He remembered the two Parsi ladies — they were right behind him and had asked him to move up quickly. At the top he saw nine or ten people. Apart from the Parsi ladies the others were all Hindus. He recalled seeing Malikbhai on the ground floor before he went up, but had not seen him at the top. He saw the Parsi ladies admiring the view, but did not speak to them. He heard the clock strike first, and a little afterwards he heard the chimes. He had then gone down and saw two of his friends playing in front of the High Court. He heard the sound of the first body hitting the ground, and saw the second body falling when it was about midway. Upon cross-examination, Hemachand said he was near the ladies when they were at the top of the tower, and he did not notice if either of them was wearing spectacles. They were the only Parsis on the tower with him. There were no other Parsis, only Hindus, and he did not see any Parsi children up there. Asked by a member of the jury if he'd spotted anyone on the tower when he saw the second body falling, Hemachand said he had seen no one. And yes, the ladies appeared cheerful when he saw them.

Purbhooshunker Pudumsey, a book-keeper, said he was at the tower at 3 or 3.15 p.m. that afternoon. Four or five Muslim women and a Muslim man and a boy also went up with him. There were one or two Marwaris as well at the top. Three or four other men (friends of the accountant general's peon) also came up after he reached the top. He was looking towards the harbour from the viewing gallery and he could not say if any Parsi men, women or children came up. Cross-examined, he said he hadn't gone around the tower but stayed at one spot, looking at the steamers, Hog Island and Elephanta Island in the distance. He had seen no women in distress or frightened, nor had he observed any Parsi gentleman, with his clothes disordered, rushing downstairs turban in hand. When he was about to go down, the police had come up and asked him not to leave as a robbery had been committed. He was kept in custody and released around midnight after his statement was recorded.

Luxuman Narayan, a peon, testified to having seen several people when he had gone to the tower that day, but could not give the exact number. He had been accompanied by a boy named Babajee Sudoo. He remembered seeing the bania boy (Parbhooshunker), Malikbhai and Syed Lal, the havildar Atmaram, and Aslajee. He also saw the two Parsi ladies coming up along with Dowlut. He could not say where Aslajee was when the ladies came up. Aslajee had been wearing a black coat, white pantaloons and a turban of the kind usually worn by Parsis. He could not recall if he had seen anyone coming up as he was descending. When asked if he'd noticed any Parsi children at the top before he went down to the clock room, Narayan said he had not seen any. To the best of his belief, he told the court, the only people at the top when he went to see the clock room were the two Parsi ladies, Malikbhai, Syed Lal and the bania boy. He heard no 'noise, cries, or screams, or shouting', neither did he see 'two Mussulmans or Khojas' while he was on the tower. He had not been detained by the police, he told the judge, but went to see Superintendent MacDermott at his bungalow the day after the incident on being told to do so by Dowlat. Babajee Sudoo was examined by the advocate general and confirmed all that Narayan had said. He gave a statement a few days after the incident, but did not see it being taken down in writing, the thirteen-year-old schoolboy told the court. A police sepoy had come to his house to take him away for questioning.[8]

Two of the men who went to the tower with Dowlut Luxmon, also gave largely similar testimonies. Vithoo Babajee and Narayan Raghoo were sure that they had not seen any

Parsi children at the tower. Dowlut, however, claimed to have seen two children, who had preceded them up the tower. He had not taken particular notice of the kids, but he thought they were a boy and a girl. He could not identify them, and they were not dressed in clean clothes. He was not sure of the time, but he had left his office at 3 p.m., so it would have to be some time after that. He also could not be sure of the exact time when each of the several people he saw at the top of the tower came down.

The university havildar, Atmaram Babajee, was examined next. He was a crucial witness, and the prosecution and defence lawyers questioned him at great length and in minute detail about the events leading up to the deaths of the two women. His recollection of events of that day did not vary much from the statement he had made to the police, except for the very crucial point that he had seen Aslajee coming down near the entrance to the clock room as he went up. Questioned by the acting advocate general, the havildar said he had never seen the Parsi before and had to move to one side to let him pass. He next saw Aslajee at the police station and had recognized him. The only problem here was that in his initial statement to the police, Atmaram had not made any mention of the Parsi – a point Superintendent MacDermott would also confirm.

Atmaram was also sure that no Parsi children had been to the tower that afternoon (the police statement did not mention the children, as their existence came to light only a week after the incident), nor had he seen any Khojas or Muslims (besides those he had earlier mentioned) that afternoon. He'd not heard any screams or cries either. Any sound in the tower carried easily, Atmaram told the court, and if a man had been talking in the clock room he could be easily heard on the top of the tower. He had locked the library door immediately after he heard that the women had fallen from the tower, but could not say if anyone had come through the door before it was locked. Asked by one of the jurors if he'd taken the policemen straight up to the top of the tower, Atmaram said he had led them up by the main tower staircase and they had examined each floor and room in the tower. He did not know the deceased women and had never seen them at the university in the twenty-one years that he had worked there.

A very important witness then took the stand, and many in the courtroom might have wondered if the testimony of eleven-year-old Nawazbai Shapurjee Engineer could only be taken with a generous measure of salt. Opinion was divided on whether any Parsi children were actually at the tower that day, or if they'd been put up only to incriminate Aslajee. On being examined by Basil Lang, the little girl said that she and her sister Sirinbai, left her house at Cowasjee Patel Street (about a kilometre away) at 2.30 p.m. with her sister Sirinbai, Ardeshir and Cowasjee to go to the tower. Making their way up, they saw five or six persons of different castes going up. Two Muslim boys, around fourteen to sixteen years old, who were behind them, had made it to the top ahead of her, and there were two Marwaris as well. Later, two women from the oilmen caste came up and the Marwaris went down. After the clock struck 3 p.m., a Parsi (Aslajee) and two Muslims, about twenty-five years of age, came up. She saw them having a conversation. The two Muslim men then went down, followed by the women of the oilmen caste and the two Muslim boys. The two Parsi ladies had then come up and began walking around the tower. Aslajee was walking behind them. Having gone around the tower three or four times, the ladies went down, followed by Aslajee, when the clock chimed a quarter past three. Nawaz and her companions were still looking around when the two ladies came up again. Their clothes were in disorder, their sarees being entirely off their bodies and held in their hands. She noticed that the thinner of the two was wearing her *mathabana*, but not the stouter one. The latter woman was also not wearing her spectacles, which she had on when Nawaz had first seen her. The thin-looking woman (Phirojbai) told the stouter one, 'There are Parsi children here; come here.' As the women came and stood near her, Aslajee came running up and the stout woman muttered, '*Mare re, mare re*' (an expression often used to show sorrow or fear, helplessness or despair).[9] The ladies then went around to the side facing the High Court, still followed by the accused, but Nawaz had not noticed if Aslajee's coat was then buttoned or unbuttoned. The clock struck 3.30 p.m. just then, and as she listened to the chimes, she saw Aslajee, coat unbuttoned and *pagri* in hand, walking away quickly. However, she could not say what he or the ladies had been doing, as they'd been out of her sight. She then descended from the tower, and on her way down saw five or six people coming up, including someone she thought was a 'Portuguese'. On being shown the Bengali babu, she said it might have been him, but she could not be sure. Later, she had seen the bodies lying on the ground, and as she stood watching, a Parsi had asked her if the ladies were related to her. She had been very much afraid, and on reaching home that evening had told her mother about the incident at the tower. Some six or seven days later, she had been taken to the office of a lawyer (Adair Craigie of Craigie, Lynch & Owen) where her statement was taken down in writing.[10] The two Parsi boys, Ardeshir and Cowasjee, also testified, in much the same vein.

The defence refused to give any credence to these claims. To any impartial observer, they countered, it must be evident that the three children had been tutored. Their recollections were similar in almost every point, and this was impossible unless they'd gone over it again and again, as they would a classroom lesson. Aslajee, now in the fight of his life, was predictably furious. The Parsis were out to get him, he told the court, and the kids were only parroting what their elders had taught them. At the coroner's inquiry he'd observed a Parsi gentleman pointing him out to one of the children, who had then identified him as being on the tower. The identification parade in the coroner's office, where he was made to stand with men who were shorter than him had been flawed, but his protests had been summarily dismissed. Aslajee's contention that the identification process had been rigged found support from an unexpected quarter. The defence produced a police sepoy to buttress their claim. Shaik Mahomed Shaik Mohideen confirmed that he'd seen a Parsi pointing out Aslajee to one of the boys who was about to give evidence before the coroner.

To compound an already muddled case, there was another witness whose account seemed to suggest that at least one of the ladies had jumped from the tower deliberately. Abdul Kadar Khan, a court clerk, was standing on the veranda of the translator's office on the third floor of the High Court that afternoon. Examined by the advocate general, Khan said he'd seen the two ladies on the top of the tower above the clock. This was at 3.35 p.m. He knew the time as he had gone on the veranda to adjust his watch with the tower clock. One of the ladies was holding the other by the chest. He saw a Parsi on the tower, standing about four feet behind the women. While he was looking on, he saw the lady who was being held by the chest falling down in the front of the clock. The accused was the Parsi whom he saw on the tower, and he had seen him in the court earlier that day. He had been frightened when the women fell, Khan said, and rushed downstairs. He had passed through the translator's office on his way down and all the clerks were in, but he was too scared to tell anyone what he had just seen. He'd only mentioned the matter to some people after three or four days, but he could not be sure of the date – at which point the judge expressed surprise that a lawyer's clerk could not remember such a vital detail.

Cross-examined by Jardine, Khan said he had kept quiet about the matter as he knew he would then have to go to the police and would be 'annoyed' by them. A few days later, at the translator's office, hearing some people talk about the involvement of some Muslims in the matter, he had told them that it was not so, as he had seen what had happened on the tower. They had urged him to go and make a statement to MacDermott, or go to Craigie's office and make an affidavit. He told them he was confident that the Bombay Police were quite capable of finding out any murder or crime and it was not necessary for him to tell them.

When asked to confirm what exactly the women were

doing when he saw them, Khan said they were facing each other, and one of them was holding the other by the chest. They were standing inside the parapet wall and not on the wall. He'd seen them struggling for about five to ten seconds, while the Parsi man was standing behind them, looking on, he said. It appeared to him that one of the ladies wanted to throw herself over and the other one was holding her back. Neither woman had her foot on the wall, but one of them fell over first, with the other holding on. After he saw the ladies on the ground, he had wanted to go up the tower but had been stopped by Luckia, the peon from his office, who was also there. Luckia said people were talking about Khojas being responsible for the tragedy and Khan could be mistaken for a Khoja and arrested if he was found upstairs. Khan had then gone back to his office.

If those in the courtroom were still not confused as to what had really happened on the tower there was further conflicting testimony to contend with. Framroz Dosabhoy, assistant weaving master at the Swadeshi Mills, said he was walking on the university road that afternoon when he took out his watch to compare it with the tower clock. It was then 3.30 p.m. by the tower clock. Looking up, he saw what looked to him like a bundle falling from the High Court side of the tower. He was wondering what it was when he spotted a man pushing or throwing out something over the parapet wall. He could not identify the man or his sect. There were two or three people on the east side of the tower at this time, but he could not say if they were male or female. After the second object fell, he went away as he had to attend a wedding. He did not give the matter much thought as the thing he saw falling only looked like a bundle.

Cross-examined by Jardine, Dosabhoy said he was not sure about the two or three people he saw on the tower, but the one who pushed the bundle over was definitely a man. The man had been wearing some sort of headgear, but he could not say if it was a helmet or a worsted cap or something else. He did not think the bundle that fell resembled a human being. He did not see where the second bundle was before it was pushed over as he was then looking at his watch. When he saw it being pushed over, it was on the parapet wall. He'd seen people rushing towards the tower after the bundle fell, but did not connect it with what he had just seen. He had made a statement to Inspector Stanford, partly in broken English and partly in Marathi, and was not sure if he'd been correctly understood. The jury then asked several questions regarding the headgear worn by the man Dosabhoy had seen on top of the tower, which he answered.

Dadabhoy Pestonjee, the shigram driver, was then questioned by Basil Scott as to what he'd done after seeing the bodies on the ground. Pestonjee confirmed that he had been assisted by three other Parsis to move the bodies of the deceased to the library porch. He had attempted to cover up the body of the younger lady which was almost bare, but had not done anything to the dress of the stouter woman. Crucially, he testified to having seen three Parsi children standing nearby when he saw the bodies, and he had asked them if they were related to the deceased.

Pestonjee, on being questioned by Jardine, said he had made a statement to the police at 1 a.m. the next day, but had said nothing about having seen the children. Neither had he said anything about them when examined before the coroner. However, he later told the Magistrate that he had seen 'two or three grown-up Parsees with turbans and coats on, and three small Parsee boys' while he was standing by the bodies. He had not said anything about having spoken to them as he had not been asked. This was the first he had identified them, Pestonjee told the court. But yes, he'd seen them earlier in the court corridor since the trial began. He said he'd never been asked either by the police or the coroner about any Parsi children. He had not been specifically asked in the police court to identify them, but they had identified him.

The medical professionals who examined the bodies of the two women told the court their story on 10 January. Here too there was no unanimity, with the Indian doctors (all Parsi) disagreeing with Dr Sidney Smith, the coroner's surgeon, on the cause of death and the nature of the wounds on the corpses. Dr Sorabjee Nadirshaw and Dr Framjee Divecha had been the first of the medical fraternity to examine the bodies. This was done around 5.30 p.m. in the University Hall at the request of Superintendent MacDermott, who only wished to ascertain if the ladies had been assaulted or molested in any manner. The doctors were not allowed to examine the backs of the women. Both men arrived at the same conclusion: the marks on both victims were inconsistent with a fall from a great height and were definitely scratch marks caused by fingernails in the course of an attempted rape. Dr Nadirshaw was convinced that the marks on the breasts of the elder woman (Bachoobai), supposedly indentations made by the silver buttons of her jacket or blouse, were made by the fingernails of an assailant. In his opinion, the marks on the women, both on the thigh and breasts, were not caused by the fall from the tower. The scratch marks on the thigh of the younger woman (Phirojbai) were the result of an indecent assault and could not have been formed even by her climbing the parapet of the tower, he maintained. There were one hundred fingernail marks on the thigh, he told the court, and these had been caused by someone attempting to separate the legs of the victim. He also disagreed with the report of the coroner's surgeon that there were traces of dust in the scratch marks. He had certainly not noticed any dust in the scratches when he viewed them, he told the court.

Dr Divecha too would not attribute the marks on the victims to the fall from the tower, despite the presence of sharp stones on the roadway where the bodies fell. The thigh bones were fractured by the fall, but there were no other marks that could be caused by the body hitting the telephone wire or any other obstruction on the way down. He was convinced that the scratch marks pointed to an attempted rape. In his opinion, the marks could not have been made through the deceased's clothing, unless the material was very thin. Dr Divecha also said that he had been unable to make a full examination of the bodies as he was stopped by Deputy Commissioner Gell who had just then arrived at the hall.

A third Parsi doctor, Ardeshir Hormusjee Gaswalla, was also called to give evidence. He began reading from prepared notes, which he said were made just before the coroner had begun his examination. The defence objected to this, and the judge asked him to put away the notes. On cross-examination by Jardine, he admitted that he had not sought Dr Smith's permission to be present at the post-mortem. He was not asked to be present, but merely went out of 'curiosity'. Still, Gaswalla claimed to have 'assisted in the autopsy' by bringing 'two or three pieces of glasses' (he probably meant lenses). But his mind was made up: the marks he saw on the corpses were definitely scratch marks. When asked if he had ever seen similar marks on anyone he replied: 'Yes. When children were struggling [with one another].' The judge, who apparently did not take him seriously, asked Gaswalla if he could produce similar scratches on his hand. The witness attempted to do this, without success, and was asked by the judge (now laughing) to try harder. He failed again, and then said the marks could only be made by someone with long fingernails.[11]

The only medical opinion that really counted was that of the coroner's surgeon. Dr Sidney Smith was questioned very closely by the advocate general on the observations made in his report.[12] The surgeon said he had conducted the autopsy on the two bodies in the house on Frere Road a day after the incident at the tower. Dr Rustomjee Bharucha, a friend of the Godrej family, Dr Smith's two Hindu assistants and the corpse-bearers were the only people present during the autopsy. After describing the injuries found on Phirojbai's body, Dr Smith said they could have been caused only by the fall. The marks were caused by the bodies 'impinging on the rough gravel and could not have been made with fingernails. During the course of his work, he had seen a lot of injuries caused by fingernails and so was certain the marks on the women were not scratch marks. They were wider and deeper, and the skin not being broken, there was no escape of blood. In his opinion, they 'did not appear to be such as would have been caused by a man attempting to outrage [a woman]'.

There were three- or four-dozen indentations on the inner and outer sides of Phirojbai's right thigh, and there was dust in the indentations. These marks might have been caused by the fall, as the body in all probability had rolled over after hitting the ground, he told the court. While Bachoobai's body had fallen on the right side, the marks on her left breast could have been caused by the body rolling over on the gravel, or by her climbing over the parapet wall. The body would not necessarily have remained on its face when rolling over after the fall as a muscular contraction may again have caused it to roll over onto its back.

Dr Smith was questioned again about any signs of an attempted assault on the women, to which he replied: 'There was nothing to justify that an outrage had been committed; whether an attempt had been made, I cannot say.' He had not seen any marks on the body to lead him to that conclusion. If such an attempt had been made, he would have expected to see marks on both thighs, not just the right thigh. The rupture of the hymen of the younger woman, in his opinion, took place after death. As to the rent in her trousers, Dr Smith thought it might have been caused by the fall, or by her body hitting a projection of the building or the telephone wire. He did not know Dr Gaswalla and had noticed him only at the coroner's court. Dr Smith had definitely not seen him at the autopsy; he had certainly not come near the table. The piece of glass he asked for was handed to him by his attendant, not by Dr Gaswalla, he told the court.

Dr Smith's testimony probably saved Aslajee. The coroner's surgeon was a man of wide experience, and his opinion certainly weighed more with the English jury as opposed to that of the Parsi doctors who had, it must be said, only made a brief examination of the bodies. Dr Gaswalla's antics during the post-mortem (if he was indeed there) and his subsequent testimony could also not have impressed either judge or jury.

The Parsi doctors were apparently not vocal enough in testifying. Their replies to questions from counsel, the *Times of India* correspondent wrote, were made in a very low voice that was not audible to the reporters and could only be heard by the jury. Even the judge, who was seated not too far from the witnesses, had to frequently order them to speak up.

Aslajee's bête noire Jamsetjee Enty, who claimed to have seen the suspect being hauled away by Superintendent MacDermott, did not cut much ice with either judge or jury. Cross-examined by the defence, Enty said he thought Aslajee had committed the crime as the latter had 'a very fierce face, his eyeballs protruding and his lips trembling so that he could not speak. His face at the time was not favourable to his innocence.' This was probably a little over the top and was pooh-poohed by Superintendent MacDermott. Aslajee eyes were not protruding nor were his lips trembling when he was led to the roadway, the officer retorted. He did not appear to be frightened and had in fact volunteered the information that he had been up to the tower and had seen the two ladies there. When questioned by a member of the jury, Enty said he took it for granted that the superintendent understood Gujarati as he did not ask him to translate what the prisoner had said. There were witnesses who could corroborate his statement, Enty told the court. The judge, who seemed to have made up his mind that Enty was not a credible witness, asked him to leave.

As was the norm in criminal cases, the police had charges of high-handedness and bribery levelled against them. MacDermott was alleged to have taken a bribe from Aslajee, and had apparently also slapped one of the witnesses. The policeman denied these 'fabrications'. He also rubbished all of Enty's claims. When he took Aslajee out on to the road, there was a lot of noise and excitement, as they were followed by a rabble of 200 people, and he could not say if Enty was in that crowd. He claimed to have not laid a hand on the prisoner, as it would have been improper of him to do such a thing. He would never have allowed Enty to question Aslajee as that would have been improper and against the rules. In short, Enty was a liar. No spectacles or pieces of clothing had been found when the police had searched the tower; nor was there any evidence of a struggle in any of the rooms or on the terrace, he told the court. The telephone wire had snapped a few feet from the tower, and he thought the tear in the trousers of one of the ladies might have been caused by the 'rebound of the body from the wire'. When asked why he had let Aslajee go that night, MacDermott said there had been 'no evidence in his possession at 3 o'clock in the morning' to justify keeping him or indeed any of the other witnesses in custody.

Aslajee for his part put up a stout defence from the dock. He had nothing to hide, he said. He had been to the university grounds after he heard that the ladies had fallen from the tower. There he had told a Parsi gentleman that he had been with them up at the tower. He had told the police all that he knew, and had been released later that night. He had followed MacDermott's instruction to attend the inquest and had always made himself available to the police for questioning.

Enty was a liar, he maintained, and had been put up by the Parsis to frame him. 'I am ruined in money and reputation,' he told the court. There was a conspiracy against him, and it had been 'got up' by the Parsis.[13]

The seven-day trial finally drew to a close on 13 July. Summing up the case for the prosecution, Basil Lang told the jury that it was their duty to determine whether or not the accused was guilty of the crime charged against him or had any hand in causing the death of the Parsi ladies. It was open to the jury to consider whether the ladies went to tower with the intention of committing suicide. He reminded them that while the havildar Atmaram had testified to seeing the prisoner making his way down when he was going up, they should remember that he did mention this in his statement to the police, and the jury would be 'justified in taking this important circumstance into their consideration'. The jury had heard the children's testimony and the manner in which they had answered the questions put to them in cross-examination, and it was up to them to 'determine the weight to be attached' to their evidence. The girl Nawazbai had given her evidence in a straightforward way, and it was for the jury to judge whether it was 'satisfactory'. It was for the jury to decide if there was anything unlikely in what the children had said.

As for the medical evidence, the prosecutor said, it was impossible to reconcile the opinions of the doctors. The Parsi doctors had said positively that they saw evidence of an outrage or an attempt to outrage, while Dr Smith was equally positive the other way. Remarking on fact that the elder lady's mathabana and the younger lady's kushti were missing, he said they might have been lost during the course of a struggle. They would also have to consider whether the fall from the tower 'was not the result of a struggle in which they were engaged'. As for the evidence of the policeman Shaik Mohideen, who said he had seen a Parsi man pointing out Aslajee to the children, Lang said he 'thought the jury would not believe the policeman'.

The chief evidence against Aslajee, the prosecutor reminded the jury, was that of the Parsi children. If the jury did not believe the evidence, the case must fail. But they should still consider whether the evidence, coupled with other evidence in the case, was not sufficient to sustain the minor charge – that of abetment of suicide. It was possible that the second lady was thrown over, he said, but that was for the jury to decide.

Speaking for Aslajee, Jardine asked the jury to consider the circumstances of the grave charges levelled against the accused. Jardine thought that the evidence of the Parsi children 'was not to be believed' – as, if the jury 'did not believe in the existence or presence of the two Khojas on the tower, the whole testimony of the children fell to the ground'. Further, he reminded the jury, if the medical evidence failed to point to any attempt at rape, then the reason for the flight to the top of the tower followed by the prisoner 'fell to pieces'. The theory of the prosecution, he said, was that two young ladies had been 'outraged in a certain fashion by two Khojas and as they were running away up the tower, the accused followed them, and was then said to have thrown one or both of them from the top of the building'. He asked the jury to consider the improbability of the occurrence, for considering the number of people who had been there, it was almost like a 'public thoroughfare'. Moreover, if rape had been attempted in one of the rooms below the tower and the ladies had run upstairs, was it credible that the accused would follow them up to the top where he knew there were many people present? Would the accused not have run downstairs and tried to get away as fast as he could? It had been overwhelmingly proved by the evidence laid before the court, Jardine said, that there were no Khojas on the tower that day and 'though the entire city had been ransacked for evidence, nothing had been found to prove who those Khojas were'.

The prosecution, Jardine went on, had asked the jury to believe that for fifteen minutes the Parsi children were the only ones on the tower when the tragedy took place; and that, he thought, 'was a good deal for the jury to be expected to believe'. If the children had indeed seen the ladies coming up with their disordered dresses, followed by the suspect, would they not, out of the natural curiosity of children, have followed the ladies? And would the ladies have left the side of the children if something had been done to them? It was all too incredible to believe, Jardine said, and on those grounds alone he asked the jury to regard the children's evidence as false. They would have to consider, he told the jury, whether the evidence of the children had been 'merely got up to bring home the crime to an unfortunate and innocent man'.

The proceeding had now been underway for a few hours and the court at this stage rose for 'tiffin'. After it had reassembled, Jardine, presumably aided by a full belly, resumed his address with vigour. He had analysed the evidence a good deal, he told the jury, and based on the strength and veracity of it, would ask them 'to believe that there were no Khojas on the tower, and that the children were not on the tower at the time they stated'. As to the suggestion that an outrage had been committed, he pointed out that the prosecution had not been able to produce a single witness who had heard any scream or cries; nor had a search of the premises turned up any traces of a struggle. As for the evidence of the Parsi doctors, he did not wish to say that they had 'not given their correct opinions, but thought that they had started with the idea that an outrage had been committed and having made an examination had been unable to get it out of their mind'. He could not make out how the doctors had concluded that in a case of rape, only nail marks would be found on the right leg and not on the left. On this point, he told the jury, he would prefer to believe the evidence of Dr Smith, who was a doctor with much greater expertise than any of the Parsi medical men.

Asking the jury to 'dispel from their minds that the girls were not virtuous', Jardine asked them to consider what possible reasons the girls could have had for coming to the tower by themselves. The facts of the case, he thought, pointed to the ladies having committed suicide, something 'being in their minds to induce them to leave their homes clandestinely'. Considering the evidence, he told the jury, 'They must come to the conclusion that the case, which had been a most instructive one as showing the manner in which the witnesses had come forward and perjured themselves in giving evidence … had not been made out by the prosecution.' In India, Jardine reminded the jury, 'false evidence sprang up like a mushroom in a single night and probably would lead to the sacrifice of a human life'. Keeping this in mind, he could 'await the result of their verdict with confidence'.[14]

Finally, it was for the judge to sum up the case for the jury. To those nine gentlemen sitting in a hot and crowded courtroom through hours of testimony, the trial must have been something of an ordeal. Some of the jurymen did question the witnesses from time to time, but what they thought of the answers is anybody's guess. Despite the numerous accounts of what had transpired at the tower, a clear and unambiguous picture was yet to emerge. It was left to the judge to guide the jury through the maze of contradictory evidence before they arrived at a verdict.[15]

Justice Farran began by telling the jury that it would be impossible for him to address them without giving his opinion on the matter, but asked them not be guided by anything that was not supported by evidence. The only safe verdict they could bring in, if the jury found Aslajee guilty of murder, was the one on the third count: that he had murdered either Bachoobai or Phirojbai, but that they were unable to say which girl had met her death at the hands of the accused. His Lordship did not think there was any evidence that pointed to abetment of suicide, and if the jury brought in a verdict of murder under the alternative count, it would then be referred to the High Court, as per the law. The deaths of the ladies, Justice Farran thought, were caused either by their falling or jumping from the tower. He thought it improbable that anyone in broad daylight would have thrown them down from the tower with the 'almost certainty of being caught like a rat in a trap'. From the conflicting nature of the evidence, he could see nothing to show that they might not have fallen from the tower; they all knew that if one of them had climbed over the parapet and had fallen over, the other, in attempting to save her, could have been pulled over.

As for the medical evidence, His Lordship said, assuming that all the doctors were equally truthful, the jury should remember that Dr Smith had made his examination in broad daylight while the Indian doctors had only seen the bodies in the evening, partly with the help of lights. It was very difficult, he said, to decide evidence when two doctors with very little experience pledged themselves against Dr Smith, who was highly experienced. There was no evidence of rape, the judge remarked, but if the jury considered that the marks on the women were those of fingernails, then the case assumed a different aspect altogether. But if they could not form on opinion on this, then they should consider the case irrespective of the medical evidence, though it was 'not to be forgotten that Dr Smith had never seen such marks on the thighs of a woman on whom rape had been attempted. It, was therefore, to be determined how one hundred such marks came on the legs of the girl'.

The other evidence in the case, he pointed out, was all contradictory: One, that the ladies had been subjected to some form of violence; and the other, that they fell from the tower. It was for the jury to decide on which side they found 'a preponderance of evidence of a creditable nature'. It was up to the jury to decide whether they believed the evidence of Superintendent MacDermott on the allegations against him. As to the presence of people on the tower, he pointed out that the statement of the clerk Abdul Kadar that he had not seen anyone on the tower was at variance with that of other witnesses, who claimed to have seen people on the tower when the ladies fell. Abdul Kadar's position at the High Court veranda was such that he could have easily seen the tower, and if what he said was true, it negated the evidence of the witnesses who claimed to have seen two or three people on the tower from the roadway. Then there was also the conflicting evidence of the Parsi children, who swore they were the only ones on the tower except for the accused when the ladies fell. It was for the jury to determine, His Lordship said, which evidence they wanted to believe. As for Nawazbai's evidence, and the contention that she and the two boys had been tutored, His Lordship found that wherever the girl's story varied, that of the boys also varied in the same detail and in the same manner; all this 'led a person to believe that there was someone behind the scenes'. Commenting on the testimony of Framroz Dosabhoy, who claimed to have seen someone throwing a bundle over the top of the parapet while there were two or three other people where the children were standing, his Lordship said he could not reconcile that with the evidence of the children. It would be 'a long time', he told the jury, before he could believe the prosecution's suggestion that the children had stood on something to raise themselves above the parapet. The judge also asked the jury to keep in mind the age and character of the witnesses. When an excitable witness was being examined, he said, it was possible for them to believe that they saw more than what they did. Human memory, the judge added, was not a machine and varied according to the individual, pointing out that Framroz had in his testimony contradicted himself within two minutes regarding what the time was when he had stopped to check his watch.

Finally, Enty's evidence had not favourably impressed the court, the judge said. His Lordship then made a startling revelation – he had received two anonymous letters that morning, which led him to believe that there were some people who were anxious that Enty's evidence should be corroborated, even though that gentleman had stated that he did not know if anyone in the crowd had heard what he said to the prisoner. There were some people, Justice Farran told the jury, who after repeating a line and telling it to somebody else, were so convinced of its truth that they got to believe it themselves.

Concluding his three-hour-long summing-up, Justice Farran said that having heard the testimony of the various witnesses, it was now up to the jury to consider on which side the truth lay. If they believed that no crime was committed, then it was their duty to acquit the accused. But if they believed that an infamous crime had in fact been perpetrated, they should consider if the evidence was sufficient to prove the prisoner's guilt.

The nine good men and true seemed to have made up their minds already, and without leaving the jury-box for discussions delivered a verdict of 'not guilty'.[16] Maneckjee Aslajee's nearly four-month-long ordeal had finally ended and he was immediately released from custody. It is not known if he thanked the jury, but those worthy gentlemen were presumably much relieved, for they were now excused from jury duty for a period of two years.

The 'not guilty' verdict was greeted by howls of protest from the Parsi community. The police were accused of having conducted a shoddy investigation, and there were calls for a retrial. Public opinion mattered enormously in a case like this, and (in the absence of Facebook and X) a picture postcard featuring the Rajabai Tower, flanked by images of the two ladies, was printed and circulated to drum up support for the cause. A petition seeking an independent inquiry into the case was also sent to the authorities in Delhi. However, Sir William Lee-Warner, secretary to the Government of India, found no merit in the case, and it was accordingly dismissed.

Not that there was no dissenting opinion among the Parsis. In a letter to the editor of the *Jam-e-Jamshed*, Sorabjee Bengalee,[17] a journalist, philanthropist and member of the Bombay Legislative Council, strongly deprecated the noise and din generated by the Parsi community over the tragedy. Castigating the *Jamshed* and other newspapers for encouraging the spread of baseless allegations against the accused, he called for a stop to the agitation against Aslajee. While the English press appreciated his courage in standing up to his own people, Bengalee's views did not endear himself to his co-religionists.[18]

Another Parsi stalwart who did not subscribe to the foul-play theory was the 'Lion of Bombay', Sir Phirozeshah Mehta, who viewed the whole tragedy as nothing but an unfortunate accident. He, too, risked the ire of his community by refusing to lead a delegation seeking an inquiry into the incident.[19]

The relentless publicity (it was also discussed in the British Parliament) and the innuendos about Bachoobai greatly distressed Ardeshir Godrej. Calling out the poor investigation into the case in a letter to the *Times of India*, he maintained that the two women had no reason to commit suicide. The untimely death of his young wife left its mark on him. Always a reticent man, Ardeshir withdrew further into his shell following the tragedy. He never married again, choosing instead to devote his time and energy to laying the groundwork for what would in time become one of India's largest industrial houses.

———

What became of Maneckjee Aslajee is not known. I could not dig up anything about him, though some accounts describe him as the son of a millionaire whose deep pockets served to pervert the course of justice, at least in the eyes of many Parsis. The community did not forget the two women, though. They duly set up a Rajabai Tower Tragedy Fund, which donated 9,628 rupees to build a block in memory of the two ladies at the K.N. Bahadurji Sanatorium in Deolali.

Acknowledgements

This book couldn't have been written without the prodding and encouragement of several friends and well-wishers, following the publication of my first book, *Tales of Crimes Past*. Foremost among them is the indefatigable P. Vishnu Kamath, who kept at me to finish this work at moments when my interest flagged. Thanks are also due to Santosh Nair, fellow author and one my few friends from newspaper days, who introduced me to my editor, Teesta Guha Sarkar. It was Teesta who got the ball rolling to get this work published, and I cannot thank her enough. My sincere thanks for the encouragement I received from Juggernaut Books's Chiki Sarkar, to Chaharika Uppal who edited this work and also to the entire Juggernaut team for helping me see this book through.

Mumbai city historian Deepak Rao's contribution to this book must be acknowledged. His insights into the workings of the Bombay police and the several anecdotes have served to spice up this work. My friend *India Today* journalist and author Dhaval Kulkarni's X posts on Mumbai also provided valuable leads and interesting tidbits on some of the cases featured in this book. I would also like to thank Joseph Victor and his colleagues at the Asiatic Society of Mumbai for patiently attending to my requests and helping me locate all the necessary newspaper files in the Society's splendid archives.

Last, but not the least, my long-suffering wife Asha (who hardly reads) and my daughter Arunima (who reads too much) deserve thanks for simply putting up with mercurial me all these years! Nothing I do is complete without them.

A Note on the Author

A Mumbaikar-turned-Bengalurian, Sunil Nair is a copy editor by profession. For over two decades, he has worked on the copy desks of the *Indian Express*, *Business Standard*, *Economic Times*, *Sunday Observer* and *Reuters*, among others. A passionate curio-junkie and book-collector, his interests include history, heritage conservation, international affairs and defence.

Notes

1. The Bombay House Heist

1. Jehangir Sohrab Bharucha took over from his British predecessor A.E. Caffin on 15 August 1947. Interestingly, both men were batchmates who had given their police exams together in 1923. Bharucha, a dog-lover and champion boxer, came from an affluent family in Surat and had studied at Oxford. His tenure as police commissioner was a challenging one and included the probe into the assassination of Mahatma Gandhi in 1948 and the refugee troubles that arose post-Partition in 1947. He also had issues with the reorganization of the police force following the decision to merge the Bombay State police and the Bombay City police, which would make the city police commissioner subordinate to the state's inspector general of Police, and stepped down in May 1949. He ended an illustrious career as the DIG, Northern Range, Ahmedabad, and retired to Poona. Sadly, for someone who dearly loved his canine friends, he died of a dog bite in 1977.

2. Vaidyanath Sami, DCP, Crime Branch, CID (1930–68), was also responsible for the arrests in the famous Kalbadevi shooting case (14 September 1946), which he investigated when he was a deputy inspector, along with George W. Quilter, superintendent of Crime Branch, CID, who later retired to Australia. Sami's daughter is the famous singer, Usha Uthup.

3. *The Times of India*, 11 January 1949.

4. 'Alleged Dacoity in Bombay. Rs 40,000 Recovered', *The Times of India*, 15 January 1949.

5.   K.L. Gauba, *Sensational Trials of Crime*, Hind Pocket Books (P)
     Ltd, Delhi, pp. 49–50.

2. The Alavandar Murder Case

1.   Gem & Co., which was set up by M.C. Cunnan and S.
     Venkatarangam in 1928, is still very much around in George Town.
     It now deals only in pens, and customers don't flock to the store
     as they did in the good old days 60 years ago. Still, it commands
     a certain clientele, and gets visitors from around the country and
     overseas. The store is famous for its hand-crafted Gama pens,
     which find many takers among the younger generation, for most
     of whom writing with a fountain pen is a unique experience.

2   The Indo–Ceylon Express was also known as the Boat Mail as
     it connected Madras with Dhanushkodi from where passengers
     would take a ferry to Talaimannar in Ceylon, from where another
     train went to Colombo. It completed 100 years of service in 2014
     and still runs as the Rameswaram (Boat Mail) Express. It was one
     of the earliest trains to be equipped with vestibule carriages, in
     1898. In the late 1800s, the railway portion of the route within
     India was from Madras to Tuticorin (a 22-hour journey), where
     passengers embarked on the boat mail steamer to Colombo. In
     1914, after the Pamban bridge was built, the route was changed
     from Madras to Dhanushkodi. A shorter ferry service then took
     passengers to Talaimannar. The 35-kilometre ferry ride was much
     shorter than the 270-kilometre Tuticorin–Colombo route.

3.   'Menon Confesses to Gruesome Murder', *Indian Daily Mail*,
     13 September 1952, https://eresources.nlb.gov.sg/newspapers/
     digitised/page/indiandailymail19520913-1.1.1, accessed 20
     February 2026.

4.   'P.P. Menon Confesses Separating Head & Body', *Indian
     Daily Mail*, 19 September 1952, https://eresources.nlb.gov.sg/
     newspapers/digitised/page/indiandailymail19520919-1.1.2,
     accessed 20 February 2026.

5.   'Alavandar Murder Case Charge-Sheet', *Indian Daily Mail*,

30 September 1952, https://eresources.nlb.gov.sg/newspapers/ digitised/page/indiandailymail19520930-1.1.3, accessed 20 February 2026.

6. 'Menon's Wife Refuses to Give Evidence', *Indian Daily Mail*, 7 November 1952, https://eresources.nlb.gov.sg/newspapers/ Digitised/Article/indiandailymail19521107-1.2.18?ST=1&AT =search&k=Alavandar&QT=alavandar&oref=article, accessed 20 February 2026.

7. '"Confessional Statement" a Compelled One, Says Devaki', *Indian Daily Mail*, 22 December 1952, https://eresources.nlb. gov.sg/newspapers/Digitised/Article/indiandailymail19521222- 1.2.26?ST=1&AT=search&k=Alavandar&QT=alavandar&oref =article, accessed 20 February 2026.

8. 'P.P. Menon on Hunger-Strike!', Indian Daily Mail, 18 November 1952, https://eresources.nlb.gov.sg/newspapers/Digitised/Article/ indiandailymail19521118-1.2.7?ST=1&AT=search&k=Alavanda r&QT=alavandar&oref=article, accessed 20 February 2026.

9. The Swaminadhans were a distinguished family. Dr Subbarama Swaminadhan, a doctor of law from Harvard University, was a brilliant lawyer who practised both in London and Madras. His wife Ammu Swaminadhan took part in the Independence movement and was as member of the Constituent Assembly. Later, she became a member of the Rajya Sabha from Madras. The couple had equally gifted children. Their elder daughter Lakshmi gained fame as Captain Lakshmi Sehgal of Subhas Chandra Bose's Indian National Army, while the younger, Mrinalini, was a talented dancer who married Indian space pioneer Vikram Sarabhai. While the elder son Govind was a noted barrister and later the advocate general of Tamil Nadu, the younger son, Subbaram, became a director of Mahindra and Mahindra.

10. Ayilam Subramania Panchapakesan Ayyar (1899–1963) was born in a small village in the Palakkad district of what is now the state of Kerala. Entering the Indian Civil Service after his education at Oxford, he served in the judiciary for many years. Till Independence in 1947, around a quarter of the ICS served in the

judiciary to become District, Sessions and High Court judges. The rationale behind transferring officers to the judicial branch after about 10 years of service was that they had first-hand experience of working with the people and had greater insights into the workings of the administration, having served on the ground as assistant and sub-collectors in the districts. A.S.P. Iyyar was of a literary bent and authored many works, including *The Layman's Bhagavad Gita*, *Three Men of Destiny* and *Baladitya*, a romantic fiction based on Indian history. He was never popular with the British, whom he derided often, and they denied him promotions, keeping him as a district judge for long years. Finally, after Independence, he got his much-deserved elevation as the first permanent Indian Chief Justice of the Madras High Court. His son A.P. Venkateswaran too followed the family tradition of public service, going on to become India's foreign secretary for a short stint in 1986–87 in the Rajiv Gandhi government.

3. The Dadar Triple Murder

1. *The Times of India*, 19 October 1888.
2. Ibid.
3. S.M. Edwardes, *The Bombay City Police: A Historical Sketch 1672–1916*, Humphrey Milford, Oxford University Press, 1923.
4. 'Horrible Triple Murder at Dadar', *The Times of India*, 19 October 1888, p. 5.
5. *The Times of India*, 20 October 1888.
6. *The Times of India*, 19 October 1888.
7. *The Times of India*, 19 October 1888
8. *The Times of India*, 22 October 1888.
9. *The Times of India*, 20 October 1888.
10. *The Times of India*, 22 October 1888.
11. Ibid.
12. *A biographical sketch of Sardar Mir Abdul Ali, Khan Bahadur Head of the Detective Force Bombay*, Bombay Gazette Steam Printing Works, 1896, p. 213.

4. The de la Hey Murder

1. Over a three-month raiding career spanning 30,000 nautical miles (56,000 kilometres), the *Emden*, under its brilliant commander Captain Karl Friedrich Max von Müller, destroyed two Allied warships and sank or captured sixteen British steamers and one Russian merchant ship. A further four British ships were captured and released, and one British and one Greek ship were used as colliers. It was finally battered into submission after a gun battle with the Australian light cruiser HMAS *Sydney*, with Captain Müller finally beaching his ship on North Keeling Island to save the lives of his crew. The *Emden* also has the distinction of having added a word to the Tamil and Sinhala languages, where 'emden' means tough, and also manipulative and crafty, while in the Malayalam vocabulary an 'emandan' is something big and powerful.

2. Lord Pentland was also responsible for paving the way for the talented S. Ramanujan's journey to Cambridge. As head of Madras University and the government in 1914, he facilitated the grant of a scholarship of 250 pounds a year along with passage and outfit for the mathematical genius. Despite his differences with Annie Besant over the question of Home Rule, he was sympathetic to Indians. He endeared himself to the servants at Government House by providing them larger and well-ventilated houses, organizing night classes to teach them English, and introducing a provident fund for their welfare. (Lord Pentland, pp. 156, 168–69)

3. Lady Pentland, *The Right Honourable John Sinclair*, Methuen & Co. Ltd, 1928, p. 154.

4. Ibid., p. 155.

5. 'An Extraordinary Case', *Pinang Gazette and Straits Chronicle*, 29 October 1919, p. 3, https://eresources.nlb.gov.sg/newspapers/digitised/article/pinangazette19191029-1.2.10, accessed 22 February 2026.

6. Lady Pentland, *The Right Honourable John Sinclair*, Methuen and Co. Ltd, 1928, p. 149.

7. 'An Extraordinary Case', *Pinang Gazette and Straits Chronicle*, 29 October 1919, p. 3, https://eresources.nlb.gov.sg/newspapers/ digitised/article/pinangazette19191029-1.2.10, accessed 22 February 2026.

8. Pasupuleti Parankusam Naidu began his career as a clerk in the office of the chief engineer for irrigation, Madras, in 1887. He joined the police department in 1890 as a fourth-grade police inspector. Appointed deputy commissioner of police, Madras, in 1911, he played a major role in maintaining law and order in the city during the First World War years, when food shortages and rising prices led to unrest and rioting. In 1919, he became the first Indian police commissioner of Madras. A recipient of several honours during his career, Naidu was awarded the title of Rao Bahadur in 1904 and Dewan Bahadur in 1914, and the prestigious King's Police Medal in 1920. He retired in 1921, but continued to remain active in public life, serving as district commissioner of the Boy Scouts in Madras and vice-president of the Indian Officers' Association. His portrait is on display at the Tamil Nadu Police Museum, Chennai.

9. 'The Shooting Tragedy', *Pinang Gazette and Straits Chronicle*, 1 November 1919, p. 8, https://eresources.nlb.gov.sg/newspapers/ digitised/article/pinangazette19191101-1.2.58, accessed 22 February 2026.

10. Vellore Lakshmanaswamy Ethiraj (18 July 1890–18 August 1960) was the first Indian to be appointed crown prosecutor in British India. A formidable criminal lawyer, he later served as president of the Madras Bar association. One of his greatest successes was the Lakshmikanthan murder case in which he defended Tamil film actors M.K. Thyagaraja Bhagavathar and N.S. Krishnan. Sir C.P. Ramaswami Iyer, law member of the Viceroy's Executive Council, and dewan of Travancore, described Ethiraj's advocacy as 'a marvel of the 20th Century'.

11. P.B. Vachha, *Famous Judges, Lawyers, and Cases of Bombay*, N.M. Tripathi, 1962, p. 311.

12. 'The Newington Murder', *The Andhra Patrika*, 4 February 1920.

13. P.B. Vachha, *Famous Judges, Lawyers, and Cases of Bombay*, N.M. Tripathi, 1962, p. 313.

14. 'De La Hey Murder Case' *The Straits Times*, 3 February 1921, p. 7; 'Mrs De La Hey's claim' *Pinang Gazette and Straits Chronicle*, 18 Apr 1922, p. 11, https://eresources.nlb.gov.sg/newspapers/digitised/article/straitstimes19210203-1.2.60?qt=de,%20la,%20hey,%20murder&q=de%20la%20hey%20murder, https://eresources.nlb.gov.sg/newspapers/digitised/article/pinangazette19220418-1.2.82?qt=de,%20la,%20hey,%20claim&q=de%20la%20hey%27s%20claim, accessed 22 February 2026.

5. The Lloyds Bank Robbery

1.   *The Bombay Chronicle*, 21 April 1951.

2.   According to Mumbai city police historian Deepak Rao, Lawrence Cardoso's funeral was attended by hundreds of mourners, including scores of taxi drivers. His son A.L. Quadros would later become the general secretary of the Mumbai Taximen's Union.

3.   *The Bombay Chronicle*, 21 April 1951.

4.   Ibid.

5.   *The Townsville Daily Bulletin*, 21 April 1951, https://trove.nla.gov.au/newspaper/article/63134581, accessed 21 February 2026.

6.   Released in 1950, the film is based on the real-life exploits of the so-called tri-state gang that robbed banks across the states of North Carolina, Virginia and Maryland. It was later banned in Mumbai.

7.   'Life Sentence for Three Accused', *The Times of India*, 7 October 1952.

6. The Kishori Case

1.   K.L. Gauba, *Battles at the Bar*, N.M. Tripathi, Bombay, 1956, p. 91.

2   Ibid., p. 92.

3.   'Sentence of Indian Actress Upheld', *Indian Daily Mail*, 23

February 1952, https://eresources.nlb.gov.sg/newspapers/
Digitised/Article/indiandailymail19520223-1.2.33, accessed 22
February 2026.

4. Khushboo Narayan, 'A House for Hamida Banu', *The Indian
    Express*, 2 April 2017, https://indianexpress.com/article/lifestyle/
    life-style/a-house-for-hamida-begum-4595520/, accessed 22
    February 2026.

7. The Temple View Murders

1. Samuel T. Sheppard, *Bombay place-names and street-names*, The
    Times Press, Bombay, 1917, p. 90.
2. Another famous canine of the Bombay Police Dog Squad which
    had been formed in 1959, was an Alsatian named Major. He had
    been brought over from England by Inspector (later DCP) Basil
    Kane of the Crime Branch, who had been sent to the UK to
    learn dog handling under the supervision of Scotland Yard's Dog
    Training Centre.
3. 'Family of Three & Maidservant Done to Death', *The Times of
    India*, 24 October 1967, p. 1.
4. Mumbai Police, *Urbs Primus in Indis*, Commissioner of Police,
    Mumbai.
5. *The Times of India*, 26 October 1967.

8. The Tragedy of Elokeshi

1. Narasingha P. Sil, *Problem Child of Renascent Bengal: The Babu of
    Colonial Calcutta*, K.P. Bagchi & Company, 2017, pp. 11–13.
2. Sanjoy Ghose, 'The Tarakeshwar case: When the "theatre" in the
    court room was more interesting than Shakespeare's Othello',
    Bar and Bench, 25 October 2020, https://www.barandbench.
    com/columns/when-the-theatre-in-the-court-room-was-more-
    interesting-than-shakespeares-othello, accessed 22 February 2026.
3. 'Queen vs Nobin Chunder Banerjee', *Bengal Law Reports (1874)*,
    Vol. 13, pp. 20–22.

9. The Jehangir Mansion Murders

1.   'Four aged people done to death', *The Times of India*, 5 February 1971; *Parsiana*.
2.   *The Times of India*, 3 February 1971.
3.   *The Times of India*, 5 February 1971.
4.   Matka is a form of gambling where bets are placed on chits drawn from a matka (earthen pot). Ratan Khatri later told the police that he had in fact been approached by Daruwala who requested him to inaugurate a factory that he claimed to have set up. A colourful character who arrived penniless in Bombay from Karachi after the Partition of India in 1947, Khatri was said to have made an enormous fortune from gambling. Khatri reigned as the city matka boss till the 1990s, when he 'retired' from the business. He died in his house in south Mumbai in May 2020, at the age of eighty-eight.
5.   R.S. Kulkarni, *Crimes, Criminals and Cops*, Vikas Publishing House, New Delhi, 1989, p. 46.

10. The Khambekar Street Poisoning Case

1.   S.M. Edwardes, *The Bombay City Police: A Historical Sketch, 1672–1916*, Oxford University Press, 1923, p. 91.
2.   Ibid, p. 81. Edwardes noted that the police investigation into the case was, 'obstructed by the collateral relatives of the family, who made every effort to render the inquiry abortive and were assisted by the whole Memon community'.
3.   *A Biographical Sketch of Sardar Mir Abdul Ali, Khan Bahadur, Head of the Detective Force, Bombay*, Bombay Gazette Steam Printing Works, 1896, p. 235.

11. The Parel Trunk Murder

1.   'Mysterious Occurrence at Parel', *The Times of India*, 25 November 1887.
2.   *The Times of India*, 19 December 1887.

3.   *The Times of India*, 12 December 1887.

4.   *The Times of India*, 19 December 1987.

5.   *A Biographical Sketch of Sardar Mir Abdul Ali, Khan Bahadur, Head of the Detective Force, Bombay*, Bombay Gazette Steam Printing Works, 1896, p. 201.

12. The DeGa Poisoning Case

1.   'Family of Eight Poisoned at Bombay: Report from the Times of India', *Maitland Mercury and Hunter River General Advertiser*, 2 January 1873, 18 November 1872, p. 1, https://trove.nla.gov.au/newspaper/article/18769785

13. The Umerkhadi Double Murder

1.   'A Murderous Assault', *The Times of India*, 26 June 1884.

2.   Ibid. The term 'pedri sookhta' or 'peder-sokteh', which roughly translates to 'burned father' in Persian, has offensive connotations, and could be construed as a term of abuse. It has its origins in the days when the Arabs tried to convert the Persians (who were then Zoroastrians and therefore fire-worshippers) to Islam. The head of a family that refused to convert would have his tongue cut, or he would be set on fire. If the father survived, he would be called a 'peder-sokteh' or 'burnt father'. His children would be made slaves and were also referred to in the slave-owner's household as 'peder-sokteh'.

3.   *The Times of India*, 30 June 1884.

4.   Ibid.

5.   *A Biographical Sketch of Sardar Mir Abdul Ali, Khan Bahadur, Head of the Detective Force, Bombay*, Bombay Gazette Steam Printing Works, 1896, p. 125.

14. Jambulingam – South India's Robin Hood

1.   *The Straits Times*, 13 June 1923.

2.   'From the Archives (October 5, 1921): Dacoit's Escape', *The Hindu*, 5 October 2021, https://www.thehindu.com/archives/from-the-archives-october-5-1921-dacoits-escape/article36827601.ece, accessed 20 February 2026.

15. The Nanavati Case

1.   The INS *Kunjali* is not a sailing ship but a building which serves as the navy's detention centre, housing naval ratings serving time for theft and other misdemeanours or to cool off after a wild night on the town. It is also the home of the naval band and its training school.
2.   I have been told that copies of the *Blitz* featuring the Nanavati case are now eagerly sought-after 'collector's items'.
3.   *Blitz*, 17 October 1959; Interestingly, this issue also carried, next to the report of Sylvia's testimony, an advertisement for Parle's Gluco biscuits, with the line, 'Is your husband a good provider?' exhorting the wife to welcome her tired spouse home after a long day's work with 'six crisp, golden-brown Gluco biscuits'.
4.   Bachi Karkaria, *In Hot Blood: The Nanavati Case that shook India*, Juggernaut Books, New Delhi, 2017, pp. 93–95.
5.   'Love/Death and Scandal in Bombay', *Man's World*, August 31, 2016, https://www.mansworldindia.com/lifestyle/entertainment/love-death-and-scandal-in-bombay-nanavati-case-inspired-film-rustom-the-real-story, accessed 22 February 2026.

16. Raman Raghav: The Terror of Bombay

1.   Alex Fialho later served as a senior police inspector in the Crime Branch and then as ACP, Colaba division. Post-retirement, he settled in Bandra with his family. He passed away in November 2020, aged ninety-two.
2   R.S. Kulkarni, *Crimes, Criminals and Cops*, Vikas Publishing, 1989, pp. 122–23.
3.   Khushwant Singh, *Portrait of a Serial Killer: Uncollected Writings*,

Aleph Book Company, 2015, pp. 18–19.

4. Ibid, pp. 20–21.

5. R.S. Kulkarni, *Crimes, Criminals and Cops*, Vikas Publishing, 1989, pp. 144–47.

17. The Simla Train Hold-Up

1. Sunil Nair, *Tales of Crimes Past: A Casebook of Crimes in Colonial India*, Hachette India, New Delhi, 2022, pp. 79–98.

2. Papua Rao Naidu, *The History of the Railway Thieves in India: With Illustrations and Hints on Detection*, Vintage Books, Delhi, 1996, p. 149.

18. The Shakereh Murder Case

1. Vinamra Mathur, 'Explained: The murder of Shakreh Khaleeli, the arrest of Swami Shraddhanand, and the legal notice for their documentary', *Firstpost*, 25 April 2023, https://www.firstpost.com/entertainment/explained-the-murder-of-shakereh-khaleeli-the-arrest-of-swami-shraddhanand-and-the-legal-notice-for-their-documentary-dancing-on-the-grave-12503392.html, accessed 21 February 2026.

2. Shyam Prasad S., 'High Court denies Swami Shradanand murdered wife's property', *Bangalore Mirror*, 26 March 2017, https://bangaloremirror.indiatimes.com/bangalore/cover-story/high-court-denies-swami-shradanand-murdered-wifes-property/articleshow/57831570.cms, accessed 21 February 2026.

3. Suchitra Kalyan Mohanty, 'Shakereh murder case: SC refuses to entertain plea of Swamy Shraddananda', *The New Indian Express*, 5 Decemeber 2025, https://www.newindianexpress.com/nation/2025/Dec/05/shakereh-murder-case-sc-refuses-to-entertain-plea-of-swamy-shraddananda-2, accessed 21 February 2026.

19. The Mystery of the Rajabai Tower Deaths

1. *The Times of India*, 27 April 1891.
2. Ibid.
3. Ibid.
4. 'Extraordinary Tragedy at the Rajabai Tower', *The Times of India*, 27 April 1891, pp. 5-6.
5. *The Times of India*, 28 April 1891.
6. 'The Rajabai Tower Tragedy', *The Times of India*, 30 April 1891.
7. 'The Trial of Maneckjee Aslajee', *The Times of India*, 9 July 1891, pp. 5-6.
8. Ibid.
9. 'The Trial of Maneckjee Aslajee', *The Times of India*, 9 July 1891, p. 6.
10. *The Times of India*, 9 July 1891.
11. 'The Trial of Maneckjee Aslajee', *The Times of India*, 11 July 1891, p. 3.
12. 'The Trial of Maneckjee Aslajee', *The Times of India*, 13 July 1891, p. 8.
13. 'The Trial of Maneckjee Aslajee', *The Times of India*, 13 July 1891, p. 8.
14. 'The Trial of Maneckjee Aslajee', *The Times of India*, 14 July 1891, pp. 5-6.
15. 'The Trial of Maneckjee Aslajee', *The Times of India*, 14 July 1891, p. 6.
16. Ibid.
17. As a social activist, Sorabjee Bengalee was among the few who sought improved conditions for workers. In 1878, he drafted a bill for the Bombay Legislative Council that proposed to limit the working hours for men, women and children in Bombay's textile mills to 11, 10 and nine, respectively. Although he was unable to generate sufficient support to introduce his bill, he continued to argue for pro-labour legislation. Through his newspaper, *Rast Goftar*, he publicized the abject working conditions of mill workers. As a member of the Factory Commissions of 1884 and 1890, he

also argued for a weekly holiday and reduced working hours for factory workers.

18. *Life of Sorabjee Bengallee*, Times of India Press, 1893, pp. 65-67.
19. Bakhtiar Dadabhoy, *Sugar in Milk: Life of Eminent Parsis* Rupa Publications Pvt. Ltd, New Delhi, 2008, p. 162.

Cambridge Elements

Elements in Public Economics
edited by
Robin Boadway
Queen's University
Frank A. Cowell
The London School of Economics and Political Science
Massimo Florio
University of Milan

PUBLIC HEALTH CARE

Luigi Siciliani
University of York

Kurt Brekke
Norwegian School of Economics

Mathias Kifmann
University of Hamburg

Odd Rune Straume
University of Minho

CAMBRIDGE
UNIVERSITY PRESS

Shaftesbury Road, Cambridge CB2 8EA, United Kingdom

One Liberty Plaza, 20th Floor, New York, NY 10006, USA

477 Williamstown Road, Port Melbourne, VIC 3207, Australia

314–321, 3rd Floor, Plot 3, Splendor Forum, Jasola District Centre,
New Delhi – 110025, India

103 Penang Road, #05–06/07, Visioncrest Commercial, Singapore 238467

Cambridge University Press is part of Cambridge University Press & Assessment,
a department of the University of Cambridge.

We share the University's mission to contribute to society through the pursuit of
education, learning and research at the highest international levels of excellence.

www.cambridge.org
Information on this title: www.cambridge.org/9781009578769

DOI: 10.1017/9781108652537

First published 2025

A catalogue record for this publication is available from the British Library

ISBN 978-1-009-57876-9 Hardback
ISBN 978-1-108-71818-9 Paperback
ISSN 2516-2276 (online)
ISSN 2516-2268 (print)

Public Health Care

Elements in Public Economics

DOI: 10.1017/9781108652537
First published online: March 2025

Luigi Siciliani
University of York

Kurt Brekke
Norwegian School of Economics

Mathias Kifmann
University of Hamburg

Odd Rune Straume
University of Minho

Author for correspondence: Luigi Siciliani, Luigi.siciliani@york.ac.uk

Abstract: This Element discusses the role of the government in the financing and provision of public health care. It summarises core knowledge and findings in the economics literature, giving a state-of-the-art account of public health care. The first section is devoted to health system financing. It provides policy rationales for public health insurance which rely on both equity and efficiency, the coexistence of public and private health insurance, how health systems deal with excess demand, and the effect of health insurance expansion. The second section covers the provision of health care and the effect of policy interventions that aim at improving quality and efficiency, including reimbursement mechanisms, competition, public–private mix, and integrated care. The third section is devoted to the market for pharmaceuticals, focusing on the challenges of regulating on-patent and off-patent markets, and discussing the main incentives for pharmaceutical innovation.

Keywords: health care, health financing, healthcare provision, pharmaceuticals, public

JEL codes: I1, I11, I13, I14, I18

ISBNs: 9781009578769 (HB), 9781108718189 (PB), 9781108652537 (OC)
ISSNs: 2516-2276 (online), 2516-2268 (print)

Contents

1 Introduction

Most health spending in high-income countries is public. In 2021, 73% of health expenditure was publicly funded across thirty-eight OECD countries. There is heterogeneity across countries in public health expenditure, which reflects a range of institutional arrangements. Public health expenditure was higher and equal to 84–86% in Denmark, Norway, and the United Kingdom, 79% in France and Germany, and 77% in Ireland. It was 74–75% in Australia and Italy, 72–73% in Canada, Poland, and Spain, and 68% in Peru. In the US, where only people older than sixty-five years old and the poor are covered by publicly funded insurance (Medicare and Medicaid), public health expenditure is still 56% of the total. It was 55% in Indonesia, 54% in China, and 50% in Mexico (OECD, 2023). In most countries, public health insurance provides universal coverage for a core set of health services. This is the case for Australia, Austria, Canada, Greece, Ireland, Italy, Japan, Korea, the Nordic Countries, New Zealand, Portugal, and Spain (OECD, 2023).

What is the rationale for such a high proportion of public health spending? The role of public financing in the health sector is incredibly varied across institutional settings and involves many design issues. The very first issue relates to the choice between public and private insurance. If a private insurance model is chosen, this can be mandatory or voluntary. If a public insurance model is chosen, then private health insurance is still likely to coexist along with public insurance and this coexistence is multifaceted. Moreover, within any health insurance system (public or private) policymakers must choose or regulate the extent to which patients are exposed to co-payments, which again can vary significantly across countries and institutional settings. Countries that do not choose to rely on co-payments will still have to manage the excess demand of health care, which can translate into long waiting lists and waiting times unless such demand is matched with increased supply and health spending. We discuss these issues in a systematic way in Section 2.

In more detail, in Section 2.1, we provide the policy rationales for public health insurance which rely on both equity and efficiency arguments. Some countries rely on multi-payers to cover the population and potentially compete with each other. In Germany, these are non-profit insurers, so-called sickness funds, in the Netherlands health insurers operate under private law, with most working on a not-for-profit basis. In Switzerland, health insurers are private companies. In these countries, the health insurance market is heavily regulated, and insurers cannot charge premiums based on individual risk. 66% of health spending is public in the Netherlands, but only 37% in Switzerland. We discuss these systems in Section 2.2.

Despite public health insurance being universal in many countries, voluntary private health insurance coexists with public health insurance with a range of different functions. Private health insurance can be duplicative covering the same services as under public insurance, but with quicker access, greater choice of provider, and amenities. Private health insurance can be supplementary for services not covered by public insurance, or complementary to cover out-of-pocket payments not covered by public health insurance. The heterogeneity of these arrangements and the coexistence of public and private health insurance are discussed in Section 2.3.

Health systems with public health insurance exhibit excess demand in many countries. One policy lever to deal with such excess demand is to introduce co-payments. Most countries with a high proportion of health spending only make limited use of co-payments, and these are used to both raise the funding for and affect the utilisation of health services. Section 2.4 reviews several conceptual issues and empirical evidence related to the effect of co-payments on the demand of health care. In some health systems, the combination of public insurance with tight capacity constraints leads to long waiting lists and waiting times for patients. Section 2.5 argues that waiting times act as a non-monetary price that brings together the demand for and supply of health services, and reviews related empirical literature.

Although most OECD countries have universal coverage, several countries have expanded public health insurance to cover segments of the population who were previously uninsured (e.g., Indonesia, Taiwan, Thailand, and Peru). These policy reforms give an opportunity to test the fundamental question on the extent to which public health insurance expansion improves access to care and health, and provides financial protection through reductions in out-of-pocket payments. These are reviewed in Section 2.6.

Although many countries rely on public health insurance, this does not automatically mean that these health systems will rely on public providers to treat patients. Indeed, several OECD countries have a mix of public and private (non-profit or for-profit) providers to treat publicly funded patients. Regardless of the public–private mix in provision, health systems have to decide how to reimburse healthcare providers for the care they provide and the regulatory setting in which they operate. They also have to decide the architecture of the health sector, and the extent to which healthcare providers compete with each other for segments of healthcare services or they integrate across different types of care along the patient pathway.

We discuss the provision of health care in Section 3. Many policy interventions within a publicly funded health sector aim at improving the quality and efficiency of healthcare providers, whether public or private. Section 3.1

discusses different reimbursement mechanisms that have been traditionally adopted across OECD countries, such as activity-based financing, cost reimbursement, capitation and fee for service, and the effect they have on provider behaviour. One recent development in provider reimbursement is Pay for Performance, which aims at paying directly for dimensions of quality. Although appealing, this approach raises several design issues that are discussed in Section 3.2.

Provider behaviour can be affected not only by financial incentives but also by the market structure in which providers operate. Section 3.3 reviews the literature on provider competition and patient choice and the effect that it can have on quality and efficiency. Although we discuss separately reimbursement mechanisms and provider competition, these themes are interconnected. For example, the effect of provider competition depends on the reimbursement mechanisms, and countries can introduce activity-based financing as part of broader pro-competition reforms.

Across the OECD countries, providers also differ systematically by ownership status. Some providers are public while others are private non-profit or private for-profit, and the mix of providers can differ substantially across countries. Section 3.4 reviews the literature investigating the effect of ownership status on quality and efficiency. Last, the increase in the number of multi-morbidity patients driven by an ageing population has stimulated policy reforms that encourage the integration of care within the health sector and between the health and other sectors with the aim of improving coordination of care and patient experience. Section 3.5 reviews key concepts and some limited but growing evidence. Again, although we discuss integrated care on its own, this topic connects other themes discussed in the section. Integrated care can be seen as an alternative to competition, or can coexist with competition if providers compete to offer integrated packages. Integrated care has to be reimbursed in some way and several countries have experimented with bundled payments covering several types of care under one reimbursement tariff.

The market for pharmaceuticals is characterised by several features that are to some extent distinct from healthcare provision covered in Section 3 or other product markets. The pharmaceutical industry is one of the most research-intensive ones and is characterised by high fixed (sunk) costs and low marginal costs. Drug demand is the result of a complex decision-making process that involves the prescribing physician and, in some cases, the dispensing pharmacy. We therefore discuss pharmaceuticals separately in Section 4. To give pharmaceutical firms incentives for drug innovation, most countries offer patent protection that allows them to sell the drug at a price higher than the marginal cost. The combination of inelastic demand and market power poses several regulatory challenges for policymakers who are concerned about securing wide access to drugs at affordable prices and ensuring that pharmaceutical firms have sufficient incentives for developing new and beneficial drug treatments. The section discusses the main policy options in light of economic theory and available empirical evidence. Section 4.1 focuses on on-patent markets, while Section 4.2 on off-patent markets, which pose distinct regulatory challenges. Last, Section 4.3 discusses the main incentives for pharmaceutical innovation.

2 Financing of Health Systems

2.1 Public Health Insurance

Public health insurance is pervasive across OECD countries. Many countries have universal public health coverage for a core set of services. Countries with 100% of the population covered by public health insurance include Australia, Austria, Canada, Greece, Ireland, Italy, Japan, Korea, the Nordic Countries, New Zealand, Portugal and Spain (OECD, 2023). In Germany, public coverage of the population was 89% in 2021 with the remaining 11% covered by primary private health insurance coverage. In the United States, 38% of the population was covered by public health insurance through the Medicare programme covering the population older than sixty-five years old and Medicaid covering the poor; 53% of the population has (voluntary) private health insurance with the remaining 9% remaining uncovered in 2021 (OECD, 2023). In the Netherlands and in Switzerland, 100% of the population is covered through primary private health insurance, which is mandatory.

The policy rationale for public health insurance is often motivated by equity considerations and has a strong redistributive and solidarity component. Many health systems pursue the objective that access to care should be based on need and not ability to pay. Health systems based on a National Health Services (also known as the Beveridge model), such as in England, Italy and Norway, tend to rely more on income taxation to finance the health system through income tax revenues that are not earmarked. Other health systems, such as France and Germany, are based on social health insurance (also known as the Bismarckian model) with salary contributions from employees and employers, though some countries such as France have expanded over time the tax base towards total income, not only earned income.

Publicly funded health systems redistribute resources both across health states and income levels (Cremer and Pestieau, 1996). They redistribute income from individuals with good health, who have a low probability of falling ill and requiring health care, to those in poor health with a high probability of falling ill. Moreover, for a given level of health, they redistribute from high- to low-income individuals or households given that health systems are mostly financed through income taxation or proportionate salary contributions.

The redistributive component is strengthened if there is a negative correlation between income and health risk (Cremer and Pestieau, 1996), which is in line with empirical evidence showing that individuals with lower socioeconomic status have poorer health. The 'veil of ignorance' argument can also be applied in the health context (Rawls, 1971). If individuals do not know ex ante whether they will be in poor health or good health, they may be favourable to a health system that redistributes resources across health risks. From a political economy perspective, there may be limits to the extent to which governments can pursue redistribution, and these limits are stronger in institutional contexts where public insurance coexists with (duplicative) private health insurance. If high-income individuals buy private health insurance, they contribute to the public health system through taxation but may not use public health care, which in turn reduces their political support for expanding publicly funded health services (Epple and Romano, 1996).

Public health insurance systems are mostly financed by taxes, social health insurance contributions, or a mix of both. Both forms of finance implicate redistribution from individuals in good health to those in poor health. The degree of income distribution, however, differs. Tax financing, when structured progressively, ensures that higher-income individuals contribute a larger share relative to their income, which can promote equity in healthcare financing. In particular, this applies if health care is financed mostly by direct taxation in the form of a progressive income tax. By contrast, indirect taxes (such as sales taxes) tend to be regressive, disproportionately impacting lower-income individuals. To what extent these forms of taxation are efficient depends on how they keep tax distortions to a minimum, considering the restrictions introduced by the need to raise revenue and the equity objectives for the distribution of the tax burden (Auerbach and Hines, 2002). This calls for a comprehensive assessment of a country's tax system.

Social health insurance contributions are typically income-related and thus similar to income taxation. However, social insurance systems may have ceilings on contributions, which introduces a regressive element into healthcare financing as higher-income individuals are exempt from higher payments beyond a certain threshold (Evans, 2002). For example, this holds for Germany where high-income individuals can also switch to private health insurance beyond an income threshold. Social health insurance contributions may also be levied only on labour income which may disproportionately distort labour supply. An overall assessment, however, should take into account how the tax system is designed, for example, whether social insurance contributions can be deducted from income tax and the extent of progressivity of the income tax.

Overall, both ways of finance can ensure that those who need health care can obtain it. If more income distribution is desired, then financing health care via progressive income taxation is the preferred way. A further aspect is that tax financing combines in one authority both the incentive and the capacity to contain costs to a greater extent than social health insurance (Evans, 2002). Health care is part of the public budget and can thus be adapted more easily compared to social health insurance where contributions tend to be earmarked for health care and healthcare providers have more autonomy. Tax-financed systems may therefore come more under pressure during fiscal crises, potentially leading to reduced funding for health care and erosion of public confidence in the system (Evans, 2002). Here, social health insurance may provide more stability. On the other hand, necessary structural reforms may be more difficult to implement in social health insurance systems.

Several empirical studies have quantified the degree of inequalities in healthcare payments (Wagstaff and Van Dooerslaer, 1992; Wagstaff et al., 1999; Wagstaff and Van Dooerslaer, 2000). These studies use survey data in European countries to compute Kakwani progressivity indices that are based on the concentration curves of healthcare payments and individual income. The studies find that financing a health system through direct taxation or social insurance contributions is generally progressive. Indirect taxation is generally regressive because the consumption of poor people represents a higher proportion of their income. The review by Luyten and Tubeuf (2024), which covers high- and low-income countries, confirms these findings. Tax-based systems exhibit high progressivity, as direct taxes contribute to a favourable redistribution toward low-income households given that poorer households contribute a smaller proportion of income to finance health care. Although indirect taxes are regressive, the combined effect of direct and indirect taxation remains progressive. Social insurance systems are generally found to be progressive but in some cases may be regressive in practice due to contribution ceilings and exemptions for high-income earners. Out-of-pocket payments are systematically regressive as they disproportionately burden lower-income households, and this effect is even more marked in low-income or middle-income countries (LMICs).

There are also efficiency arguments that have been brought forward to justify government intervention in the health sector that relate to adverse selection. Economic theory predicts that in private health insurance markets where the probability of illness is private information of the individual and not observable to an insurer (adverse selection) and where insurance is voluntary, individuals with a lower probability of being ill will have only partial coverage of their medical expenses (Rothschild and Stiglitz, 1976). This is suboptimal relative to a benchmark where insurers can observe the probability of illness and offer full coverage of medical expenses.

Rothschild and Stiglitz (1976) show that with asymmetric information, the only possible stable equilibrium is a separating one where high-risk individuals are offered full coverage of the medical expenses but pay a high insurance premium that reflects their risk, while low-risk individuals have only partial coverage (and a lower premium that reflects both the lower risk and lower coverage). The authors demonstrate that this equilibrium is stable only if the proportion of low risk is sufficiently low. They also show that a pooling equilibrium where the insurer offers only one premium that pools risks across individuals and offers 100% coverage is not stable. This is because other private insurers could offer insurance contracts with partial coverage and lower premiums that low-risk individuals would find more attractive, leaving the insurer offering the pooling equilibrium with a deficit.

It can also be shown that, relative to a separating equilibrium, a Pareto improvement can be achieved by introducing compulsory public insurance with partial coverage provided that individuals are allowed to buy supplementary health insurance on top. This is because high-risk types benefit from the lower premium due to the pooling within the public insurance contract. Low-risk types are better off because the combination of public and private insurance allows an increased overall coverage compared to the separating equilibrium without intervention. However, it needs to the emphasised that this result hinges on the particular equilibrium concept used by Rothschild and Stiglitz (1976). Under other concepts, there is no scope for a Pareto improvement (Zweifel et al., 2009).

There is extensive evidence from the US suggesting that adverse selection is quantitatively important. For example, there is evidence that worse health status increases the probability of choosing insurance plans that reimburse providers based on a fee-for-service scheme, which is considered more generous relative to a managed care plan. Worse health status also reduces the probability of being uninsured (Cutler and Zeckhauser, 2000; Breyer et al., 2011). Panhans (2019) investigates the introduction of the Affordable Care Act in the US which made premiums more uniform by limiting insurers' ability to adjust the premium to reflect individual risk. The study shows that uniform pricing induced healthier individuals to forgo coverage, which increased the premium for those remaining as a result of the higher proportion of less healthy individuals.

One way to enforce a pooling equilibrium is to introduce public health insurance. For example, National Health Services are set up as a single-payer system where one public insurer provides the same coverage to the whole population and the financing is centralised therefore pooling across different health risks (in addition to pooling across income). Social health insurance systems are more varied. They can involve a single payer or multiple payers.

In France, there is one large public insurer, known as the 'Securite sociale', which covers the whole population, though co-payments can differ across segments of the population. In Germany, there is a multi-payer system where non-profit insurers, so-called sickness funds, cover the population and potentially compete with each other. Similar systems are in place in the Netherlands and Switzerland. This type of social health insurance with a multi-payer system tries to enforce a pooling equilibrium by regulating the health insurance market. We take a closer look at such systems in the next section.

2.2 Social Health Insurance with Competition

At first sight, social health insurance systems with competition resemble private insurance models. However, a key distinction remains: contributions are regulated, meaning that insurers cannot charge premiums based on individual risk—a practice known as 'community rating'. Furthermore, insurers are required to accept all applicants through open enrolment, and insurance coverage is mandatory for all or most citizens.

Advocates of such systems emphasise the potential benefits of competition in health insurance markets. According to van de Ven and van Vliet (1992), competition can help to enhance the quality of care, improve the efficiency of care, and increase responsiveness to consumer preferences. These benefits depend on insurers taking an active role in healthcare delivery, such as contracting with efficient providers and monitoring care quality.

Countries differ in the extent to which they allow health insurers to take on such a role. In Germany, collective contracting is dominant. However, sickness funds exert some influence over care delivery as selective contracting is permitted to a certain extent. Funds have incentives to maintain efficient administrative operations as they compete on the contribution rates. Cost savings can be achieved, particularly in the procurement of pharmaceuticals and mobility aids (Kifmann, 2017). In the Netherlands, health insurers are less regulated. Insurers may also contract exclusively with certain healthcare providers (Kroneman et al., 2016). In Switzerland, competition between health insurers is particularly pronounced. Individuals can choose from various managed care plans, including family doctor plans provided by physician networks, Health Maintenance Organizations comprised of group practices or small networks of physicians financially responsible for costs, and gatekeeping models (De Pietro et al., 2015).

A problem in all countries is that community rating incentivises risk selection as individuals with high expected healthcare expenditures (high risks) result in losses for insurers, while those with low expected expenditures (low risks) generate profits. This can take two forms. Direct risk selection occurs when insurers use observable characteristics correlated with risk, such as age or sex, to selectively enrol individuals, for example, by not or slowly processing their applications. Indirect risk selection involves the design of benefit packages; for example, high-risk individuals can be deterred by offering contracts with high deductibles or inferior quality care for conditions like cancer and HIV, while low-risk individuals can be attracted through policies highlighting comprehensive coverage for athletic medicine or regular check-ups that appeal to individuals who prioritise their health and fitness (Zweifel et al., 2009).

There are only a few studies on the extent of risk selection in social health insurance. Bauhoff (2012) conducted a field experiment. Fictitious individuals from different locations approached German sickness funds and requested a contract form and further information. He finds that funds are less likely to respond and follow-up with applicants from higher-cost regions. Using a similar approach for Switzerland, Baumgartner and Busato (2012) compared insurers' reactions to low risks (young applicants) willing to accept high deductibles and to high risks (old applicants) preferring low deductibles. Applicants exhibiting low-risk signals experience a shorter wait time of approximately one day for a response from an insurer, are presented with lower premiums, and frequently receive offers from a subsidiary within an affiliated group that seemingly focuses on low-risk cases. Stolper et al. (2022) assessed promotional material used by Dutch health insurers in 2019. They find that the majority of marketing initiatives are aimed at financially advantageous groups, while only a small portion of insurers' marketing efforts is directed towards actual care users.

To prevent risk selection, several regulatory measures are available. For direct risk selection, laws penalising insurers for such practices and minimising contact between insurers and the insured can be implemented and enforced. For indirect risk selection, regulating the benefit package to include minimum benefits prevents underprovision for high-risk individuals, while maximum benefits prevent overprovision for low-risk individuals. Restrictions on the co-payments and deductibles can also limit risk selection. Yet, these regulations curtail the freedom of insurers to provide benefit packages potentially in the interest of all individuals, thereby reducing the value of competition.

Risk adjustment schemes are the standard approach to address risk selection. These are transfer mechanisms that aim to equalise expected payoffs for insurers across different risk profiles. They are based on risk adjusters, that is, observable characteristics of individuals. Typically, the risk adjustment payments are based on the predicted healthcare expenditure conditional on these variables. As a consequence, payments are higher for individuals with characteristics that predict high healthcare expenditure such as higher age or diagnosis of a major illness. All countries mentioned have implemented such schemes. These use multiple risk adjusters such as age, gender, income type, region, health indicators derived from diagnostic data, and pharmaceutical use.

2.3 Duplicative, Supplementary, and Complementary Private Health Insurance

Amongst OECD countries, it is common for public health insurance to cover 100% of the population. Yet, within the same countries private health insurance coexists alongside public health insurance. For countries where private health insurance is not primary, voluntary private health insurance can be duplicative, supplementary or complementary.

Private health insurance *duplicates* coverage of health services already provided by public insurance in countries such as Australia, Ireland, Spain and the United Kingdom. The key feature of private insurance is that it promises quicker access to health services, greater degree of choice of doctors and providers, and better amenities (e.g., a single rather than shared room in a hospital). Individuals therefore have to assess prospectively whether the benefits from quicker access, greater choice and better amenities by private providers are worth the premium charged by private health insurers (Barros and Siciliani, 2011). In several countries, private health insurance coverage remains relatively small. For example, in 2021 only 11% of the population in Mexico and the UK had duplicative private health insurance (OECD, 2023). Similarly, this figure was 15% in Spain and 17% in Greece.

Low coverage of duplicative private health insurance is not surprising. Given that individuals are already covered by public insurance, only a relatively small proportion of the population decides to buy additional insurance. This can include for example individuals with relatively high income, high need or risk aversion, or who have insurance provided through their employer as an additional benefit. Moreover, given that private health insurance is voluntary, some individuals may prefer to pay for private health care out of pocket if they find private health insurance premiums too high relative to the coverage offered. Duplicative private health insurance is instead high in Australia and Ireland with 54% and 47% of the population holding private health insurance in 2021 (OECD, 2023), respectively, possibly due to long waiting times and access issues in the public universal health system. Furthermore, in both countries, the state subsidises private health insurance (Hall et al., 2020; Turner and Smith, 2020).

Private health insurance is *supplementary* instead when it covers health services not covered by public health insurance. For example, public coverage of dental services varies significantly across countries, and this can be targeted by private insurance. The Netherlands has one of the largest supplementary private health insurance markets covering about 85% of the population. The coverage offered by private insurance could be duplicative and supplementary at the same time, as is often the case in Australia (OECD, 2023).

Last, private health insurance can be *complementary*, which refers to insurance to cover out-of-pocket payments sustained within a public insurance system. In France and Belgium, 96% and 98% of the population had complementary health insurance, which is mostly private. Coverage can be varied. For example, in France about 54% of the population have private insurance on an individual basis, 35% through the employer, and 7% is instead state-funded insurance for low-income households. The key feature of this insurance is that it covers expenses for care not fully covered by a different insurance scheme. When deciding whether to buy complementary insurance, individuals have to trade off the cost in terms of the premium paid to the insurer against the benefits of financial protection from the out-of-pocket payments arising when utilising services under the public insurance scheme.

These examples illustrate how public and private insurance coexist within health systems, but the role and the size of private health insurance varies significantly across countries.

2.4 Co-payments

Economic theory can offer insights into the design and use of co-payments. In a seminal contribution, Zeckhauser (1970) determines the optimal co-payments in a health insurance model where insured patients can choose healthcare consumption. In the absence of co-payments, patients have an incentive to consume health care up to the point where the marginal benefit is equal to zero (and therefore below the marginal cost). Ideally, patients should receive a fixed payment just covering the optimal amount of health care given their health state. This solution, however, is not feasible in a situation in which insurance companies cannot exactly identify the medical condition of the individual. Instead, insurance needs to reimburse part of actual healthcare expenditure to provide protection. In this situation known as 'moral hazard', a trade-off between risk spreading and incentives emerges. Health insurance theory suggests that the optimal co-payment is positive and set such that it trades off the benefit from insurance against excessive consumption. It can be useful to vary co-payments for different classes of disease to optimally deal with this trade-off.

This theoretical finding assumes that it is the patient who rationally chooses health care. In many health systems, however, access to health care is mediated by healthcare professionals. Some health systems have excess capacity and providers are reimbursed through fee-for-service mechanisms. In such scenarios, providers' financial incentives may align with those of the patients, and this may lead to a high level of healthcare consumption.

Many publicly funded systems have however capacity constraints and access to health care is limited by rationing or long waiting lists. Moreover, healthcare professionals in some countries are salaried. Primary care providers are paid by capitation and secondary care providers have limited capacity that restricts the number of patients they can treat. If the opportunity cost of public funds is high, the health care provided to patients at the margin may be such that the health benefit is higher than treatment costs even in the absence of co-payments. Therefore, whether co-payments increase or reduce expected utility within a publicly funded health system depends on whether they encourage beneficial care or unnecessary care (Siciliani, 2014). Policy initiatives in favour of introducing co-payments argue that they will reduce unnecessary care and help finance the health systems. Policy initiatives that remove co-payments argue that they improve access to care. Moreover, co-payments can increase inequalities if poorer individuals are less likely to afford them further increasing unmet needs.

Given the potential impact of co-payments on access and utilisation, it is not surprising that a large body of empirical evidence has investigated the effects of co-payments. In most studies, moral hazard is identified with a positive effect of insurance on healthcare use. A key study in this area is the RAND health insurance experiment that randomised individuals in the US in groups facing different coinsurance rates ranging from zero to 25%, 50%, and 95%, until the threshold limit of US$1,000 per family (Manning et al., 1987). A main result was that individuals with higher coinsurance had lower levels of healthcare spending. In particular, the difference between zero and 25% coinsurance rate was striking. According to the estimates by Manning et al. (1987), medical expenses were 19% lower in the plan with the 25% coinsurance rate. For higher levels of coinsurance, medical expenses tended to fall further but the effect was less pronounced. Other studies have largely confirmed a positive effect of health insurance coverage on the use of health care (see McGuire (2011) for a survey). Further causal evidence was obtained from the Oregon Health Insurance Experiment which analysed the state of Oregon's expansion of its Medicaid programme through random-lottery selection from a waiting list. Finkelstein et al. (2012) find evidence of higher healthcare utilisation for formerly uninsured low-income adults. For example, the probability of hospital admission increased by 2.1 percentage points or 30%, while the number of emergency department visits by 0.41 visits or 40%.

The interpretation of the empirical findings is controversial. Sometimes it argued (or implicitly assumed) that the extra healthcare consumption generated by insurance is inefficient (see, e.g., Feldman and Dowd, 1991). However, this reasoning neglects the 'access motive' of health insurance. As Nyman (1999a) pointed out, a significant portion of efficient health care can only be consumed if made affordable by insurance. An example is liver transplantations which would be unaffordable for many patients without insurance. The key mechanism is that insurance requires only a comparatively small premium as few people require a liver transplant. Furthermore, De Meza (1983) and Nyman (1999b) have emphasised that insurance involves a transfer of purchasing power from the healthy to the sick state. Assuming that health care is a normal good, demand will therefore increase when insurance is available and, at least to some extent, this extra demand is efficient. Nyman et al. (2018) provide a decomposition of the demand expansion due to the insurance, labelling the extra demand due to the income transfer 'efficient moral hazard'. For individuals with a priority condition such as cancer or diabetes, they find that this effect is in the range of 13–29% (depending on the subgroup considered) of the additional health care due to insurance.

For an overall assessment of co-payments, it is also important to examine the effects of insurance on health and other outcome variables. In the RAND health insurance experiment, the reduction in services induced by cost sharing had no adverse effect on health for the average adult. However, the poorest and sickest 6% of the sample at the beginning of the study had better outcomes under the free plan for four of the thirty conditions measured (Brook et al., 2006). Baicker et al. (2013) examined the health effects of the Oregon Medicaid expansion. It improved self-reported health and reduced depression, while no statistically significant effect was found on physical health measures (blood pressure, cholesterol, glycated haemoglobin), employment, or earnings.

There is also evidence from other countries. Using difference-in-difference methods, Ma et al. (2020) evaluate the effect of a policy in Ireland which removed co-pays for GP visits for patients who are older than seventy years. The study finds that removing co-payments increased the probability of seeking GP care, and reduced perceived stress, in particular amongst poorer, sicker and single patients. Di Giacomo et al. (2022) use a regression discontinuity design to test the effect of eliminating co-payments for non-invasive screening prenatal tests. The study shows that following the elimination of the co-payment the probability of a non-invasive prenatal test increased by 5.5 percentage points.

An interesting finding of the RAND health insurance experiment was that with higher coinsurance, individuals reduced both medically appropriate and inappropriate hospital admission rates and inpatient days (Siu et al., 1986). This puts into question the ability of patients to rationally choose health care. Such limitations are taken up by Baicker et al. (2015) who develop a model that considers that patients make mistakes which they call 'behavioural hazard'.

Concretely, patients may both under- and overestimate the benefits of treatments when demanding health care. They show that the optimal co-payment according to the standard moral hazard is too high in the first case and too low in the second. Their analysis provides a theoretical foundation for value-based health insurance design where optimal co-payments are set to correct behavioural mistakes (Chernew et al., 2007). In particular, the co-payment should be lower for underused high-value care. An example is co-payments for effective diabetes medications with low adherence.

The studies covered so far in this section focus on *ex-post* moral hazard, which refers to the effect of insurance and co-payments on actions taken by patients after they fall ill, such as healthcare utilisation. A more limited empirical literature has a focus on *ex-ante* moral hazard, which refers to actions taken by individuals before they get ill. Examples include lifestyle choices, such as exercising, smoking or diet, or secondary prevention, for example, screening. De Preux (2011) compares trends in the lifestyle of individuals before and after the age of sixty-five when individuals become eligible for Medicare, and finds no clear effect on alcohol or smoking, but some reductions in physical activity. Similarly, Simon et al. (2017) use difference-in-difference methods to test the effect of the Affordable Care Act on preventive and health behaviour and found no evidence that it affected risky health behaviours. Barbaresco et al. (2015) found that the same reform reduced body mass index but had no effect on preventive care utilisation and increased risky drinking.

2.5 Waiting Times

Several health systems are characterised by public health insurance and limited capacity, which translates into an excess demand for health services (OECD, 2020). Patients are therefore put on a waiting list and can wait a significant time before accessing health care. Waiting times in turn generate dissatisfaction for patients since they postpone health benefits from treatment, may induce a deterioration of the health status of the patient, can prolong suffering and generate uncertainty.

A demand-supply framework can be used to understand the determinants of waiting times. In the absence of price rationing, waiting times act as a non-monetary price (or a disutility) that brings demand for and supply of health services together (Iversen, 1997; Martin and Smith, 1999). Longer waiting times reduce demand because at the margin a longer wait induces patients to opt for care in the private sector where waiting times are typically shorter if patients have private health insurance or if they are willing to pay out of pocket. Some patients may give up treatment if they find it more time-consuming to engage with the public system as a result of longer waiting times. On the supply side, longer waiting times induce providers to increase volume either because waiting times are often used as performance indicators or because providers have altruistic concerns towards patients and feel responsible for patients waiting for a long time. At the health system level, policymakers may also be willing to allocate more resources to healthcare providers when waiting lists grow, which can be the subject of intense political debate.

Several empirical studies have tested the extent to which waiting times reduce demand and increase supply. Evidence from England suggests that demand is generally inelastic with an elasticity of −0.1 or −0.2 using both cross-sectional and panel data. An increase in waiting times by 10% reduces demand by 1 or 2%. The estimates for the supply elasticity vary across studies and range from around -0.1 to 3 (Martin and Smith, 1999, 2003; Gravelle et al., 2003; Martin et al., 2007). A key econometric concern is that waiting times are endogenous as they simultaneously affect demand and supply, which can be addressed through an instrumental variable approach (e.g., using exogenous determinants of the demand to instrument waiting times in the supply equation, and using exogenous determinants of the supply to instrument waiting times in the demand equation). Demand estimates for Italy also suggest an elasticity of about −0.1 (Riganti et al., 2017) while the elasticity is higher for Australia possibly due to the larger private sector and a significant proportion of the population who holds private health insurance (Stavrunova and Yerokhin, 2011).

A key policy concern with long waiting times is that they do not only deter access, but they can ultimately worsen health outcomes, which could also further increase healthcare utilisation. Moscelli et al. (2016a) find no evidence that waiting times in England are associated with higher in-hospital mortality for coronary bypass but they find a weak association between waiting times and emergency readmission following a surgery. Nikolova et al. (2016) find that long waits in England reduce health-related quality of life for hip and knee replacement patients, as measured by patient-reported outcome measure, but no effect was found for varicose veins and inguinal hernia. Godøy et al. (2024) show that in Norway long waiting times for orthopaedic surgery do not increase healthcare utilisation (e.g., due to worsened health status) but have persistent reductions in labour supply through an increase in work absences and permanent disability receipt. An econometric concern in estimating the relation between waiting times and outcomes is an omitted variable due to unobserved patient characteristics if, for example, more urgent patients are both prioritised on the waiting list and have worse health outcomes, which can be addressed through an instrumental variable approach based on measures of congestion (Godøy et al., 2024).

Several policies have been introduced to reduce waiting times. The most common policy is to introduce maximum waiting time guarantees, which can be used as a performance indicator for providers (OECD, 2013). Propper et al. (2008a, 2010) use difference-in-difference methods with Scotland as a control group to show that the introduction of maximum waiting time targets in England combined with tough penalties for providers not adhering to these targets reduced waiting times significantly without affecting quality proxied by thirty-day mortality.

A second common policy is to stimulate provider competition. Propper et al. (2008b) show that the introduction of internal markets in England which involved splitting purchasers and providers of health services reduced waiting times, but this came at the cost of poorer quality as proxied by higher heart attack mortality. Ge et al. (2024) show instead that the introduction of patient choice which was intended to stimulate competition across providers did not affect waiting times and volume of visits in Norway. Another policy to reduce waiting times is to encourage individuals to hold private health insurance (e.g., through tax rebates), which in turn could reduce demand for public health care and reduce waiting times. Yang et al. (2024) show that in Australia, where about 45% of the population held private health insurance in 2022, increasing coverage by one percentage point has only a small reduction in waiting times (0.34 days). To address possible reverse causality and omitted variable bias they use an instrumental variable approach based on average house prices, which correlates with income and wealth.

With given capacity, one policy to minimise the total disutility from waiting is to enhance waiting time prioritisation, which involves reducing waiting times for patients with higher urgency, need and severity and increasing waiting times for those with lower urgency, need and severity (Gravelle and Siciliani, 2008). Waiting times differ systematically across treatments with waiting times for more urgent procedures (such as coronary bypass) being substantially lower than less urgent ones (such as hip and knee replacement, or cataract) across different OECD countries (OECD, 2013). Gutacker et al. (2016a) show that prioritisation for a given treatment is limited: patients with higher pain and reduced mobility while waiting for a hip replacement in England wait only a few days less than patients with lower pain and higher mobility. Askildsen et al. (2010) show that the introduction of the maximum recommended waiting time in Norway that could differ by health condition did not appear to improve prioritisation. Moreover, there is some evidence of mis-prioritisation with patients with lower socioeconomic status waiting longer for publicly funded care than patients with higher socioeconomic status in England (Laudicella et al., 2012; Moscelli et al., 2018c), Norway (Kaarboe and Carlsen, 2014; Monstad et al., 2014) and Australia (Johar et al., 2013; Sharma et al., 2013).

2.6 Public Health Insurance Expansion in Low- and Middle-Income Countries

Several low- and middle-income countries have expanded public health insurance to cover segments of the population who were uninsured, often individuals working in the informal sector. This has been achieved by either introducing universal schemes or schemes targeting the poor. Policy objectives included improving access to care and reducing out-of-pocket and catastrophic payments.

One example is the universal public health insurance scheme that was introduced in 2001 in Thailand and extended coverage to eighteen million uninsured citizens (about a fourth of the population). This was combined with supply-side policy measures, such as gatekeeping of primary care and capitation-based budgets, to ensure additional public health spending was cost-effective (Limwattananon et al., 2015). Before the reform, tax-financed public insurance covered the poor, children, elderly and disabled, which comprised 32% of the population. 21% of the population was covered by private health insurance that was subsidised by the government. Civil servants were also covered by insurance. Using a difference-in-different design with public sector employees as the control group, Limwattananon et al. (2015) find that individuals covered by public insurance, mostly workers in the informal sector, experienced reductions in out-of-pocket payments by 28% on average, and by 42% at the 95th percentile of the health spending distribution.

Public health insurance can affect both utilisation and out-of-pocket payments, but the effect can vary depending on the country. Bauhoff et al. (2011) evaluate the impact of expanding health insurance for the poor in Georgia. Using a regression-discontinuity design based on an eligibility threshold, they find that public insurance for the poor reduced out-of-pocket spending for outpatients and inpatient care but did not affect utilisation.

Sparrow et al. (2013) evaluated the effect of introducing a new social insurance scheme for the poor in Indonesia where formal insurance coverage was limited due to many people working in the informal sector, about 60% of the labour force. In this case, the study found that outpatient utilisation improved but that out-of-pocket spending did not decrease, which can be explained by the complementarity between care covered by insurance and additional care demanded that was not covered. Bernal et al. (2017) evaluate the effect of a policy in Peru that introduced health insurance for the poor aimed at individuals outside the formal labour market. Using a regression discontinuity design based on eligibility criteria, the study found an increase in several measures of curative care, such as the likelihood of receiving medicines, a medical analysis being performed, a visit to a hospital, and receiving surgery. However, out-of-pocket spending increased, and this was due to higher consumption of medicines, hospital visits or surgeries not covered by the insurance scheme, and more awareness of their health needs.

Only a few studies are able to assess the effect of public health insurance on health outcomes. Chen et al. (2007) evaluate the introduction of National Health Insurance in Taiwan in 1995, which increased population coverage from 55% to 92%. Using a difference-in-differences approach the study did not find significant effects on mortality for the previously uninsured elderly after the reform. However, Chang (2012) provides evidence of reduced mortality rates for this group by using more extensive data. Lee et al. (2010) also identify substantial reductions in mortality for deaths considered amenable to health care, particularly among the young and old. Similarly, Keng and Sheu (2013) find significant reductions in mortality rates for the elderly, in particular for women. They also examined the effects on functional limitations and self-assessed health and found that these did not significantly improve. Finally, Chou et al. (2014) used government employees who had insurance prior to the reform as a control group in a difference-in-difference analysis. National Health Insurance improved coverage for both industrial private-sector workers and farmers, the latter being characterised by lower levels of health, education, and income and low-weight infants in worse health than other infants. The study finds that the postneonatal mortality rate of infants born in farm households decreased but there is no effect on infants born in private-sector households. The findings indicate that health insurance enhances infant health outcomes among population subgroups with low levels of education, income, and overall health.

3 Provision of Health Care

This section covers several issues related to incentives of primary and secondary care providers with a focus on quality and efficiency. It first discusses different reimbursement mechanisms that have been traditionally adopted across OECD countries to reimburse providers that treat publicly funded patients. These include activity-based financing, cost reimbursement, capitation and fee for service, and the effect they have on provider behaviour (Section 3.1). It then discusses a more recent development in financing known as Pay for

Performance, which aims at paying directly for dimensions of quality (Section 3.2).

Provider behaviour can be affected not only by financial incentives but also by the market structure in which providers operate. We therefore review the literature on provider competition and patient choice and the effect that it can have on quality and efficiency (Section 3.3). The effect of provider competition is connected to reimbursement mechanisms. For example, reforms that have introduced provider competition have done so in combination with activity-based financing based on the idea that providers that increase quality are rewarded with higher revenues.

Although many countries rely on public health insurance, health systems can rely on public and private providers. Private providers can be non-profit or for-profit, and the mix of providers can differ substantially across countries. Ownership status in turn can affect the way providers take decisions and impact quality and efficiency (Section 3.4).

Last, the increase in the number of multimorbidity patients driven by an ageing population has stimulated policy reforms that encourage the integration of care within the health sector and between the health and other sectors with the aim of improving coordination of care and patient experience (Section 3.5). Integrated care can be seen as an alternative to competition, or can coexist with competition if providers compete to offer integrated packages. A key issue is how to pay for integrated care and several countries have experimented with bundled payments covering several types of care under one reimbursement tariff.

3.1 Financial Incentives and Provider Behaviour

Within secondary care, payment systems based on fixed tariffs have become the dominant model to reimburse hospitals across OECD countries. In the early eighties, Medicare in the US introduced the Diagnosis Related Groups (DRG) system. The idea was that hospitals should be reimbursed a fixed tariff for treating a patient within a given diagnosis or treatment. DRG tariffs are commonly set to reflect past average costs with a lag of one or two years. The DRG system was then adopted in many European countries (such as France, Germany, Italy, Norway, Spain, and the UK) and other high-income countries (e.g., Canada, Australia). In some countries, the change in the reimbursement system was motivated by concerns over rapid health expenditure growth or broader efficiency considerations.

For countries starting with a fee-for-service or cost reimbursement system (e.g., US, France, and Germany), the introduction of a tariff-based reimbursement system should theoretically induce providers to contain costs within a given treatment (Ellis and McGuire, 1986). For countries where providers were reimbursed with a fixed annual budget (e.g., in the UK), moving towards an activity-based payment can induce providers to increase volume (Chalkley and Malcomson, 1998a) while maintaining incentives to keep costs down. One possible concern with a DRG tariff system is that it will induce providers to skimp on quality to save costs and increase profits. However, if patient demand responds to quality, then providers have an incentive to compete on quality to attract patients and increase revenues (Ma, 1994).

DRG reimbursement systems have been refined over time. Given that one diagnosis can be associated with several treatments, tariffs have been increasingly split to reflect the cost of each treatment. For example, a patient with cardiovascular disease could be treated with a less expensive medical treatment (e.g., beta blocker) or with a more invasive one such as a coronary bypass (McClellan, 1997). This introduces a financial incentive that induces the provider to recommend a more intensive treatment, leading to higher reimbursement and health spending (Hafsteinsdottir and Siciliani, 2010). The provision of more intensive treatment can mitigate the reductions in costs that the DRG system intended to promote. Another concern with a DRG reimbursement system is that it gives a financial incentive to avoid more complex patients (Ellis and McGuire, 1990; Kifmann and Siciliani, 2017) when these patients would instead benefit from treatment. Similarly, there are concerns that the DRG reimbursement system could lead to upcoding or, more broadly, gaming. Given that reimbursement rules are complex, such complexity can be used by the provider to allocate patients to the most remunerative tariffs (upcoding). Other forms of gaming or manipulation include billing services that were not delivered, and splitting or unbundling of a treatment episode into separate ones which lead to additional reimbursement (Kuhn and Siciliani, 2009).

Most countries reimburse providers either based on a DRG system, costs or through fixed budgets. Mixed reimbursement rules are less frequent but possible. One example is Norway, where a mixed payment system is used. The DRG tariff is decided every year and has been varying between 40% and 60% of the average cost. Hospitals also received a block grant component to cover the remaining costs (Brekke and Straume, 2017). Mixed payment systems can be theoretically appealing. While a full DRG-based reimbursement system could give excessive incentives to increase volume and a fixed budget would give weak incentives, a mixed payment system can balance these two concerns (Ellis and McGuire, 1986). In England, there has also been a move away from Healthcare Resource Groups (the English version of DRGs) towards a 'blended' (mixed) payment where, for example, services for Accidents and Emergencies, have about 30% of their costs reimbursed.

The design of reimbursement mechanisms for primary care providers in publicly funded systems faces similar challenges to those identified for secondary care. The institutional details however differ. Primary care providers in several European countries have been reimbursed either by capitation mechanisms, fee for service or a mix of capitation and fee for service. Under capitation, the primary care doctor or organisation receives a fixed payment for each person registered in the practice, which is often risk-adjusted (e.g., in England). Under a fee-for-service system, primary care physicians are reimbursed a fee for each visit (e.g., in France, Belgium). Some countries use a mixed system combining fee-for-service for each visit with a capitation payment (e.g., Denmark and Norway). Depending on the institutional setting, primary care providers can work in solo practices or larger organisations where GPs are employed by larger primary care practices. One concern with capitation is that providers may skimp on quality or services because reimbursement does not vary with the care provided. However, this concern can in theory be mitigated if patients have free choice of primary care provider and providers compete on quality to attract patients and increase revenues. In contrast, fee-for-service systems could incentivise excessive visits and lead to unnecessary treatments.

Several empirical studies have tested the effects of introducing or changing a DRG reimbursement system. The findings are generally mixed. DRG systems affect incentives on the utilisation of health care, while an effect on quality is more difficult to detect. Using difference-in-differences methods, Dafny (2005) exploits an exogenous change in hospital tariffs within the US Medicare program. The prospective payment eliminated DRGs that related to the patient's age (e.g., the patient is older than seventy years), which effectively led to an increase in the tariff for about half of the DRGs, while the remaining were unaffected For the DRGs in the treatment group, the tariff increased by about 12%, while it remained the same in the DRGs in the control group. The study found that the increases in tariff did not increase quality. However, it let to upcoding in the form of a higher proportion of young patients who were coded as having complications. The upcoding effect was stronger in for-profit hospitals than in non-profit ones.

Farrar et al. (2009) investigate the introduction of Healthcare Resource Groups (HRG) in England. The HRG system replaced a reimbursement scheme where hospitals were allocated an annual fixed budget with a marginal revenue for additional treatments of zero. The study uses difference-in-difference methods with Scotland as the control group. It finds that the introduction of a DRG tariff in England had no effect on quality (mortality and readmissions) but improved efficiency by accelerating growth in volume, reducing the length of stay, and increasing the proportion of patients admitted as day cases.

Batty and Ippolito (2017) investigate the effect of State laws in California in the US that limited how much hospitals could charge uninsured patients, also known as 'fair pricing' laws. The reform in 2007 implied a reduction in the tariff received by hospitals for uninsured patients by 25–30% from 2007/8 in California. Using a difference-in-differences design with other US states as the control group, the study finds that length of stay reduced by up to 0.3 days or 7.3%. There was no effect on quality as measured by avoidable mortality and incidence of preventable in-hospital complications.

Shin (2019) exploits an exogenous shock in the DRG tariff that was generated by a change in the definition of urban and rural areas. In 2005 Medicare prospective payment system changed its definition of payment areas from the Metropolitan Statistical Areas to the Core-Based Statistical Areas generating substantial exogenous area-specific tariff shocks. The areas that were originally rural received a higher tariff when they were redefined as urban areas. The study shows that the DRG tariff increase had no effect on the volume of admissions, treatment intensity, and quality of care.

Some studies investigate the effect of relative tariff changes within a diagnosis with multiple treatments. Foo et al. (2017) investigate the effect of tariff changes in California on the probability of a caesarean delivery. The study shows that an increase in hospital tariff difference between caesarean section and vaginal birth by one standard deviation ($5,805 in 2004–2011) increases the probability of a caesarean section by 31%. Papanicolas and McGuire (2015) focus on hip replacement surgery in England. The study examines the change in the difference in hospital tariff reimbursement between uncemented and cemented hip replacement. Using Scotland as a control group, where the tariff was the same across both types of surgery, it finds that the proportion of uncemented procedures increases by 20 percentage points.

Januleviciute et al. (2016) exploit variations in DRG tariffs in Norway in 2003–2007 created by the changes in national average past treatment cost. Using fixed-effect models, the study shows that a 10% increase in tariff leads to 0.8–1.3% increase in the volume of patients treated for medical DRGs but does not affect the volume for surgical DRGs. The study also provides evidence of upcoding. A 10% increase in the tariff ratio between patients with and without complications increases the proportion of patients coded with complications by 0.3–0.4 percentage points.

Overall, these studies suggest that financial incentives do affect provider behaviour in particular in relation to healthcare utilisation as measured by volume and length of stay. The effects on quality are more difficult to detect. The empirical evidence also highlights that DRG reimbursement mechanisms can have unintended effects in the form of upcoding patients in more remunerative groups.

3.2 Pay for Performance

Traditional reimbursement systems based on activity-based payments have limitations because they ultimately do not reward directly what matters to patients, which is improvements in health. A relatively recent policy development is the introduction of pay-for-performance (P4P) schemes that incentivise quality improvements directly, which has been facilitated by information systems that routinely record patient records.

We can identify two main types of P4P schemes that encourage improvements in quality. The first type links financial incentives to measures of health, such as mortality, readmission rates or patient-reported health outcome measures. The second type links financial incentives to process measures of quality. Examples of schemes that incentivise reductions in mortality are the US Premier Hospital Quality Incentive Demonstration in 2003 (Werner et al., 2011), Hospital Value-Based Purchasing in 2012, and Advancing Quality in 2008 in England (Sutton et al., 2012). These focus on specific conditions and procedures such as heart failure, acute myocardial infarction, stroke, hip fracture, pneumonia, and coronary bypass where the mortality rate is relatively high. Mortality rates can be measured as in-hospital mortality or as thirty-day mortality. The latter is arguably a better indicator as low-quality care can affect mortality also after the patient has been discharged from the hospital, which is instead not captured by in-hospital mortality.

Many treatments have negligible or very low mortality risk. For these treatments, a second common indicator is twenty-eight-day emergency readmission rates, which measures whether the patient is readmitted to the originating or some other hospitals following hospital discharge. Examples include elective (non-emergency) hip and knee replacement, where mortality is negligible. Readmissions are also collected for emergency care, as for mortality, and examples include again heart failure, stroke, hip fracture and pneumonia. One scheme that incentivised reductions in readmission rates is the Hospital Readmission Reduction Programme introduced by Medicare (Mellor et al., 2017).

The main advantage of using mortality and readmission rates is that they are routinely collected and therefore easily available. To ensure meaningful comparability across providers, however, these indicators need to be risk-adjusted to control for differences in patients' casemix. The presence of significant unobserved severity would invalidate any comparison across providers.

The use of emergency readmission rates for conditions where the mortality rate is high can also be problematic. This is because providers with high quality that achieve lower mortality are likely to have more severe patients who survive who in turn are more likely to be readmitted as an emergency. This can generate a bias in the measure of readmission rates, as hospitals with high readmission rates could be those with higher quality and lower mortality. Laudicella et al. (2013) show that readmission rates can suffer from mortality selection bias using data from England for patients who were admitted in an emergency for a fractured hip (see Lisi et al., 2020, for a theoretical analysis).

One limitation of both mortality and readmission indicators is that they only capture health at the lower end of the health distribution, and they are not necessarily representative of the average patient experience. This can be addressed by the collection of Patient-Reported (health) Outcome Measures (PROMS). For example, in England since 2009, PROMS data have been collected for hip replacement, knee replacement, hernia and varicose veins (though data collection for the last two has been discontinued). Health measures are collected both before and six months after the surgery, which allows to compute the average health gain at the provider level (also risk-adjusted for patient characteristics). Health is measured both with the EQ-5D and procedure-specific indicators such as the Oxford hip and knee score that measure different dimensions of pain and patient mobility.

One criticism to P4P based on the measures of health, such as mortality, readmissions, and PROMS, is that health outcomes depend not only on the quality of care provided by physicians but also on patient engagement with their own care (for example, physiotherapy and physical rehabilitation, or lifestyle choices). Therefore, lack of performance is not directly attributable to healthcare providers. A second type of indicator that addresses this issue is the use of process measures of quality that are under more direct control of the provider. Two examples from England are the Best Practice Tariff for stroke and hip fracture patients. For stroke, three dimensions of care were financially incentivised: whether the patient has rapid brain imaging, whether the patient is admitted to an acute stroke unit, and if the patient requires the medicine alteplase (if clinically appropriate to dissolve blood clots) (Kristensen et al., 2016). For hip fracture, providers received a bonus (of about £1350 in 2013) if all these nine processes were provided: surgery within thirty-six hours; shared care by surgeon and geriatrician; care protocol agreed by geriatrician, surgeon and anaesthetist; preoperative cognitive function assessment; postoperative cognitive function assessment; perioperative assessment by geriatrician; geriatrician-led multidisciplinary rehabilitation; secondary prevention including falls; bone health assessment.

Pay for performance has also been applied in the context of primary care. A notable example is the Quality and Outcome Framework in England which in 2004 introduced a scheme which incentivised quality based on 146 indicators that led to an increase in revenues for GPs by 28% in two years (Sutton et al., 2010). The indicators were organised around disease areas (such as diabetes, coronary heart disease, hypertension) and incentivised the proportion of primary care patients registered in the GP practice that had their blood pressure and cholesterol checked, and their body mass index for diabetes or similar indicators for other conditions.

Economic theory has highlighted several potential issues arising when using P4P schemes. A common concern with P4P is that it causes tunnel vision. Consider a multitasking framework, where some dimensions of quality are contracted for while others are not. Then, financially incentivising some dimensions of quality may improve performance in the dimensions that are contracted but reduce performance in the dimensions of quality that are not contracted (Holmstrom and Milgrom, 1991; Eggleston, 2005). The extent to which P4P crowds out non-contracted dimensions of quality depends on the degree of substitution in provider costs or in patient health benefits between different quality dimensions (Kaarboe and Siciliani, 2011). The presence of cost or benefit substitution between quality dimensions generally reduces the power of the incentive scheme and the extent to which they should be used to incentivise quality. Another common criticism to P4P is that financial incentives may crowd out intrinsic motivation or altruism (Siciliani, 2009). Last, P4P could induce providers to game the performance indicators depending on the complexity of their design (Kuhn and Siciliani, 2009).

Several empirical studies have assessed the effects of introducing P4P in the health sector. For example, Gupta (2021) investigates the effect of the introduction of the Hospital Readmission Reduction Programme which financially penalised hospitals whose risk-adjusted readmission rates were above the average. The penalties were about 5% of the revenues for the conditions included in the scheme (heart attack, heart failure and pneumonia). Using a difference-in-difference design, where hospitals whose readmission rates are below the average are used as a control group, the study finds that the penalty scheme reduced readmission rates by one percentage point or 5% and also reduced one-year mortality, which was not incentivised, by 0.5 percentage points or 2%. However, part of the reduction in emergency readmissions was due to hospitals having changed their admission protocols at the emergency departments though such reductions had no harmful effect on the affected patients.

A different study compares whether performance should be measured with health outcomes or with process measures of quality. Mohanan et al. (2021) conduct a field experiment in Karnakata, a rural area in India, where private obstetric care providers were randomised in three groups, a control group, a treatment group that rewards health outcomes, and another that rewards process measures of quality. Health outcomes are measured through postpartum haemorrhage, sepsis, preeclampsia, and neonatal death. Instead, process measures of quality are measured through pregnancy care, childbirth care, counselling for postnatal maternal care, newborn care, and counselling for postnatal newborn care. The study finds that providers contracted with a P4P scheme both achieved similar levels of improvements in maternal health. However, the contract payment was substantially smaller for the P4P scheme that rewarded process measures of quality.

Sutton et al. (2010) investigate the extent to which the introduction of the Quality and Outcome Framework for primary care in England affects process measures of quality that were not financially incentivised by the P4P scheme. The study finds that there was no evidence of effort diversion and that instead there was some evidence of positive spillovers onto unincentivised factors for groups of patients that were targeted by the scheme. Gravelle et al. (2010) provide evidence that the same incentive scheme induced some gaming of the performance indicators, as measured by the number of 'exception' reports which affected the number of eligible patients in the denominator of the performance indicators.

Several reviews have summarised the existing evidence on the effectiveness of P4P in the health sector. Within the hospital sector, Cashin et al. (2014) suggest that providers respond only to a small extent to such incentive schemes. Mendelson et al. (2017) find that the largest improvements are concentrated in providers whose baseline performance is lower, but that consistent positive associations with improved health have not been demonstrated. For ambulatory care, there is more consistent evidence that process measures of care have improved. Milstein and Schreyogg (2016) suggest that P4P schemes across OECD countries are highly heterogeneous in design, and that some of the moderate positive effects are also due to public reporting and increased awareness of data recording rather than financial incentives.

One possible explanation for the mixed findings so far is that, with few exceptions, the payments made to reward higher quality (or to penalise lower quality) are still relatively small, often below 5% of the revenues. The small payments may be the result of multitasking concerns and are consistent with the theory which suggests that the power of the incentive scheme should be low-powered when qualities are substitutes (Holmstrom and Milgrom, 1991). But the small payments may also be the reason for the small take up in quality. One possible solution is to ensure that performance indicators have broader coverage of key areas of care based on best practices and available empirical evidence. In those cases, there may be a stronger rationale for increasing the size of the bonus as suggested for example by Kristensen et al. (2016) in relation to a P4P scheme on stroke patients which covered all key dimensions of validated process measures of quality.

Most P4P schemes have a focus on improving quality. Some P4P schemes instead aim at incentivising efficiency. In England, one Best Practice Tariff gave a bonus payment in 2010 if patients were admitted to hospitals as day case treatment or as day surgery therefore avoiding a more expensive overnight hospital admission. The scheme selected thirty-two treatments that were previously identified by the British Association for Day surgery and the British Association for Ambulatory Emergency Care. Using difference-in-difference and synthetic control methods, Gaughan et al. (2019) found that the policy had a positive impact only on fourteen out of the thirty-two treatments, and had no effect on the others. Kreutzberg et al. (2023) show that due to the pressure to reduce health spending, thirteen OECD countries are implementing financial incentive schemes to encourage an increase in the proportion of day surgeries.

3.3 Provider Competition and Patient Choice

Provider competition is a systemic feature of health systems across several OECD countries. In countries such as Germany, France, Italy and the US, hospitals compete on quality to attract patients and increase provider revenues. Other countries, such as England and Norway, had historically limited patient choice and competition but over time have introduced a series of reforms that allowed patient choice with the purpose of stimulating provider competition (Siciliani et al., 2022). In England, a payer-driven competition was introduced with the 1990 NHS internal market reforms. Public hospitals became NHS Trusts which competed for contracts with NHS purchasers. In 2006, patient choice was introduced with the patient being offered a choice of at least four providers, and then expanded in 2008 to choice of any qualified provider. Patient choice was further supported by public reporting of a range of clinical quality measures, such as risk-adjusted mortality, and indicators related to patient experience, such as cleanliness or user rating.

The policy motivation behind introducing or facilitating provider competition is that it will improve the quality of care. The idea is that if providers are reimbursed through activity-based financing (e.g., based on Diagnosis Related Groups) and patients can freely choose the provider based on quality considerations, then providers will have a stronger incentive to invest in quality to attract patients and increase revenues. Economic theory suggests that competition increases quality when tariffs are fixed, the marginal cost of treating patients is constant and providers are profit-oriented. A higher price mark-up (DRG tariff minus treatment costs) and a higher responsiveness of demand to quality strengthen the incentive to compete and increase quality (Gaynor, 2007).

The theoretical predictions of the effect of competition on quality are instead ambiguous in the presence of capacity constraints that feature several publicly funded health systems and when providers are altruistic and their objective function contains patient health and quality in addition to profit considerations. If the marginal treatment costs increase in volume, for example, due to capacity constraints, and providers work at a negative profit margin due to altruistic considerations, then more competition could reduce quality as effectively providers compete to avoid rather than to attract additional patients. If the profit margin is negative, then hospitals make more losses by attracting additional patients, which weakens the incentive to compete on quality (Brekke et al., 2011a).

Several empirical studies have tested the effect of competition on quality. Using an instrumental variable approach, Bloom et al. (2015) show that more competition across providers, as measured by the number of public hospitals within a catchment area, enhances quality, as measured by are reduction of heart attack mortality, and that this driven by better quality of the management of the hospital. One additional hospital reduces mortality by 1.5 percentage points. To address possible omitted variable bias, the number of hospitals is instrumented with a measure of political marginality, the idea being that constituencies where political parties are closer to a winning margin, they are less likely to close hospitals because it is politically unpopular.

Using quasi-difference-in-differences methods, several studies have exploited the expansion of patient choice in 2006 (Cooper, 2011; Gaynor et al., 2013). They test whether hospitals in areas with more providers, therefore facing more competition by other providers, improved health outcomes more quickly when the patient choice policy was expanded relative to areas with fewer hospitals. An increase in competition by 10% reduces heart attack mortality by 2.9%. Using similar methods, Moscelli et al. (2018a) found that competition also reduced hip fracture mortality, in addition to heart attack mortality, but had no effect on stroke mortality. These studies use health outcomes for emergency conditions, such as heart attacks, as a proxy for quality to mitigate possible selection concerns due to unobserved dimensions of severity. If more severe patients choose hospitals with higher quality, hospitals in more competitive areas may have a higher mortality and appear to be of lower quality while this reflects a higher patient severity.

Moscelli et al. (2021) focus on non-emergency treatments, and deal with possible unobserved severity through a two-stage residual inclusion approach. Using a similar difference-in-difference approach, the study finds that competition had no effect on thirty-day mortality for patients in need of coronary artery bypass grafting (CABG) and it increased readmission rates (lower quality) for patients who had hip and knee replacement surgery. Cooper et al. (2018) provide evidence that competition by private providers treating publicly funded patients increases efficiency, as measured by a reduction in the preoperative length of stay for patients having hip and knee replacements, though private providers treated healthier patients leaving the sicker patients to the public hospitals. Earlier studies in England found that competition increased heart attack mortality when the tariffs paid by the purchasers to the hospitals were not fixed but negotiated with health authorities (Propper et al., 2004, 2008b), and reduced waiting times (Propper et al., 2008b) in the 1990s. This can be explained by purchasers negotiating with hospitals mostly on price and waiting times, while clinical quality indicators were not available. Therefore, competition reduced clinical quality.

The evidence from other European countries is mixed. In the Netherlands, where tariffs are negotiated for some non-emergency treatments, Rocs et al. (2020) find that price deregulation in a competitive environment (where hospitals are located close to several other hospitals) did not affect quality as measured by readmission rates for hip replacement patients. In Italy, Berta et al. (2016) find that competition did not affect quality as measured by mortality and readmission rates for coronary bypass.

In Norway, Brekke et al. (2021) use a similar identification strategy as in Gaynor et al. (2013) and find that following the 2001 choice reform, hospitals facing a more competitive environment (as measured by more providers in the hospital catchment area) had lower heart attack mortality rates relative to hospitals facing a less competitive environment, but no effect was found for stroke mortality. The study also finds that exposure to competition reduces all-cause mortality and shortens the length of stay, but increases readmissions, though these effects are small in magnitude. In France, Or et al. (2022) focus on surgical procedures for breast cancer (breast reconstruction after mastectomy and sentinel lymph node biopsy) and find that the likelihood of receiving these procedures is higher in hospitals located in more competitive areas.

There are several studies from the US investigating the effect of hospital competition for publicly funded patients covered by Medicare and Medicaid. A first seminal study by Kessler and McClellan (2000) suggests that competition reduced heart attack mortality and costs after a DRG system was introduced in 1983. It reduced mortality but increased costs when hospitals were reimbursed through a fee-for-service reimbursement system. Kessler and Geppert (2005) confirm that competition increases quality but suggest that this is concentrated in patients with high severity. Gowrisankaran and Town (2003) instead found that competition is associated with higher mortality for heart attack and pneumonia.

One premise for provider competition to work is that demand responds to quality. By increasing quality, the provider can attract more patients and increase revenues. The literature reviewed earlier in this section has investigated how competition affects quality. A different empirical literature has instead tested whether higher quality affects the choice of provider. This empirical approach uses conditional logit models or mixed logit models (Gaynor et al., 2016). It involves modelling individual patient choice of one provider versus other providers in the patient choice set as a function of providers' quality and the distance between each patient's place of residence and the location of the provider. The idea is that patients have a preference for both higher quality and shorter distances, and there is a trade-off between different hospital attributes.

There are several mechanisms through which quality can affect demand. The first is through word of mouth. Some hospitals develop a reputation for being of high quality, and this is communicated informally through verbal communication within social networks. The second mechanism is directed through primary care providers. In many health systems, primary care doctors act as gatekeepers and patients are required a referral from the GP to access specialist care. Primary care doctors can advise and direct patients towards providers with higher quality of care. The third mechanism is through public reporting. Health systems are increasingly keen to provide quality indicators in the public domain, which reduces search costs for patients.

Several empirical studies have investigated the effect of quality on patient choice across a range of health conditions and treatments. Gaynor et al. (2016) show that, following the introduction of patient choice reforms in 2006 in England, patients having coronary artery bypass grafting were more likely to choose hospitals with lower mortality rates. They found an elasticity of -0.05, suggesting that a 10% increase in mortality rates reduces demand by -0.5%, and that this elasticity does not differ for patients with different socioeconomic status. Patients with comorbidities instead have a higher elasticity (in absolute value) of around -0.1, which is consistent with more severe patients being more willing to travel further to avoid higher mortality.

Gutacker et al. (2016b) and Moscelli et al. (2016b) focus on hip replacement in England and show that patients were more likely to choose hospitals with greater health gains, as measured by patient-reported outcome measures (PROMs), and lower readmission rates. The study finds that a one standard deviation increase in quality, measured by PROMS, increases demand by 9.8%, and that the willingness to travel further for the same increase in quality is 1.4 kilometres (9% of the average distance travelled). Beckert et al. (2012) also focus on hip replacement and show that patients are less likely to choose hospitals with higher overall mortality rates (across all treatments within a hospital) and higher methicillin-resistant Staphylococcus aureus (MRSA) infection rates. Overall, these studies suggest that proximity to the provider remains the most important driver of patient choice, but quality considerations are also taken into account. As a result, the demand is relatively inelastic to quality.

In Germany, there is evidence that expectant mothers are willing to travel to give birth in maternity clinics with higher reported quality as measured by clinical indicators and satisfaction scores (Avdic et al., 2019). Kuklinski et al. (2021) show that colorectal resection patients are willing to travel longer for specialised hospitals. Patients in need of knee replacement travel longer to hospitals with better service quality and higher volume.

In the Netherlands, Varkevisser et al. (2012) provide evidence that patients having angioplasty are more likely to choose hospitals with a good (overall and cardiology) reputation and low heart-failure readmissions. Beukers et al. (2014) show that the choice of hospital for hip replacements is affected by information provided in the public domain on hospital waiting times and a reputation index.

In Norway, Brekke et al. (2018) show that half of patients bypassing their local hospital do so under their own initiative (as opposed to, for example, the GP's initiative), and the effect is reinforced for patients with higher educational attainment. In Italy, Bruni et al. (2021) find that patients in need of angioplasty are willing to travel further to reduce waiting times and avoid higher mortality, with stronger effects of quality for more severe patients. These general findings are also consistent with studies from the US (reviewed, e.g., in Gaynor and Town, 2011).

The studies reviewed so far focus on hospital care. There is less empirical evidence of patient choice within the context of primary care, possibly due to the difficulty of accessing data at the patient level and collecting quality indicators for primary care providers. One exception is Santos et al. (2017) who use data from the Quality and Outcome Framework in England. They find that one standard deviation increase in clinical quality would increase primary care practice size by around 17%.

3.4 Public, Private Non-profit and Private for-profit Hospitals

Countries differ significantly in the mix of public and private providers treating publicly funded patients. For example, in Germany, about 30% of hospitals are public, 35% are private non-profit hospitals and 35% are private for-profit hospitals. In France, private hospitals provide 60% of surgical treatments. In Italy, the mix between public and private providers can differ significantly across regions. Provision is instead dominated by public hospitals in England and Norway, though the proportion of patients treated by private providers has steadily increased. All hospitals are mandated to be private non-profit in the Netherlands (Siciliani et al., 2022).

This diversity in the mix between public and private (for-profit and non-profit) providers raises the question of whether one type of provision is better than the other in relation to key domains such as quality and efficiency. Economic theory has clear-cut predictions in relation to incentives towards cost containment. Private providers have stronger incentives to contain costs because any reduction in costs will translate into higher profits. Conversely, public providers have weaker incentives to contain costs if profits cannot be redistributed or if providers have a soft budget constraint where the payer can cover deficits or confiscate surpluses (Brekke et al., 2012, 2015a). On the other hand, public hospitals may experience larger excess demand and may also have an obligation to treat all the patients referred to public hospitals, which in turn could increase efficiency.

The theoretical predictions in relation to quality of care are less clear-cut. On the one hand, private providers may skimp on quality to increase profits. On the other hand, if demand responds to quality, private providers may compete more aggressively on quality to attract patients and increase revenues (Sloan, 2000; Glaeser and Shleifer, 2001; Brekke et al., 2012). Moreover, non-profit providers may attract more altruistic or motivated doctors relative to for-profit ones, which can contribute to higher quality. One common policy concern with the provision by private providers is that they will cream-skim less complex patients. Given that hospitals are commonly reimbursed by a fixed tariff system, private providers have a financial incentive to treat less complex patients and avoid the more costly ones.

There is extensive empirical evidence that has tested for differences in quality, efficiency and casemix between public and private providers. Given that hospital status tends to be time-invariant, the evidence is mostly cross-sectional in nature. The meta-analysis by Eggleston et al. (2008) reviewed thirty-one studies since 1990 in the US. It suggested that whether for-profit hospitals provide higher quality than non-profit ones depends on specific contexts such as the region, the data source, and the period of analysis, though as a whole quality seems to be lower among for-profit hospitals.

There are also several cross-sectional studies from other high-income countries. For example, Milcent (2005) shows that in France public and private not-for-profit hospitals did not differ in heart attack mortality, while private for-profit hospitals had lower heart attack mortality. At the time of the study, private hospitals were paid by fee-for-service, while public and private not-for-profit hospitals were subject to a global budget. Jensen et al. (2009) also show that in

Australia private hospitals had lower readmission and mortality rates for patients who had their *first* heart attack.

One possible methodological concern with cross-sectional models is that some dimensions of the patient's severity remain unobservable to the researcher and that more severe patients are more likely to choose hospitals with higher quality. To address this concern, Lien et al. (2008) employed an instrumental-variable approach. Whether the patient is treated by a public or private provider is instrumented with the distance between the patient's residence and the location of the closest public and private hospital. Using data from Taiwan, the study finds that public and non-profit hospitals have higher quality, measured by one-month or twelve-month mortality rates for stroke and cardiac treatment.

Moscelli et al. (2018b) use a similar approach to compare thirty-day emergency readmission rates for public and private providers that provided 133 commonly planned treatments in 2013–2014. The study finds no differences between public and private hospitals in emergency readmissions after controlling for unobserved patient severity. Using also an instrumental variable approach based on distance, Moscone et al. (2020) test for differences between public and private hospitals in Italy (Lombardy) for both emergency and planned care. They find that public and private hospitals do not differ in stroke and hip fracture mortality, mortality for coronary bypass and readmissions for knee replacement. Private hospitals have lower heart attack mortality but higher readmissions for hip replacement. Only a few studies go beyond mortality and readmission rates to measure quality. Pérotin et al. (2013) use a switching regression framework and find no differences in patient satisfaction between public and private providers in England. Chard et al. (2011) compare private and public hospitals in England and find that private hospitals have better patient-reported outcomes for hip and knee replacements, but similar outcomes for varicose veins and hernia surgery.

Although hospital status is generally time-invariant, hospitals can change status for example by converting from private for-profit to private non-profit or the other way around. Some studies in the US have employed a panel-data approach to test whether changes in hospital status affect quality while controlling for unobserved time-invariant factors. Shen (2002) finds that hospitals that changed status from non-profit to for-profit have higher heart attack mortality. Instead, there was no evidence of differences in quality for hospitals that converted from public (government) hospitals or for-profit hospitals to non-profit hospitals. Neither was there an effect for non-profit or for-profit hospitals that converted to public hospitals.

Although most of the recent literature has focused on differences in quality, there is also extensive evidence comparing efficiency between public and private providers using either a production function or a cost function approach. Using a cost function approach, Herr (2008) finds that private hospitals have higher costs than public ones in Germany at a time when private hospitals were paid a fee for service with a per diem for each patient spent in hospitals. Costs were instead similar once both types of hospitals were reimbursed under a common tariff system based on Diagnosis Related Groups (Herr et al., 2011).

Barbetta et al. (2007) use instead a production function approach. They found that private non-profit hospitals were more efficient than public ones though efficiency converged when public and private hospitals were reimbursed based on a common set of tariffs (based on Diagnosis Related Groups). Marini et al. (2008) use a panel-data approach to test whether giving public hospitals greater financial autonomy impacted costs and financial surplus and find no effect of financial autonomy on these outcomes.

Hollingsworth (2008) reviewed more than 300 studies across a range of countries and found that public and non-profit hospitals tend to be more efficient than for-profit ones but there is heterogeneity in findings across institutional settings. A more recent review by Kruse et al. (2018) for European countries has similar findings: most evidence suggests that public hospitals are at least as efficient as private hospitals.

In summary, the empirical evidence does not make a strong case for quality being systematically higher either for for-profit or non-profit hospitals. Neither does the evidence confirm that public hospitals are less efficient than private ones as predicted by standard economic theory.

3.5 Integrated Care

Driven by an ageing population, the number of individuals with chronic conditions and multimorbidity is rising. These individuals can require a complex pattern of care that involves coordination within and across the health and long-term care sector. The lack of coordination within and across sectors leads to fragmented services.

One solution to improve coordination of care is to move towards integrated care. Examples of integrated care are heterogeneous and involve integration across different segments of the health sector or sectors, such as health and social care. A frequent feature of integrated care is that it involves a bundled payment that covers different types of care under one reimbursed tariff. Integration of services can involve schemes covering segments of the population with specific needs with a focus on single disease management models or the whole population (Siciliani et al., 2022).

As an example, in the Netherlands, bundled payments for integrated care were introduced in 2010 to cover patients with type II diabetes, chronic obstructive pulmonary disease (COPD), asthma, and those at high risk of cardiovascular diseases. A 'care group' organises the care necessary for managing these diseases based on clinical standards and offers coordinated outpatient care with the aim of improving coordination, and reducing specialist visits and hospitalisation. Care groups were owned by GPs, and varied in size from 4 to 150 GPs (Schut and Varkevisser, 2017).

In Germany, Disease Management Programmes for chronic diseases were introduced in 2005 by sickness funds for patients with asthma, COPD, diabetes, and ischaemic heart disease with the aim of coordinating ambulatory services. Services were provided mostly by family physicians and specialists based on evidence-based guidelines. Another example in Germany was the 'Integrated care contracts' to cover a population for a given condition such as stroke, or procedure, such as hip replacement to overcome inter-sectoral barriers through case management and coordinated patient pathways that integrated providers horizontally (within ambulatory care) or vertically across sectors (inpatient and ambulatory care) (Kifmann, 2017).

In England, new care models were introduced with the aim of integrating health and social care and motivating providers to design better packages of care. The 'multispecialty community provider' model involved groups of GPs coming together to offer a range of services, including community and outpatient services. 'Primary and acute care systems' aimed at integrating also hospital services with primary, community, and mental health services to improve coordination and to shift care away from the more expensive secondary sector (Siciliani et al., 2022). In the US, several initiatives have integrated hospital services with other segments of the health system for example through vertical integration between hospitals and physician practices or with post-acute care rehabilitation providers (skilled nursing facilities and home health agencies) (Konetzka et al., 2018).

The economic rationale for integrated care rests on the presence of synergies in the patient's benefits through coordination of care and reduction in costs through reductions in duplications and scale and scope economies. This is then implemented through a bundled payment, which is supposed to internalise spillover effects therefore improving the efficiency of the organisation. Integrated care however changes the extent to which patients can exercise choice and the degree of competition across providers. Providers can still compete by offering different integrated services, but patient choice is restricted because different services within a package are offered by the same organisation. Whether competition reduces because of integration is a priori unclear. On one hand, demand responsiveness to each dimension of quality reduces, which reduces competition. On the other hand, providers receive higher reimbursement for each patient that they attract, which increases competition (Biglaiser and Ma, 2003; Brekke et al., 2024). Therefore, although patient choice is restricted under integrated care, provider competition does not necessarily reduce, and the benefits from integration from synergies and coordination can make patients better off.

The empirical evidence on the effect of integrated care is limited but growing. Baxter et al. (2018) provide a review to summarise the evidence on the effects of integration or coordination between healthcare services, or between health and social care on service delivery outcomes. It cautiously concluded that integrated care may enhance patient satisfaction, increase perceived quality of care, and enable access to services, but the evidence for service costs and health outcomes is limited.

Morciano et al. (2020) evaluate the efficacy of the population-based and care home site integrated care (known as Vanguard) models in England in reducing hospital utilisation using a difference-in-difference model using non-Vanguard sites as a control group. It shows that Vanguard sites had a smaller increase in emergency admissions relative to non-Vanguard sites, but there were no differences in bed days. Konetzka et al. (2018) investigate the effect of integration between hospitals and post-acute rehabilitation care provided by skilled nursing facilities or home health agencies in the US. They find that vertical integration between hospitals and skilled nursing facilities reduces rehospitalisation rates but increases Medicare payments, while other forms of integration have no effect.

Other studies that investigate possible substitution effects across and within sectors can inform policy reforms related to integrated care. Within health care, better access to primary care can reduce emergency hospitalisations. Pinchbeck (2019) exploits a policy that expanded access to primary care in England through the introduction of new primary care services. More than half were 'walk-in clinics' that were open also in the evening and at weekends with no need to make an appointment. The study shows that proximity to these convenience-oriented services results in reductions in unplanned emergency department visits by 1.5–4%. The findings therefore suggest that primary and secondary care can be substitutes. Gaughan et al. (2015) focus on the interface between health and social care in England by studying the extent to which greater supplies of nursing home beds or lower prices reduce hospital bed blocking. Hospital bed-blocking occurs when patients in a hospital are ready to be discharged to a nursing home, but no place is available so hospital care acts as a more costly substitute for long-term care. Using panel data measuring delayed discharges across Local Authorities, the study finds that delayed discharges respond to the availability of care home beds, but the effect is modest: an increase in care home beds by 10% reduces social care delayed discharges by 6–9%.

4 Pharmaceuticals

The market for pharmaceuticals, more specifically prescription drugs, is characterised by several features that distinguish it from most other product markets. Such features are found both on the demand side and on the supply side of the market.

On the demand side, public or private insurance means that the demand for prescription drugs is generally highly price-inelastic, since at most a fraction of the drug price is paid by the patient out-of-pocket. Furthermore, drug demand is not solely a result of consumer choice as for most other products, but results instead from a more complex decision-making process that also involves the prescribing physician and, in some cases, the dispensing pharmacy.

Furthermore, the pharmaceutical industry is one of the most research-intensive, which implies that the supply side is generally characterised by high fixed (sunk) costs and low marginal costs. To give pharmaceutical firms incentives for drug innovation, most countries offer patent protection that implies that innovating firms are granted monopoly status for a given period, which allows them to recover the costs of innovation by selling the drug at a price higher than the marginal cost during the patent period.

The combination of low price-elasticity of demand and considerable market power on the supply side poses several regulatory challenges for policymakers who are concerned about securing wide access to drugs at affordable prices and ensuring that pharmaceutical firms have sufficient incentives for developing new and beneficial drug treatments.

In the remainder of this section, we will describe and discuss the main policy options in the light of economic theory and available empirical evidence. In doing so, we will distinguish between on-patent markets (section 4.1) and off-patent markets (section 4.2) for prescription drugs, which pose distinctly separate regulatory challenges, and then conclude by discussing key incentives for pharmaceutical innovation (section 4.3).

4.1 Pharmaceuticals: Patented Drugs

A patent-holding producer is by definition given the exclusive right to produce and sell the drug during the patent period. However, this does not necessarily mean that the producer is insulated from competition. On the contrary, a patent-holding firm might face therapeutic competition from other drugs that have broadly similar therapeutic effects. Thus, the potential market power of a patent-holder depends in part on the existence of therapeutic substitutes.

A key policy question is whether patent-holding firms should be allowed to freely set the prices of their drugs, or whether drug prices should be regulated in some way. In the absence of sufficiently close therapeutic substitutes, which curb the market power of patent-holding firms, a general concern among policymakers is that the combination of strong market power and relatively price-inelastic drug demand leads to excessively high prices. Most countries have therefore introduced some form of price cap regulation for on-patent drugs usually related to the approval of the drug for reimbursement. The most common forms of price cap regulation are value-based pricing and international reference pricing, which will be further discussed in subsequent sections.

Another related issue is the extent to which patent-holding firms are able to price discriminate between markets (countries) with different willingness to pay for the drug, which depends in part on regulatory policies, such as the use of international reference pricing and whether or not parallel trade between different countries is prohibited. All else equal, the ability to internationally price discriminate increases the value of the patent, but also implies that countries with a high (low) willingness to pay for drug treatments pay a higher (lower) price than they would have done in the absence of such discrimination (see, e.g., Danzon et al., 2015).

4.1.1 Pricing of Patented Drugs: Static versus Dynamic Efficiency

From the viewpoint of national policy makers, the pricing of on-patent drugs entails a basic policy trade-off between dynamic and static efficiency. On the one hand, incentives for drug innovation require that the innovation costs can be recouped by revenues earned during the patent period, which implies that patent-holding firms are granted the market power to set prices sufficiently above marginal costs. On the other hand, once a patented drug has entered the market, drug purchasers have an incentive to acquire them as cheaply as possible. In particular, small countries without a significant pharmaceutical industry have a strong incentive for free-riding by imposing strict price regulation and letting payers in other countries pay for the drug innovation costs.

Considerations for drug innovation incentives apart, national policymakers also face a potential trade-off between lower costs and higher access for existing drugs. Even if a policy maker is only concerned about acquiring a drug at the lowest possible cost, it might be necessary to accept prices considerably above marginal cost in order to have access to the drug. There is robust empirical evidence of such a policy trade-off. For example, in a cross-country study on the extent and timing of the launch of new drugs, Kyle (2007) finds that, on average, the probability that a drug will be launched in a market where prices are regulated is 75% lower than the launch probability in a market with free pricing, all else equal.

4.1.2 Value-Based Pricing

Arguably the most ambitious form of price cap regulation of on-patent drugs is so-called *value-based pricing*, where the price cap is based on a monetary valuation of the therapeutic benefit offered by the drug. A relatively widespread method of value-based pricing relies on the calculation of an *incremental cost-effectiveness ratio* (ICER), where the costs and benefits of a new drug treatment are measured relative to the costs and benefits of an existing baseline treatment (in case such therapeutic substitutes exist).[1] By this method, a new drug is included in the health plan only if the price of the drug is such that the cost per additional unit of improvement in expected health benefit is below a given threshold.[2]

A main challenge of value-based pricing is the amount of information required to estimate the expected therapeutic benefit of the drug in monetary terms. In addition, the use of cost-effectiveness thresholds in value-based pricing of new drugs might also create adverse pricing incentives for existing therapeutic alternatives, since the maximum price for new drugs depends on the price of existing benchmark treatments. In particular, Brekke et al. (2022) show that an ICER-based pricing rule might have adverse effects for both payers and patients due to strategic pricing by incumbent producers and argue that the pricing of new drugs should be decoupled from the prices of existing therapeutic alternatives.

4.1.3 International Reference Pricing

A less ambitious form of price cap regulation is so-called *international refer-ence pricing* (or *external reference pricing*), where the price cap imposed by a national regulator is based on the prices of the same drug in a predefined set of other countries, usually through a simple rule in which the price cap is set equal to the lowest price or an average of the x lowest prices in this set, for example. This is a widely used price regulation scheme, particularly in Europe, and its

---

[1] See, e.g., Paris and Belloni (2013) for a description of value-based pricing in 14 OECD countries and a discussion of the pros and cons of such pricing policies.

[2] For example, the current practice in the UK is informed by the National Institute for Health and Clinical Excellence's recommendation that every new drug approved produces at least one additional QALY for every £30,000 that it costs.

popularity is almost certainly related to the very low regulatory costs, where the only information required is price information from other countries.

However, the widespread use of international reference pricing will inevitably lead to a certain degree of price harmonisation across countries. There are two concerns related to this. One concern is that it undermines drug producers' ability for international price discrimination, which reduces the value of the drug patent and is thus potentially harmful to innovation incentives.

Another concern is that it might harm low-income countries in the form of either lower drug access or higher drug prices. International reference pricing might lead to lower access because drug producers might prefer not to sell to countries with a relatively low willingness to pay for drugs to avoid low prices being 'exported' to countries with a higher willingness to pay, as shown by Geng and Saggi (2017). If drug prices in low-income countries are not set by the producers but instead determined by bargaining, international reference pricing is likely to make producers less willing to accept a low price and, conversely, make low-income countries more willing to accept higher drug prices to secure access to new drugs, as shown by Garcia Mariñoso et al. (2011). Thus, international reference pricing might cause low-income countries to face the choice between restricted access and higher prices.

However, the analysis by Geng and Saggi (2017) also highlights the importance of the choice of reference countries. If international reference pricing is based on prices in countries with much lower willingness to pay for drugs, drug producers will optimally choose to stay out of these markets, which in turn undermines the intended price-reducing effect of the international reference pricing scheme. This is also consistent with real-world practices, where international reference pricing is usually based on drug prices in relatively similar countries. Thus, the potentially detrimental effects of international reference pricing in the form of lower access to drugs are likely to be at least partly counteracted by the choice of a relatively homogeneous set of reference countries.

The widespread use of international reference pricing inevitably implies that countries use partially overlapping sets of reference countries, which means that the price cap imposed by Country A is a function of the drug price in Country B, *and vice versa*. Cross-country differences in terms of willingness to pay for drugs create an incentive for strategic choices of launch sequence by drug producers, where drug launches are delayed in countries with relatively low willingness to pay. Such strategic launch delay effects are empirically documented by Maini and Pammolli (2023), using data on pharmaceutical sales in European countries in the period 2002–2012. Based on a dynamic structural model of entry, they show that the removal of international reference pricing would reduce launch delays by up to one year per drug in some low-income European countries.

4.1.4 Parallel Imports

The use of international price discrimination by producers of patented drugs creates an incentive for arbitrage, where a drug sold in a low-price country is repackaged and sold to a high-price country by parallel traders at a price lower than the price charged by the original producer in that country. Such *parallel trade* of drugs has qualitatively the same effect as international reference pricing, in the sense that it leads to (some degree of) price convergence across countries. Thus, allowing for parallel imports could be seen as an alternative to imposing an international reference pricing scheme. Indeed, the regulatory practices on parallel trade differ. For example, parallel imports are allowed between EU countries but not from countries outside the EU, while it is largely prohibited in the US.

As for the case of international reference pricing, a potential concern with parallel imports is that it might reduce drug access in low-price countries (Roy and Saggi, 2012). In a similar vein, the possibility of parallel imports might also lead to higher prices in the source countries (i.e., the low-price countries), either through a higher regulated price (Birg, 2023) or a higher bargained price (Pecorino, 2002).

In the importing (high-price) countries, on the other hand, competition from parallel importers is likely to have a negative effect on drug prices. Such effects are empirically confirmed by Ganslandt and Maskus (2004), who use data from Sweden and find that competition from parallel importers reduces producer prices by 12–19% on average. Similar effects are also found by Duso et al. (2014), who report structural estimation results based on German data showing that parallel imports reduce prices of patented drugs by 11% on average.

However, the presence of parallel imports might also affect the impact of price cap regulation in less than obvious ways. In a theoretical analysis where retail drug prices are determined by bargaining between producers and retailers, Brekke et al. (2015b) show that the presence of parallel imports shifts bargaining power from producers to retailers, which all else equal leads to lower producer prices. However, the imposition of a price cap on producer prices weakens competition from parallel importers and therefore shifts bargaining power back towards the producers. Because of this effect, stricter price cap regulation might have a negligible, or even positive, effect on producer prices and profits in the importing country in the presence of parallel trade. This possibility is also partly confirmed in an empirical analysis using Norwegian data, where Brekke et al. (2015b) show that stricter price cap regulation leads to lower producer profits in the absence of parallel imports but has no effect on profits in the presence of parallel trade. A similar result is found by Dubois and

Sæthre (2020) who show, based on structural estimation on the same Norwegian data, that stricter price cap regulation would severely reduce retailer profits but only have a modest negative effect on producer profits in the presence of parallel trade. Overall, these results suggest that price cap regulation and allowing for parallel trade are policy complements. In the presence of parallel trade, stricter price cap regulation can potentially improve static efficiency without harming dynamic efficiency.

4.2 Pharmaceuticals: Off-patent Drugs

Once the patent term ends and the drug loses its patent protection, the producer of the drug is in principle exposed to competition from producers of copy drugs, so-called generic drugs, that contain the same active chemical ingredients as the brand-name drug. In the following we will give an overview of how generic competition is likely to affect drug prices in off-patent markets and how such competition is affected by different designs of the drug reimbursement scheme.

4.2.1 Generic Entry and Branded-Generic Competition

Off-patent pharmaceutical markets are generally characterised by two observations that are far from obvious. The first observation is that generic drugs are consistently priced below the brand-name drug without causing the latter drug to exit the market. The other observation is that, although average drug prices tend to fall after generic entry, the price of the brand-name drug has sometimes been found to increase. The latter effect is often referred to as the *generic competition paradox*.

A seminal attempt to explain the generic competition paradox is provided by Frank and Salkever (1992), who present a theoretical model where demand consists of two segments: brand-loyal and cross-price-sensitive consumers. In other words, some patients are not willing to switch from the brand-name drug to a generic alternative, while other consumers are willing to switch to a generic drug if it is offered at a lower price. Based on this model, generic entry might reduce the own-price elasticity of demand for the brand-name drug and thus lead to a higher brand-name drug price.

An arguable weakness of the Frank–Salkever model is that the existence of a brand-loyal demand segment is exogenously given and thus left unexplained. Brekke et al. (2011) use a different approach and assume that all patients are in principle willing to buy a generic drug, but that the brand-name drug is perceived to be of higher quality, for example, because of differences in advertising or physician detailing. Thus, branded-generic price differences could be explained by (perceived) vertical differentiation. Brekke et al. (2016) present a similar analysis of competition between one brand name and n generic drugs and show that increased generic competition leads to lower prices of all drugs.

In the early empirical literature on the price effects of generic entry, which is mainly based on US data, several studies find evidence of price increases for the brand-name drug (Grabowski and Vernon, 1992; Frank and Salkever, 1997; Regan, 2008), although the estimated magnitudes of these price responses are relatively small, and certainly far smaller than the branded-generic price differences. However, other studies (e.g., Wiggins and Maness, 2004) have not found evidence of any brand-name price increases in response to generic entry.

The studies considered so far the effect of generic entry at the extensive margin. However, a related question is whether generic entry at the intensive margin (i.e., an increase in the number of generic drugs) has a significant effect on drug prices. Based on US data, Regan (2008) finds only a modest negative price effect of an increase in the number of generic competitors In contrast, Granlund and Bergman (2018) report very strong price effects of generic competition at the intensive margin. Based on Swedish data, they find that increasing the number of generic competitors from one to ten has a long-run price-reducing effect of 89% for generics and 29% for brand names. These results are qualitatively in line with the theoretical results by Brekke et al. (2016) and suggest that generic drugs are not perceived as fully homogenous products.

The extent to which generic competition leads to lower prices depends on how willing patients are to switch from expensive brand names to cheaper generics. In an empirical case study on generic entry in the market for a widely prescribed drug in Japan, Ito et al. (2020) find evidence of a substantial effect of *inertia* on drug choices. Patients who used the brand-name drug before generic entry were much less likely to switch to a generic drug than patients without such a history. Such inertia might be partly caused by patient preferences but might also result from (lack of) incentives for generic substitution by the prescribing physician or the dispensing pharmacy. The role of prescribing physicians is explored by Iizuka (2012), who uses data from Japan, where physicians are able to both prescribe and dispense drugs, and shows that brand-name versus generic prescription choices depend on the financial incentives of prescribing physicians. A similar result regarding the role of dispensing pharmacies is reported by Brekke et al. (2013), who use Norwegian data to show that brand-name versus generic market shares are strongly correlated with differences in brand-name versus generic profit margins for pharmacies. These results illustrate the complexity of pharmaceutical markets, where demand is not solely determined by patient preferences.

4.2.2 Reference Pricing

A potentially major impediment to effective generic competition is the fact that patients are partly or fully insured against expenditures for drug treatment, which causes demand to be highly price-inelastic. Many patients will be reluctant to switch from the brand-name drug to a cheaper generic alternative if the difference in patient co-payment is zero or close to zero. During the last couple of decades, policymakers in many countries have therefore attempted to make generic competition more effective by designing the reimbursement scheme in a way that makes demand more elastic at higher prices. This has primarily been done through the use of *reference pricing*, which is now a widely used reimbursement scheme for off-patent pharmaceuticals.[3]

In a reimbursement scheme based on reference pricing, the (public or private) insurer reimburses a patient's drug expenditures (fully or partly) per unit of the drug up to a certain price level: the reference price. If the patient chooses to buy a drug that is priced above the reference price, the difference between the actual price and the reference price must be fully covered by the patient out-of-pocket. In principle, this makes drug demand more price-elastic at prices above the reference price.

There are two main categories of reference pricing, namely *generic reference pricing* and *therapeutic reference pricing*. Under generic reference pricing, the same reference price applies to a group of drugs that only consists of a brand-name drug and its generic alternatives. In contrast, under therapeutic reference pricing, the same reference price applies to a group of drugs that includes two or more therapeutically substitutable brand-name drugs (in addition to their generic alternatives). This means that therapeutic reference pricing can in principle apply also to on-patent drugs, which makes it somewhat more controversial than generic reference pricing.[4]

Additionally, we can also distinguish between two conceptually different ways of setting the reference price, namely *exogenous* versus *endogenous* reference pricing. In the latter scheme, the reference price is endogenously determined as a function of the actual drug prices within the relevant group of drugs (e.g., as the lowest or the average price of the drugs in the reference group). In contrast, under an exogenous reference pricing scheme, the reference

---

[3] Reference pricing as a reimbursement scheme is sometimes referred to as *internal reference pricing* in order to avoid confusion with international (or external) reference pricing, which is a price cap regulation scheme and not a reimbursement scheme.

[4] Therapeutic reference pricing is used only by a few countries, including Germany, the Netherlands, and New Zealand, which do not use direct price control mechanisms, like price cap regulation.

price is set at a certain level and does not change in response to price changes of the drugs in the reference group.

Reference pricing might affect drug prices through two different channels. In addition to a direct effect through changes in pricing incentives for a given number of drugs, there might also be indirect effects through changes in the incentives for generic entry. The theoretical literature is unanimous in the prediction that reference pricing leads to lower drug prices on average. If the reference price is endogenous, the effect is negative for all drug prices under both generic and therapeutic reference pricing (Brekke et al., 2007; Gonçalves and Rodrigues, 2018). The producers of brand-name drugs (which are generally priced above the reference price) have an incentive to reduce the price because reference pricing makes demand for brand-name drugs more price-elastic. Producers of generic drugs, on the other hand, have an incentive to reduce their prices in order to induce a reduction in the reference price and therefore make brand-name drugs relatively more expensive. The overall effect is a reduction in all drug prices.

However, the exact design of the reference pricing scheme matters. Brekke et al. (2011) analyse the effects of endogenous versus exogenous reference pricing and show that, although the average drug price falls in both cases, the latter scheme leads to an increase in generic drug prices and therefore a price convergence towards the reference price. Thus, the pro-competitive effect of reference pricing is stronger if the reference price is endogenously determined. In a related theoretical study, Ghislandi (2011) shows that the design of the reference pricing scheme might also affect the incentives for price collusion among generic competitors. More specifically, he shows that collusion is less sustainable if the (endogenous) reference price does not depend on the brand-name price.

The empirical evidence overwhelmingly supports the theoretical prediction that reference pricing has a pro-competitive effect on drug prices. For example, Brekke et al. (2011) exploit a quasi-experimental introduction of generic reference pricing (with an endogenously set reference price) in Norway and find that it led to substantial price reductions: 33% for brand-name drugs and 22% for generic drugs, on average. Kortelainen et al. (2024) estimate the effect of reference pricing on expenditures at the market level using the different timing of the introduction of reference pricing in the Nordic countries. They find that expenditure per dose decreases by 44% moving from the laxest to the strictest reference pricing regime.[5] In a survey of empirical studies from ten different

---

[5] Kortelainen et al. (2024) also consider potential adverse effects on product availability and total quantity, but find no significant effects on these outcomes due to the introduction of reference pricing in the Nordic countries.

countries, Galizzi et al. (2011) report that fourteen out of twenty-two studies found that reference pricing unambiguously led to lower prices, while the remaining eight studies found no or ambiguous effects.

In a study using Danish data, Kaiser et al. (2014) analyse the effects of a switch from exogenous to endogenous reference pricing and find strong negative price effects of around 20% on average, thus providing empirical support for the theoretical prediction of Brekke et al. (2011) regarding the pro-competitive effects of endogenous versus exogenous reference pricing.

Most of the referred empirical studies look at short-run price effects. A potential worry is that these effects might be counteracted in the longer run by changes in incentives for generic entry. In a theoretical study, Brekke et al. (2016) show that generic reference pricing leads to less generic entry and that a long-run increase in average drug prices cannot be ruled out. So far the empirical literature on reference pricing and generic entry is scant and somewhat inconclusive. Whereas Rudholm (2001) finds no significant effect of reference pricing on generic entry using Swedish data, Moreno-Torres et al. (2009) find a weak negative effect using Spanish data. In a study on the effects of price and reimbursement regulation more generally, Costa-Font et al. (2014) find that stricter regulation delays the adoption of generics. However, even if reference pricing reduces incentives for generic entry, it would arguably take a lot for such an indirect effect to outweigh the well-documented direct price-reducing effects.

4.3 Pharmaceutical Innovation

The availability of drug treatments crucially depends on pharmaceutical firms' incentives for developing these treatments in the first place. Such incentives are influenced by public policies both directly and indirectly. In an overview of different innovation policies, Kyle (2022) distinguishes between *pull* and *push* policies. Drug innovations can be incentivised by increasing the reward of the innovation (pull) or by reducing its cost (push), for example in the form of subsidies or tax breaks.

In this section we will start out by giving a brief description of the different roles played by the public sector and private agents in the development of new drug treatments, and how drug innovation is impacted by public funding, which is a key push policy. We will subsequently discuss the main pull policy, namely patent protection, and how it interacts with other regulatory instruments on the demand side of the market. Finally, we will briefly discuss some proposed alternatives to the patent system.

4.3.1 Public versus Private Involvement in Drug Innovation

Both the public and the private sector contribute to the development of new drug treatments, but generally in quite different ways. Whereas the private industry supplies most of the funds devoted to the R&D of drugs, the public sector supports most of the basic biomedical research (Sampat and Lichtenberg, 2011). The dominant role of the private sector is illustrated by Stevens et al. (2011), who document that only 9% of new drugs approved in the US between 1990 and 2007 were discovered by public sector research institutions.

However, this does not mean that public sector funding does not play an important role in pharmaceutical innovations, but rather that this role is predominantly indirect. Several studies show that the basic research undertaken by public institutions has a significant impact on private-sector drug innovation. For example, Toole (2012) finds that a 1% increase in the stock of public basic research leads to a 1.8% increase in the number of new molecular entities developed by private firms. In the same vein, Sampat and Lichtenberg (2011) find that public funding plays an indirect role in almost half of the new drugs approved, as measured by patent citations to government publications or public-sector patents. There is also evidence of a positive effect of more targeted public funding, in the form of research grants targeted to specific diseases, on private sector development of drug treatments for such diseases. For example, Blume-Kohout (2012) finds that a 10% increase in targeted funding yields eventually a 4.5% increase in the number of related drugs.

As stressed by Kyle (2022), the effectiveness of public funding and push policies in general rely crucially on the functioning of governments and relevant public agencies. Importantly, the efficient allocation of research funds requires extensive information acquisition and processing in order to identify the desired innovations and the necessary levels of funding. There are also other agency problems related to publicly funded R&D, such as susceptibility to political lobbying, which has been shown to affect the allocation of biomedical research funding in the US (e.g., Hedge, 2009).

4.3.2 Patent Protection

The predominant pull policy is patent protection, which grants a market reward to innovating firms in the form of market exclusivity for a given length of time. The rationale behind the patent system is at least to some extent supported by empirical evidence.[6] For example, Gaessler and Wagner (2022) exploit variation in the duration of market exclusivity for new drug development projects,

---

[6] See Kyle (2022) for a more thorough overview of the empirical evidence.

where this duration is lower in case of patent invalidation, and present estimates showing that a one-year loss in market exclusivity reduces the probability of drug approval by almost 5 percentage points. However, the evidence for a positive relationship between patent protection and drug innovation seems to be stronger for developed than for developing countries. For example, Kyle and McGahan (2012) find that the association between patent protection and R&D effort (as measured by the number of clinical trials) varies by country income level. They find evidence of a strong positive relationship for diseases that are prevalent in high-income countries, but do not find evidence of a similar relationship for diseases that are more prevalent in poorer countries.

Similar empirical evidence also exists for the relationship between patent protection and the diffusion of newly developed drugs. In a cross-country study on drug launches, Cockburn et al. (2016) find that longer and stronger patent protection leads to significantly quicker launches and thus accelerates the diffusion of new drugs. Qualitatively similar effects of patent protection on drug launches are also found by Dai and Watal (2021), but only for middle- and high-income countries. For low-income countries, patent protection does not seem to affect the availability of new drugs. Policies that grant market exclusivity for new drugs are also used to incentivise the development of more specific types of treatment. One example is the development of so-called 'orphan drugs' that are used to treat rare diseases (that affect a very small share of the population). A specific policy to stimulate the development of such drugs was first introduced in the US by the Orphan Drug Act of 1983, granting an exclusive seven-year marketing right. A similar policy was later adopted by the European Union, granting ten years of market exclusivity for orphan drugs. Sarpatwari et al. (2018) document that the number of drugs for treating rare diseases has increased substantially since the Orphan Drug Act was introduced. However, they also show that for a large (and increasing) share of newly developed orphan drugs, the orphan exclusivity expires before the relevant patent, suggesting perhaps that specific policies to stimulate the development of orphan drugs are to some extent superfluous. One contributing factor is that a relatively large share of orphan drugs without exclusivity lacks generic competition, since the low demand for such drugs makes generic entry less profitable.[7]

Although there is clear empirical evidence that patent protection stimulates drug innovation, the general effectiveness of the patent system depends on the degree of alignment between private and social incentives for drug innovation.

---

[7] In the study by Sarpatwari et al. (2018), around 60% of the orphan drugs whose market exclusivity had expired were without generic competition.

There are several market distortions that potentially make this alignment less than perfect. For example, the lack of insurance in developing countries likely contributes to the underinvestment in so-called neglected diseases (Kyle and McGahan, 2012). On the other hand, insurance can also create problems of ex-post moral hazard and thus lead to overconsumption and excessive pharmaceutical spending (Danzon and Pauly, 2002). Private incentives for drug innovation can also be distorted by the fact that some treatments generate externalities, leading to underconsumption in the case of positive externalities, which applies to vaccines (Geoffard and Philipson, 1997), and overconsumption in the case of negative externalities, which applies to antibiotics (Bennett et al., 2015).

Finally, there are also several potential distortions created by imperfect information about drug quality that might affect reimbursement decisions by payers and prescription decisions by physicians, which in turn might distort the incentives for developing the most effective treatments (Kyle, 2022). We will return to this issue in Section 4.3.4 when discussing incentives for developing me-too versus breakthrough drugs.

4.3.3 Price Regulation and Parallel Trade

In addition to the direct effects of the design of the patent system, innovation incentives might also be indirectly influenced by different regulatory policies that affect the value of a drug patent, such as price regulation, the design of reimbursement schemes, and policies on parallel trade.

Intuitively, price regulation reduces the value of a drug patent, all else equal, and is therefore likely to reduce incentives for drug innovation. Vernon (2005) identifies two theoretical mechanisms whereby price regulation might harm R&D incentives; firstly, through a lower expected return on R&D investments because of lower future profits, and secondly, through a higher marginal cost of R&D investments due to a cash flow effect caused by lower current profits. Based on quasi-structural estimations of US data, he also performs simulations showing that the introduction of price regulation (at the 'average level' in non-US markets) would reduce industry-level R&D spending by up to around 30%.

A related and much-debated issue is whether innovation incentives are negatively affected by parallel trade. Intuitively, parallel imports from low-price countries could undermine the patent-holder's ability to charge a high price in countries with a high willingness to pay for the drug and therefore reduce the value of the patent. However, this view has been challenged by Grossman and Lai (2008), who show that the possibility of parallel trade might induce the source countries to relax price regulation in order to ensure access to the drug, which in turn might increase the value of the patent and thereby stimulating innovation incentives. However, later studies have shown that this result hinges on the degree of policy commitment (Bennato and Valletti, 2014) and only holds if the trading countries are sufficiently similar in terms of drug demand (Reisinger et al., 2019).

The empirical evidence on the relationship between parallel trade and drug innovation is still lacking.

4.3.4 Me-too versus Breakthrough Drugs

A widely expressed concern is that too many resources are spent on developing so-called 'me-too' drugs with little therapeutic value added as compared to more innovative drugs. Indeed, 85–90% of new drugs have been shown to yield little or no advantages over existing therapeutic alternatives (Santos et al., 2019). Such concerns have also been given a theoretical foundation by González et al. (2016), who construct a model in which drugs can be both horizontally and vertically differentiated, and show that pharmaceutical firms have socially suboptimal incentives for spending resources on breakthrough innovations rather than me-too innovations. A similar conclusion is also reached by Brekke et al. (2022) based on a different type of framework.

Additional empirical evidence is provided by Kyle (2018), who analyses the relationship between therapeutic value and market rewards for new drugs, and finds that this relationship is weak. Given that the process of developing breakthrough drugs involves both higher costs and considerably more uncertainty, a lack of sufficient market rewards for breakthrough drugs suggests that drug innovation incentives are distorted in the direction of me-too drugs.

The market rewards for breakthrough versus me-too drugs might be affected by price regulation and reimbursement schemes. In particular, Bardey et al. (2010) have suggested that therapeutic reference pricing might be an effective instrument for steering resources away from me-too innovations and towards breakthrough innovations. The argument seems intuitively appealing. Under therapeutic reference pricing, me-too drugs will be subject to the same reference price as existing therapeutic alternatives, which leads to stronger therapeutic competition and therefore reduces the profitability of such drugs. As a result, pharmaceutical firms will have relatively more to gain by developing innovative drugs for which there are no existing therapeutic alternatives. However, Straume (2023) shows that this argument crucially relies on the premise that breakthrough innovations constitute a feasible option. If, instead, the relevant choices for an innovator consist of various degrees of differentiation from an existing drug within a given therapeutic category, therapeutic reference pricing has the opposite effect and leads to less differentiation (i.e., more me-too innovations).

4 3.5 Alternatives to the Patent System

Despite its potential limitations, the patent system is currently the dominating method of stimulating pharmaceutical innovations. The most commonly suggested alternatives to patents are patent buyouts (Kremer, 1998) or advanced market commitments (AMCs) (Kremer and Glennerster, 2004), where pharmaceutical firms are offered a certain monetary payment in return for unlimited access to a new drug. These types of *innovation prizes* have the appealing feature that they in principle overcome the problems of static inefficiency which is inherent in the current patent system, where patent-holding firms extract the patent rent by charging prices well above marginal costs. On the other hand, there are considerable problems related to informational asymmetries between payers and innovators in the design of such alternatives, which arguably make them less feasible in practice.

A closely related alternative to innovation prizes, which has been recently advocated, is to change the payment scheme for drugs, within the current patent system, from uniform pricing to two-part tariffs. Under a pricing scheme based on two-part tariffs, the (public or private) insurer pays a fixed fee in addition to a (much lower) per-unit price for the drug. Similarly to an innovation prize, a two-part tariff would in principle ensure drug access at a much lower marginal price and thereby alleviate the problem of static inefficiency without harming dynamic efficiency. The pros and cons of such an alternative payment scheme have recently been studied by Brekke et al. (2022), who find that the use of two-part tariffs, in addition to improving static efficiency, is also likely to steer innovation incentives away from me-too innovations and more towards the innovation of breakthrough drugs.

5 Conclusion

This Element has discussed the role of the government in health system financing and provision of public health care. Public health insurance is pervasive in high-income countries and growing in low and middle-income countries, and this is justified on both equity and efficiency grounds. Private health insurance coexists with public health insurance across a range of institutional arrangements. The interface between public and private insurance differs extensively across countries depending on whether private insurance is duplicative, complementary or supplementary. Countries also differ in the extent to which they experience and manage excess demands through co-payments or management of the waiting list. Such diversity of institutional settings gives extensive research opportunities for investigating and understanding the complexities of the health sector and health system financing. The Element also shows that the behaviour of healthcare providers responds to a range of financial incentives, and therefore its design can contribute to improving the quality and efficiency of health systems. Following the COVID-19 pandemic, health systems are under renewed pressure to increase the efficiency of health spending. Rigorous theoretical frameworks and existing evidence can inform future policy developments on both financing and provision. Last, the Element has highlighted a diverse set of interventions for regulating pharmaceutical markets, addressing both on-patent and off-patent drugs. For on-patent drugs, it highlighted the tension between, on the one hand, ensuring access to new and effective medicines and maintaining innovation incentives, and, on the other hand, managing expenditure growth and implementing regulatory measures for price control and cost containment. For off-patent drugs, the focus has been on the role of competition from generics and the impact of price interventions, such as direct price regulation or reference pricing schemes. Finally, the Element explored alternatives to the current patent system to enhance the rewards for innovation while ensuring that drugs remain accessible and affordable. These issues remain at the forefront of policy discussions to improve access to drugs around the globe.

References

Askildsen, J. E., Holmås, T. H., and Kaarboe, O., 2010. Prioritization and patients' rights: Analysing the effect of a reform in the Norwegian hospital sector. Social Science & Medicine, 70(2), pp. 199–208.

Askildsen, J. E., Holmås, T. H., and Kaarboe, O., 2011. Monitoring prioritisation in the public health-care sector by use of medical guidelines: The case of Norway. Health Economics, 20(8), pp. 958–970.

Auerbach, A. J. and Hines, J. R., 2002. Taxation and economic efficiency. In A. J. Auerbach and M. Feldstein, eds., Handbook of Public Economics. Amsterdam: Elsevier, pp. 1347–1421.

Avdic, D., Moscelli, G., Pilny, A., and Sriubaite, I., 2019. Subjective and objective quality and choice of hospital: Evidence from maternal care services in Germany. Journal of Health Economics, 68, p. 102229.

Baicker, K., Taubman, S. L., Allen, H. L., et al., 2013. The Oregon experiment – effects of medicaid on clinical outcomes. New England Journal of Medicine, 368(18), pp. 1713–1722.

Baicker, K., Mullainathan, S., and Schwartzstein, J., 2015. Behavioral hazard in health insurance. The Quarterly Journal of Economics, 130(4), pp. 1623–1667.

Barbaresco, S., Courtemanche, C. J., and Qi, Y., 2015. Impacts of the Affordable Care Act dependent coverage provision on health-related outcomes of young adults. Journal of Health Economics, 40, pp. 54–68.

Barbetta, G. P., Turati, G., and Zago, A. M., 2007. Behavioral differences between public and private not-for-profit hospitals in the Italian national health service. Health Economics, 16(1), pp. 75–96.

Bardey, D., Bommier, A., and Jullien, B., 2010. Retail price regulation and innovation: Reference pricing in the pharmaceutical industry. Journal of Health Economics, 29, pp. 303–316.

Barros, P. P. and Siciliani, L., 2011. Public and private sector interface. In Handbook of Health Economics (Vol. 2). Amsterdam: Elsevier, pp. 927–1001.

Batty, M. and Ippolito, B., 2017. Financial incentives, hospital care, and health outcomes: Evidence from fair pricing laws. American Economic Journal: Economic Policy, 9(2), pp. 28–56.

Bauhoff, S., 2012. Do health plans risk-select? An audit study on Germany's Social Health Insurance. Journal of Public Economics, 96(9–10), pp. 750–759.

Bauhoff, S., Hotchkiss, D. R., and Smith, O., 2011. The impact of medical insurance for the poor in Georgia: A regression discontinuity approach. Health Economics, 20(11), pp. 1362–1378.

Baumgartner, C. and Busato, A., 2012. Risikoselektion in der Grundversicherung. Schweizerische Ärztezeitung, 93, pp. 510–513.

Baxter, S., Johnson, M., Chambers, D., et al., 2018. The effects of integrated care: A systematic review of UK and international evidence. BMC Health Services Research, 18, pp. 1–13.

Beckert, W., Christensen, M., and Collyer, K., 2012. Choice of NHS-Funded hospital services in England. The Economic Journal, 122(560), pp. 400–417.

Bennato, A. R. and Valletti, T., 2014. Pharmaceutical innovation and parallel trade. International Journal of Industrial Organization, 33, pp. 83–92.

Bennett, D., Hung, C.-L., and Lauderdale, T.-L., 2015. Health care competition and antibiotic use in Taiwan. Journal of Industrial Economics, 63(2), pp. 371–393.

Bernal, N., Carpio, M. A., and Klein, T. J., 2017. The effects of access to health insurance: Evidence from a regression discontinuity design in Peru. Journal of Public Economics, 154, pp. 122–136.

Berta, P., Martini, G., Moscone, F., and Vittadini, G., 2016. The association between asymmetric information, hospital competition and quality of health-care: Evidence from Italy. Journal of the Royal Statistical Society Series A: Statistics in Society, 179(4), pp. 907–926.

Beukers, P. D., Kemp, R. G., and Varkevisser, M., 2014. Patient hospital choice for hip replacement: Empirical evidence from the Netherlands. The European Journal of Health Economics, 15, pp. 927–936.

Biglaiser, G. and Ma, C. T. A., 2003. Price and quality competition under adverse selection: Market organization and efficiency. RAND Journal of Economics, 34(2), pp. 266–286.

Birg, L., 2023. Pharmaceutical regulation under market integration through parallel trade. Canadian Journal of Economics, 56, pp. 1322–1346.

Bloom, N., Propper, C., Seiler, S., and Van Reenen, J., 2015. The impact of competition on management quality: Evidence from public hospitals. The Review of Economic Studies, 82(2), pp. 457–489.

Blume-Kohout, M. E., 2012. Does targeted, disease-specific public research funding influence pharmaceutical innovation? Journal of Policy Analysis and Management, 31(3), pp. 641–660.

Brekke, K. R., Königbauer, I., and Straume, O. R., 2007. Reference pricing of pharmaceuticals. Journal of Health Economics, 26, pp. 613–642.

Brekke, K. R., Siciliani, L., and Straume, O. R., 2011a. Hospital competition and quality with regulated prices. Scandinavian Journal of Economics, 113(2), pp. 444–469.

Brekke, K. R., Holmås, T. H., and Straume, O. R., 2011b. Reference pricing, competition, and pharmaceutical expenditures: Theory and evidence from a natural experiment. Journal of Public Economics, 95, pp. 624–638.

Brekke, K. R., Siciliani, L., and Straume, O. R., 2012. Quality competition with profit constraints. Journal of Economic Behavior & Organization, 84(2), pp. 642–659.

Brekke, K. R., Holmås, T. H., and Straume, O. R., 2013. Margins and market shares: Pharmacy incentives for generic substitution. European Economic Review, 61, pp. 116–131.

Brekke, K. R., Siciliani, L., and Straume, O. R., 2015a. Hospital competition with soft budgets. The Scandinavian Journal of Economics, 117(3), pp. 1019–1048.

Brekke, K. R., Holmås, and Straume, O. R., 2015b. Price regulation and parallel imports of pharmaceuticals. Journal of Public Economics, 129, pp. 92–105.

Brekke, K. R., Canta, C., and Straume, O. R., 2016. Reference pricing with endogenous generic entry. Journal of Health Economics, 50, pp. 312–329.

Brekke, K. R. and Straume, O. R., 2017. Competition policy for health care provision in Norway. Health Policy, 121(2), pp. 134–140.

Brekke, K. R., Holmås, T. H., Monstad, K., and Straume, O. R., 2018. Socio-economic status and physicians' treatment decisions. Health Economics, 27(3), pp. e77–e89.

Brekke, K. R., Canta, C., Siciliani, L., and Straume, O. R., 2021. Hospital competition in a national health service: Evidence from a patient choice reform. Journal of Health Economics, 79, p. 102509.

Brekke, K. R., Dalen, D. M., and Straume, O. R., 2022. Paying for pharmaceuticals: Uniform pricing versus two-part tariffs. Journal of Health Economics, 83, p. 102613.

Brekke, K. R., Dalen, D. M., and Straume, O. R., 2023. The price of cost-effectiveness threshold under therapeutic competition in pharmaceutical markets. Journal of Health Economics, 90, p. 102778.

Brekke, K. R., Siciliani, L., and Straume, O. R., 2024. Competition, quality and integrated health care. Journal of Health Economics, 95, p. 102880.

Breyer, F., Bundorf, M. K., and Pauly, M. V., 2011. Health care spending risk, health insurance, and payment to health plans. In Handbook of Health Economics. Elsevier BV, pp. 691–762.

Brook, R. H., Keeler, E. B., and Lohr, K. N. 2006. The Health Insurance Experiment – A Classic RAND Study Speaks to the Current Health Care Reform Debate, RAND. www.rand.org/content/dam/rand/pubs/research_briefs/2006/RAND_RB9174.pdf.

Bruni, M. L., Ugolini, C., and Verzulli, R., 2021. Should I wait or should I go? Travelling versus waiting for better healthcare. Regional Science and Urban Economics, 89, p. 103697.

Cashin, C., Chi, Y. L., Borowitz, M., and Thompson, S., 2014. Paying for Performance in Healthcare: Implications for Health System Performance and Accountability. Berkshire: McGraw-Hill Education.

Chalkley, M. and Malcomson, J. M., 1998a. Contracting for health services with unmonitored quality. The Economic Journal, 108(449), pp. 1093–1110.

Chalkley, M. and Malcomson, J. M., 1998b. Contracting for health services when patient demand does not reflect quality. Journal of Health Economics, 17(1), pp. 1–19.

Chang, S., 2012. The effect of Taiwan's national health insurance on mortality of the elderly: Revisited. Health Economics, 21(11), pp. 1257–1270.

Chard, J., Kuczawski, M., Black, N., and Van der Meulen, J., 2011. Outcomes of elective surgery undertaken in independent sector treatment centres and NHS providers in England: Audit of patient outcomes in surgery. British Medical Journal, 343: d6404, https://www.bmj.com/content/343/bmj.d6404.

Chen, L., Yip, W., Chang, M. C., et al., 2007. The effects of Taiwan's National Health Insurance on access and health status of the elderly. Health Economics, 16(3), pp. 223–242.

Chernew, M. E., Rosen, A. B., and Fendrick, A. M., 2007. Value-based insurance design. Health Affairs, 26(2), pp. w195–w203.

Chou, S. Y., Grossman, M., and Liu, J. T., 2014. The impact of national health insurance on birth outcomes: A natural experiment in Taiwan. Journal of Development Economics, 111, pp. 75–91.

Clemens, J. and Gottlieb, J. D., 2014. Do physicians' financial incentives affect medical treatment and patient health? American Economic Review, 104(4), pp. 1320–1349.

Cockburn, I. M., Lanjouw, J. O., and Schankerman, M., 2016. Patents and the global diffusion of new drugs. American Economic Review, 106, pp. 136–164.

Cooper, Z., Gibbons, S., Jones, S., and McGuire, A., 2011. Does hospital competition save lives? Evidence from the English NHS patient choice reforms. The Economic Journal, 121(554), pp. F228–F260.

Cooper, Z., Gibbons, S., and Skellern, M., 2018. Does competition from private surgical centres improve public hospitals' performance? Evidence from the English National Health Service. Journal of Public Economics, 166, pp. 63–80.

Costa-Font, J., McGuire, A., and Varol, N., 2014. Price regulation and relative delays in generic drug adoption. Journal of Health Economics, 38, pp. 1–9.

Cremer, H. and Pestieau, P., 1996. Redistributive Taxation and Social Insurance. International Tax and Public Finance, 3, pp. 281–295. https://doi.org/10.1007/BF00418945.

Cutler, D. M. and Zeckhauser, R. J., 2000. The anatomy of health insurance. In Handbook of Health Economics (Vol. 1). Amsterdam: Elsevier, pp. 563–643.

Dafny, L. S., 2005. How do hospitals respond to price changes? American Economic Review, 95(5), pp. 1525–1547.

Dai, R. and Watal, J., 2021. Product patents and access to innovative medicines. Social Science & Medicine, 291, p. 114479.

Danzon, P. M. and Pauly, M. V., 2002. Health insurance and the growth in pharmaceutical expenditures. Journal of Law and Economics, 45(S2), pp. 587–613.

Danzon, P. M., Towse, A., and Mestre-Ferrandiz, J., 2015. Value-based differential pricing: Efficient pricing for drugs in a global context. Health Economics, 24(3), pp. 294–301.

De Meza, D., 1983. Health insurance and the demand for medical care. Journal of Health Economics, 2(1), pp. 47–54.

De Pietro, C., Camenzind, P., Sturny, I., et al., 2015. Switzerland: Health system review. Health Systems in Transition, 17(4), pp. 1–288.

De Preux, L. B., 2011. Anticipatory ex ante moral hazard and the effect of Medicare on prevention. Health Economics, 20(9), pp. 1056–1072.

Di Giacomo, M., Piacenza, M., Siciliani, L., and Turati, G., 2022. The effect of co-payments on the take-up of prenatal tests. Journal of Health Economics, 81, p. 102553.

Dubois, P. and Sæthre, M., 2020. On the effect of parallel trade on manufacturers' and retailers' profits in the pharmaceutical sector. Econometrica, 88, pp. 2503–2545.

Duso, T., Herr, A., and Suppliet, M., 2014. The welfare impact of parallel imports: A structural approach applied to the German market for oral anti-diabetics. Health Economics, 23, pp. 1036–1057.

Eggleston, K., 2005. Multitasking and mixed systems for provider payment. Journal of Health Economics, 24(1), pp. 211–223.

Eggleston, K., Shen, Y. C., Lau, J., Schmid, C. H., and Chan, J., 2008. Hospital ownership and quality of care: What explains the different results in the literature? Health Economics, 17(12), pp. 1345–1362.

Ellis, R. P. and McGuire, T. G., 1986. Provider behavior under prospective reimbursement: Cost sharing and supply. Journal of Health Economics, 5(2), pp. 129–151.

Ellis, R. P. and McGuire, T. G., 1990. Optimal payment systems for health services. Journal of Health Economics, 9(4), pp. 375–396.

Epple, D. and Romano, R. E., 1996. Ends against the middle: Determining public service provision when there are private alternatives. Journal of Public Economics, 62(3), pp. 297–325.

Evans, R. G., 2002. Financing healthcare: Taxation and the alternatives. In E. A. Mossialos, A. Dixon, J. Figueras, and J. Kutzin, eds., Funding Health Care: Options for Europe. Buckingham: Open University, pp. 31–58.

Farrar, S., Yi, D., Sutton, M. et al., 2009. Has payment by results affected the way that English hospitals provide care? Difference-in-differences analysis. British Medical Journal, 339, pp. 1–8.

Feldman, R. and Dowd, B., 1991. A new estimate of the welfare loss of excess health insurance. American Economic Review, 81(1), pp. 297–301.

Finkelstein, A., Taubman, S., Wright, B., et al., 2012. The Oregon health insurance experiment: Evidence from the first year. The Quarterly Journal of Economics, 127(3), pp. 1057–1106.

Foo, P. K., Lee, R. S., and Fong, K., 2017. Physician prices, hospital prices, and treatment choice in labor and delivery. American Journal of Health Economics, 3(3), pp. 422–453.

Frank, R. G. and Salkever, D. S., 1992. Pricing, patent loss and the market for pharmaceuticals. Southern Economic Journal, 59, pp. 165–179.

Frank, R. G. and Salkever, D. S., 1997. Generic entry and the pricing of pharmaceuticals. Journal of Economics & Management Strategy, 6, pp. 75–90.

Gaessler, F. and Wagner, S., 2022. Patents, data exclusivity, and the development of new drugs. Review of Economics & Statistics, 104, pp. 571–586.

Galizzi, M. M., Ghislandi, S., and Miraldo, M., 2011. Effects of reference pricing in pharmaceutical markets: A review. Pharmacoeconomics, 29, pp. 17–33.

Ganslandt, M. and Maskus, K. E., 2004. Parallel imports and the pricing of pharmaceutical products: Evidence from the European Union. Journal of Health Economics, 23, pp. 1035–1057.

Garcia Mariñoso, B., Jelovac, I., and Olivella, P., 2011. External referencing and pharmaceutical price negotiation. Health Economics, 20, pp. 737–756.

Gaughan, J., Gravelle, H., and Siciliani, L., 2015. Testing the bed-blocking hypothesis: Does nursing and care home supply reduce delayed hospital discharges? Health Economics, 24, pp. 32–44.

Gaughan, J., Gutacker, N., Grašič, K., et al., 2019. Paying for efficiency: Incentivising same-day discharges in the English NHS. Journal of Health Economics, 68, p. 102226.

Gaynor, M., 2007. Competition and quality in health care markets. Foundations and Trends® in Microeconomics, 2(6), pp. 441–508.

Gaynor, M. and Town, R. J., 2011. Competition in health care markets. Handbook of Health Economics, 2, pp. 499–637.

Gaynor, M., Moreno-Serra, R., and Propper, C., 2013. Death by market power: Reform, competition, and patient outcomes in the National Health Service. American Economic Journal: Economic Policy, 5(4), pp. 134–166.

Gaynor, M., Propper, C., and Seiler, S., 2016. Free to choose? Reform, choice, and consideration sets in the English National Health Service. American Economic Review, 106(11), pp. 3521–3557.

Ge, G., Iversen, T., Kaarbøe, O., and Snilsberg, Ø., 2024. Impacts of Norway's extended free choice reform on waiting times and hospital visits. Health Economics, 33(4), pp. 779–803.

Geng, D. and Saggi, K., 2017. International effects of national regulations: External reference pricing and price controls. Journal of International Economics, 109, pp. 68–84.

Geoffard, P.-Y. and Philipson, T., 1997. Disease eradication: Private versus public vaccination. American Economic Review, 87(1), pp. 222–230.

Ghislandi, S., 2011. Competition and the reference pricing scheme for pharmaceuticals. Journal of Health Economics, 30, pp. 1137–1149.

Glaeser, E. L. and Shleifer, A., 2001. Not-for-profit entrepreneurs. Journal of Public Economics, 81(1), pp. 99–115.

Godøy, A., Haaland, V. F., Huitfeldt, I., and Votruba, M., 2024. Hospital queues, patient health, and labor supply. American Economic Journal: Economic Policy, 16(2), pp. 150–181.

Gonçalves, R. and Rodrigues, V., 2018. Reference pricing with elastic demand for pharmaceuticals. Scandinavian Journal of Economics, 120, pp. 159–182.

González, P., Macho-Stadler, I., and Pérez-Castrillo, D., 2016. Private versus social incentives for pharmaceutical innovation. Journal of Health Economics, 50, pp. 286–297.

Gowrisankaran, G. and Town, R. J., 2003. Competition, payers, and hospital quality 1. Health Services Research, 38(6p1), pp. 1403–1422.

Grabowski, H. G. and Vernon, J. M., 1992. Brand loyalty, entry, and price competition in pharmaceuticals after the 1984 Drug Act. Journal of Law and Economics, 35, pp. 331–350.

Granlund, D. and Bergman, M. A., 2018. Price competition in pharmaceuticals – Evidence from 1303 Swedish markets. Journal of Health Economics, 61, pp. 1–12.

Gravelle, H., Smith, P., and Xavier, A., 2003. Performance signals in the public sector: The case of health care. Oxford Economic Papers, 55(1), pp. 81–103.

Gravelle, H. and Siciliani, L., 2008. Is waiting-time prioritisation welfare improving? Health Economics, 17(2), pp. 167–184.

Gravelle, H., Sutton, M., and Ma, A., 2010. Doctor behaviour under a pay for performance contract: Treating, cheating and case finding? *The Economic Journal*, 120(542), pp. F129–F156.

Grossman, G. M. and Lai, E. L.-C., 2008. Parallel imports and price controls. RAND Journal of Economics, 39, pp. 378–402.

Gupta, A., 2021. Impacts of performance pay for hospitals: The readmissions reduction program. American Economic Review, 111(4), pp. 1241–1283.

Gutacker, N., Siciliani, L., and Cookson, R., 2016a. Waiting time prioritisation: Evidence from England. Social Science & Medicine, 159, pp. 140–151.

Gutacker, N., Siciliani, L., Moscelli, G., and Gravelle, H., 2016b. Choice of hospital: Which type of quality matters? Journal of Health Economics, 50, pp. 230–246.

Hafsteinsdottir, E. J. G. and Siciliani, L., 2010. DRG prospective payment systems: Refine or not refine? Health Economics, 19(10), pp. 1226–1239.

Hall, J., Fiebig, D. G., and Van Gool, K., 2020. Private finance publicly subsidized: The case of Australian health insurance. In Private Health Insurance. Cambridge: Cambridge University Press, pp. 41–64.

Hedge, D., 2009. Political influence behind the veil of peer review: An analysis of public biomedical research funding in the United States. Journal of Law and Economics, 52(4), pp. 665–690.

Herr, A., 2008. Cost and technical efficiency of German hospitals: Does ownership matter? Health Economics, 17(9), pp. 1057–1071.

Herr, A., Schmitz, H., and Augurzky, B., 2011. Profit efficiency and ownership of German hospitals. Health Economics, 20(6), pp. 660–674.

Hollingsworth, B., 2008. The measurement of efficiency and productivity of health care delivery. Health Economics, 17(10), pp. 1107–1128.

Holmstrom, B. and Milgrom, P., 1991. Multitask principal–agent analyses: Incentive contracts, asset ownership, and job design. The Journal of Law, Economics, and Organization, 7(special issue), pp. 24–52.

Iizuka, T., 2012. Physician agency and adoption of generic pharmaceutical. American Economic Review, 102, pp. 2826–2858.

Ito, Y., Hara, K., and Kobayashi, Y., 2020. The effect of inertia on brand-name versus generic drug choices. Journal of Economic Behavior & Organization, 172, pp. 364–379.

Iversen, T., 1997. The effect of a private sector on the waiting time in a national health service. Journal of Health Economics, 16(4), pp. 381–396.

Januleviciute, J., Askildsen, J. E., Kaarboe, O., Siciliani, L., and Sutton, M., 2016. How do hospitals respond to price changes? Evidence from Norway. Health Economics, 25(5), pp. 620–636.

Jensen, P. H., Webster, E., and Witt, J., 2009. Hospital type and patient outcomes: An empirical examination using AMI readmission and mortality records. Health Economics, 18(12), pp. 1440–1460.

Johar, M., Jones, G., Keane, M. P., Savage, E., and Stavrunova, O., 2013. Discrimination in a universal health system: Explaining socioeconomic waiting time gaps. Journal of Health Economics, 32(1), pp. 181–194.

Kaarboe, O. and Siciliani, L., 2011. Multi-tasking, quality and pay for performance. Health Economics, 20(2), pp. 225–238.

Kaarboe, O. and Carlsen, F., 2014. Waiting times and socioeconomic status: Evidence from Norway. Health Economics, 23(1), pp. 93–107.

Kaiser, U., Mendez, S. J., Rønde, T., and Ullrich, H., 2014. Regulation of pharmaceutical prices: Evidence from a reference price reform in Denmark. Journal of Health Economics, 36, pp. 174–187.

Keng, S.-H. and Sheu, S.-J., 2013. The effect of national health insurance on mortality and the SES-health gradient: Evidence from the elderly in Taiwan. Health Economics, 22(1), pp. 52–72.

Kessler, D. P. and McClellan, M. B., 2000. Is hospital competition socially wasteful? The Quarterly Journal of Economics, 115(2), pp. 577–615.

Kessler, D. P. and Geppert, J. J., 2005. The effects of competition on variation in the quality and cost of medical care. Journal of Economics & Management Strategy, 14(3), pp. 575–589.

Kifmann, M., 2017. Competition policy for health care provision in Germany. Health Policy, 121(2), pp. 119–125.

Kifmann, M. and Siciliani, L., 2017. Average-cost pricing and dynamic selection incentives in the hospital sector. Health Economics, 26(12), pp. 1566–1582.

Konetzka, R. T., Stuart, E. A., and Werner, R. M., 2018. The effect of integration of hospitals and post-acute care providers on Medicare payment and patient outcomes. Journal of Health Economics, 61, pp. 244–258.

Kortelainen, M., Markkanen, J., Siikanen, M., and Toivanen, O., 2024. The effects of price regulation on pharmaceutical expenditure and availability. CEPR working paper DP18497.

Kremer, M. R., 1998. Patent buyouts: A mechanism for encouraging innovation. Quarterly Journal of Economics, 113, pp. 1137–1167.

Kremer, M. and Glennerster, R., 2004. Strong Medicine: Creating Incentives for Pharmaceutical Research on Neglected Diseases. Princeton: Princeton University Press.

Kreutzberg, A., Eckhardt, H., Milstein, R., and Busse, R., 2023. International strategies, experiences, and payment models to incentivise day surgery. Health Policy, 140, p. 104968.

Kristensen, S. R., Siciliani, L., and Sutton, M., 2016. Optimal price-setting in pay for performance schemes in health care. Journal of Economic Behavior & Organization, 123, pp. 57–77.

Kroneman, M., Boerma, W., Van Den Berg, M., et al., 2016. The Netherlands: Health system review. Health Systems in Transition, 18(2), pp. 1–239.

Kruse, F. M., Stadhouders, N. W., Adang, E. M., Groenewoud, S., and Jeurissen, P. P., 2018. Do private hospitals outperform public hospitals regarding efficiency, accessibility, and quality of care in the European Union? A literature review. The International Journal of Health Planning and Management, 33(2), pp. e434–e453.

Kuhn, M. and Siciliani, L., 2009. Performance indicators for quality with costly falsification. Journal of Economics & Management Strategy, 18(4), pp. 1137–1154.

Kuklinski, D., Vogel, J., and Geissler, A., 2021. The impact of quality on hospital choice. Which information affects patients' behavior for colorectal resection or knee replacement? Health Care Management Science, 24, pp. 185–202.

Kyle, M. K., 2007. Pharmaceutical price controls and entry strategies. Review of Economics & Statistics, 89, 88–99.

Kyle, M. K., 2018. Are important innovations rewarded? Evidence from pharmaceutical markets. Review of Industrial Organization, 53, pp. 211–234.

Kyle, M. K., 2022. Incentives for pharmaceutical innovation: What's working, what's lacking. International Journal of Industrial Organization, 84, p. 102850.

Kyle, M. K. and McGahan, A. M., 2012. Investments in pharmaceuticals before and after TRIPS. Review of Economics & Statistics, 94, pp. 1157–1172.

Laudicella, M., Siciliani, L., and Cookson, R., 2012. Waiting times and socioeconomic status: Evidence from England. Social Science & Medicine, 74(9), pp. 1331–1341.

Laudicella, M., Donni, P. L., and Smith, P. C., 2013. Hospital readmission rates: Signal of failure or success? Journal of Health Economics, 32(5), pp. 909–921.

Lee, Y.-C., Huang, Y. T., Tsai, Y. W., et al., 2010. The impact of universal National Health Insurance on population health: The experience of Taiwan. BMC Health Services Research, 10(1), pp. 1–8.

Lien, H. M., Chou, S. Y., and Liu, J. T., 2008. Hospital ownership and performance: Evidence from stroke and cardiac treatment in Taiwan. Journal of Health Economics, 27(5), pp. 1208–1223.

Limwattananon, S., Neelsen, S., O'Donnell, O., et al., 2015. Universal coverage with supply-side reform: The impact on medical expenditure risk and utilization in Thailand. Journal of Public Economics, 121, pp. 79–94.

Lisi, D., Siciliani, L., and Straume, O. R., 2020. Hospital competition under pay-for-performance: Quality, mortality, and readmissions. Journal of Economics & Management Strategy, 29(2), pp. 289–314.

Luyten, E. and Tubeuf, S., 2024. Equity in healthcare financing: A review of evidence. Health Policy, 152, p. 105218.

Ma, C. T. A., 1994. Health care payment systems: Cost and quality incentives. Journal of Economics & Management Strategy, 3(1), pp. 93–112.

Ma, Y., Nolan, A., and Smith, J. P., 2020. Free GP care and psychological health: Quasi-experimental evidence from Ireland. Journal of Health Economics, 72, p. 102351.

Maini, L. and Pammolli, F., 2023. Reference pricing as a deterrent to entry: Evidence from the European Pharmaceutical Market. American Economic Journal: Microeconomics, 15, pp. 345–383.

Manning, W. G., Newhouse, J.P., Duan, N., Keeler, E.B., and Leibowitz, A., 1987. Health insurance and the demand for medical care: Evidence from a randomized experiment. American Economic Review, 77, pp. 251–277.

Marini, G., Miraldo, M., Jacobs, R., and Goddard, M., 2008. Giving greater financial independence to hospitals – does it make a difference? The case of English NHS trusts. Health Economics, 17(6), pp. 751–775.

Martin, S. and Smith, P. C., 1999. Rationing by waiting lists: An empirical investigation. Journal of Public Economics, 71(1), pp. 141–164.

Martin, S. and Smith, P. C., 2003. Using panel methods to model waiting times for National Health Service surgery. Journal of the Royal Statistical Society Series A: Statistics in Society, 166(3), pp. 369–387.

Martin, S., Rice, N., Jacobs, R., and Smith, P., 2007. The market for elective surgery: Joint estimation of supply and demand. Journal of Health Economics, 26(2), pp. 263–285.

McClellan, M., 1997. Hospital reimbursement incentives: An empirical analysis. Journal of Economics & Management Strategy, 6(1), pp. 91–128.

McGuire, T. G., 2011. Demand for health insurance. Handbook of Health Economics, 2, pp. 317–396.

Mellor, J., Daly, M., and Smith, M., 2017. Does it pay to penalize hospitals for excess readmissions? Intended and unintended consequences of Medicare's Hospital Readmissions Reductions Program. Health Economics, 26(8), pp. 1037–1051.

Mendelson, A., Kondo, K., Damberg, C., et al., 2017. The effects of pay-for-performance programs on health, health care use, and processes of care: A systematic review. Annals of Internal Medicine, 166(5), pp. 341–353.

Milcent, C., 2005. Hospital ownership, reimbursement systems and mortality rates. Health Economics, 14(11), pp. 1151–1168.

Milstein, R. and Schreyoegg, J., 2016. Pay for performance in the inpatient sector: A review of 34 P4P programs in 14 OECD countries. Health Policy, 120(10), pp. 1125–1140.

Mohanan, M., Donato, K., Miller, G., Truskinovsky, Y., and Vera-Hernández, M., 2021. Different strokes for different folks? Experimental evidence on the effectiveness of input and output incentive contracts for health care providers with varying skills. American Economic Journal: Applied Economics, 13(4), pp. 34–69.

Monstad, K., Engesæter, L. B., and Espehaug, B., 2014. Waiting time and socioeconomic status – An individual-level analysis. Health Economics, 23(4), pp. 446–461.

Morciano, M., Checkland, K., Billings, J. et al., 2020. New integrated care models in England associated with small reduction in hospital admissions in longer-term: A difference-in-differences analysis. Health Policy, 124(8), pp. 826–833.

Moreno-Torres, I., Puig-Junoy, J., and Borrell, J.-R., 2009. Generic entry into the regulated Spanish pharmaceutical market. Review of Industrial Organization, 34, pp. 373–388.

Moscelli, G., Siciliani, L., and Tonei, V., 2016a. Do waiting times affect health outcomes? Evidence from coronary bypass. Social Science & Medicine, 161, pp. 151–159.

Moscelli, G., Siciliani, L., Gutacker, N., and Gravelle, H., 2016b. Location, quality and choice of hospital: Evidence from England 2002–2013. Regional Science and Urban Economics, 60, pp. 112–124.

Moscelli, G., Gravelle, H., Siciliani, L., and Santos, R., 2018a. Heterogeneous effects of patient choice and hospital competition on mortality. Social Science & Medicine, 216, pp. 50–58.

Moscelli, G., Gravelle, H., Siciliani, L., and Gutacker, N., 2018b. The effect of hospital ownership on quality of care: Evidence from England. Journal of Economic Behavior & Organization, 153, pp. 322–344.

Moscelli, G., Siciliani, L., Gutacker, N., and Cookson, R., 2018c. Socioeconomic inequality of access to healthcare: Does choice explain the gradient? Journal of Health Economics, 57, pp. 290–314.

Moscelli, G., Gravelle, H., and Siciliani, L., 2021. Hospital competition and quality for non-emergency patients in the English NHS. The RAND Journal of Economics, 52(2), pp. 382–414.

Moscone, F., Siciliani, L., Tosetti, E., and Vittadini, G., 2020. Do public and private hospitals differ in quality? Evidence from Italy. Regional Science and Urban Economics, 83, p. 103523.

Nikolova, S., Harrison, M., and Sutton, M., 2016. The impact of waiting time on health gains from surgery: Evidence from a national patient-reported outcome dataset. Health Economics, 25(8), pp. 955–968.

Nyman, J. A., Koc, C., Dowd, B. E., McCreedy, E., and Trenz, H. M., 2018. Decomposition of moral hazard. Journal of Health Economics, 57, pp. 168–178.

Nyman, J. A., 1999a. The value of health insurance: The access motive. Journal of Health Economics, 18, pp. 141–152.

Nyman, J. A., 1999b. The economics of moral hazard revisited. Journal of Health Economics, 18, pp. 811–824.

OECD, 2013. Waiting Time Policies in the Health Sector What Works? OECD Health Policy Studies.

OECD, 2020. Waiting Times for Health Services: Next in Line. OECD Health Policy Studies.

OECD, 2023. Health at a Glance 2023: OECD Indicators, Paris, https://doi.org/10.1787/7a7afb35-en.

Or, Z., Rococco, E., Touré, M., and Bonastre, J., 2022. Impact of competition versus centralisation of hospital care on process quality: A multilevel analysis of breast cancer surgery in France. International Journal of Health Policy and Management, 11(4), pp. 459–469.

Panhans, M., 2019. Adverse selection in ACA exchange markets: Evidence from Colorado. American Economic Journal: Applied Economics, 11(2), pp. 1–36.

Papanicolas, I. and McGuire, A., 2015. Do financial incentives trump clinical guidance? Hip replacement in England and Scotland. Journal of Health Economics, 44, pp. 25–36.

Paris, V. and Belloni, A., 2013. Value in pharmaceutical pricing. OECD Health Working Paper no. 63.

Pecorino, P., 2002. Should the US allow prescription drug reimports from Canada? Journal of Health Economics, 21, pp. 699–708.

Pérotin, V., Zamora, B., Reeves, R., Bartlett, W., and Allen, P., 2013. Does hospital ownership affect patient experience? An investigation into public–private sector differences in England. Journal of Health Economics, 32(3), pp. 633–646.

Pinchbeck, E. W., 2019. Convenient primary care and emergency hospital utilisation. Journal of Health Economics, 68, p. 102242.

Propper, C., Burgess, S., and Green, K., 2004. Does competition between hospitals improve the quality of care? Hospital death rates and the NHS internal market. Journal of Public Economics, 88(7–8), pp. 1247–1272.

Propper, C., Sutton, M., Whitnall, C., and Windmeijer, F., 2008a. Did 'targets and terror' reduce waiting times in England for hospital care? The BE Journal of Economic Analysis & Policy, 8(2), pp. 1–25.

Propper, C., Burgess, S., and Gossage, D., 2008b. Competition and quality: Evidence from the NHS internal market 1991–9. The Economic Journal, 118(525), pp. 138–170.

Propper, C., Sutton, M., Whitnall, C., and Windmeijer, F., 2010. Incentives and targets in hospital care: Evidence from a natural experiment. Journal of Public Economics, 94(3–4), pp. 318–335.

Rawls, J., 1971. A Theory of Justice, Cambridge, MA: Belknap Press of Harvard University Press. Retrieved from https://philpapers.org/rec/RAWATO-4.

Regan, T. L., 2008. Generic entry, price competition, and market segmentation in the prescription drug market. International Journal of Industrial Organization, 26, pp. 930–948.

Reisinger, M., Saurí, L., and Zenger, H., 2019. Parallel imports, price controls, and innovation. Journal of Health Economics, 66, pp. 163–179.

Riganti, A., Siciliani, L., and Fiorio, C. V., 2017. The effect of waiting times on demand and supply for elective surgery: Evidence from Italy. Health Economics, 26, pp. 92–105.

Roos, A. F., O'Donnell, O., Schut, F. T. et al., 2020. Does price deregulation in a competitive hospital market damage quality? Journal of Health Economics, 72, p. 102328.

Rothschild, M. and Stiglitz, J., 1976. Imperfect information. The Quarterly Journal of Economics, 90(4), pp. 629–649.

Roy, S. and Saggi, K., 2012. Equilibrium parallel import policies and international market structure. Journal of International Economics, 87, pp. 262–276.

Rudholm, N., 2001. Entry and the number of firms in the Swedish pharmaceutical market. Review of Industrial Organization, 19, pp. 351–364.

Sampat, B. N. and Lichtenberg, F. R., 2011. What are the respective roles of the public and private sectors in pharmaceutical innovation? Health Affairs, 30(2), pp. 332–339.

Santos, R., Gravelle, H., and Propper, C., 2017. Does quality affect patients' choice of doctor? Evidence from England. The Economic Journal, 127(600), pp. 445–494.

Santos, A. S., Guerra-Junior, A. A., de Sousa Noronha, K. V. M., Andrade, M. V., and Ruas, C. M., 2019. The price of substitute technologies. Value in Health Regional Issues, 20, pp. 154–158.

Sarpatwari, A., Beall, R. F., Abdurrob, A., He, M., and Kesselheim, A. S., 2018. Evaluating the impact of the Orphan Drug Act's seven-year market exclusivity period. Health Affairs, 37(5), pp. 732–737.

Schut, F. T. and Varkevisser, M., 2017. Competition policy for health care provision in the Netherlands. Health Policy, 121(2), pp. 126–133.

Sharma, A., Siciliani, L., and Harris, A., 2013. Waiting times and socioeconomic status: Does sample selection matter? Economic Modelling, 33, pp. 659–667.

Shen, Y. C., 2002. The effect of hospital ownership choice on patient outcomes after treatment for acute myocardial infarction. Journal of Health Economics, 21(5), pp. 901–922.

Shin, E., 2019. Hospital responses to price shocks under the prospective payment system. Health Economics, 28(2), pp. 245–260.

Siciliani, L., 2009. Paying for performance and motivation crowding out. Economics Letters, 103(2), pp. 68–71.

Siciliani, L., 2014. Rationing of demand. In A. J. Culyer, ed., Encyclopedia of Health Economics. Amsterdam: Newnes.

Siciliani, L., Chalkley, M., and Gravelle, H., 2022. Does provider competition improve health care quality and efficiency? Expectations and evidence from Europe, Policy Brief n.48, European Observatory of Health Systems and Policies, pp. 1–35.

Simon, K., Soni, A., and Cawley, J., 2017. The impact of health insurance on preventive care and health behaviors: Evidence from the first two years of the ACA Medicaid expansions. Journal of Policy Analysis and Management, 36(2), pp. 390–417.

Siu, A. L., Sonnenberg, F. A., Manning, W. G., et al., 1986. Inappropriate use of hospitals in a randomized trial of health insurance plans. New England Journal of Medicine, 315(20), pp. 1259–1266

Sloan, F. A., 2000. Not-for-profit ownership and hospital behavior. Handbook of Health Economics, 1, pp. 1141–1174.

Sparrow, R., Suryahadi, A., and Widyanti, W., 2013. Social health insurance for the poor: Targeting and impact of Indonesia's Askeskin programme. Social Science & Medicine, 96, pp. 264–271.

Stavrunova, O. and Yerokhin, O., 2011. An equilibrium model of waiting times for elective surgery in NSW public hospitals. Economic Record, 87(278), pp. 384–398.

Stevens, A. J., Jensen, J. J., Wyller, K., et al., 2011. The role of public-sector research in the discovery of drugs and vaccines. New England Journal of Medicine, 364(6), pp. 535–541.

Stolper, K. C. F., Boonen, L. H., Schut, F. T., and Varkevisser, M., 2022. Do health insurers use target marketing as a tool for risk selection? Evidence from the Netherlands. Health Policy, 126(2), pp. 122–128.

Straume, O. R., 2023. Therapeutic reference pricing and drug innovation incentives. Economics Letters, 222, p. 110945.

Sutton, M., Elder, R., Guthrie, B., and Watt, G., 2010. Record rewards: The effects of targeted quality incentives on the recording of risk factors by primary care providers. Health Economics, 19(1), pp. 1–13.

Sutton, M., Nikolova, S., Boaden, R. et al., 2012. Reduced mortality with hospital pay for performance in England. New England Journal of Medicine, 367(19), pp. 1821–1828.

Toole, A. A., 2012. The impact of public basic research on industrial innovation: Evidence from the pharmaceutical industry. Research Policy, 41, pp. 1–12.

Turner, B. and Smith, S., 2020. Uncovering the complex role of private health insurance in Ireland. In S. Thomson, A. Sagan, and E. Mossialos, eds., Private Health Insurance. Cambridge: Cambridge University Press, pp. 221–263.

van de Ven, W. P. M. M. and van Vliet, R. C. J. A., 1992. How can we prevent cream skimming in a competitive health insurance market? In P. Zweifel and H. E. III Frech, eds., Health Economics Worldwide. Dordrecht: Kluwer, pp. 23–46.

Varkevisser, M., van der Geest, S. A., and Schut, F. T., 2012. Do patients choose hospitals with high quality ratings? Empirical evidence from the market for angioplasty in the Netherlands. Journal of Health Economics, 31(2), pp. 371–378.

Vernon, J. A., 2005. Examining the link between price regulation and pharmaceutical R&D investment. Health Economics, 14, pp. 1–16.

Wagstaff, A. and Van Doorslaer, E., 1992. Equity in the finance of health care: Some international comparisons. Journal of Health Economics, 11(4), pp. 361–387.

Wagstaff, A., Van Doorslaer, E., Van der Burg, H., et al., 1999. Equity in the finance of health care: Some further international comparisons. Journal of Health Economics, 18(3), pp. 263–290.

Wagstaff, A. and Van Doorslaer, E., 2000. Equity in health care finance and delivery. Handbook of Health Economics, 1, pp. 1803–1862.

Werner, R. M., Kolstad, J. T., Stuart, E. A., and Polsky, D., 2011. The effect of pay-for-performance in hospitals: Lessons for quality improvement. Health Affairs, 30(4), pp. 690–698.

Wiggins, S. N. and Maness, R., 2004. Price competition in pharmaceuticals: The case of anti-infectives. Economic Inquiry, 42, pp. 247–263.

Yang, O., Yong, J., and Zhang, Y., 2024. Effects of private health insurance on waiting time in public hospitals. Health Economics, 33(6), pp. 1192–1210.

Zeckhauser, R. J., 1970. Medical insurance: A case study of the tradeoff between risk spreading and appropriate incentives. Journal of Economic Theory, 2, pp. 10–26.

Zweifel, P., Breyer, F., and Kifmann, M., 2009. Health Economics, 2nd ed., Berlin: Springer Science and Business Media.

For EU product safety concerns, contact us at Calle de José Abascal, 56–1°,
28003 Madrid, Spain or eugpsr@cambridge.org.

www.ingramcontent.com/pod-product-compliance
Ingram Content Group UK Ltd.
Pitfield, Milton Keynes, MK11 3LW, UK
UKHW031425300625
460082UK00018B/258